The Truth About Relativism

Joseph Margolis

D0171218

BLACKWELL

Oxford UK & Cambridge USA

First published 1991

Basil Blackwell, Inc.
3 Cambridge Center
Cambridge, Massachusetts 02142, USA

Basil Blackwell Ltd
108 Cowley Road, Oxford, OX4 1JF, UK

Library of Congress Cataloging in Publication Data
Margolis, Joseph, 1924–
The truth about relativism / Joseph Margolis
Includes bibliographical references and index.
ISBN 0–631–17911–9 (alk. paper)
ISBN 0–631–18178–4 (pbk)
1. Relativity. 2. Protagoras. I. Title.
BD221.M33 1991
149—dc20   91–7535
                                                                        CIP
British Library Cataloguing in Publication Data
A CIP catalogue record for this book is available from the British Library.

Typeset in 10 on 12 pt Garamond
by Graphicraft Typesetters Ltd., Hong Kong
Printed in Great Britain by T.J. Press (Padstow) Ltd, Padstow, Cornwall.

This book is printed on acid-free paper.

by the same author

The Persistence of Reality

I   Pragmatism Without Foundations: *Reconciling Realism and Relativism*

II   Science Without Unity: *Reconciling the Human and Natural Sciences*

III Texts Without Referents: *Reconciling Science and Narrative*

The Truth About Relativism

man is the measure

Contents

Preface

I suppose I have been defending relativism most of my life, certainly well before I came to know the philosophical tradition. I have always had the impression, prephilosophically as well as philosophically, that its puzzles were never seriously confronted. I believe I sensed their importance before I understood them properly. In any case, I have never trusted the easy demonstration of relativism's incoherence. I concede that that may betray a pathology of my own, one that now fits me very well: namely, to take as few as possible of the established views for granted, to see whether we really couldn't do without them – always, of course, with the good sense of our being risked on the outcome.

Let me share two further thoughts. I regard the defense of relativism as a strategic part of a much larger philosophical venture that is likely to collect the strongest currents of the end of the century and to dominate the best thinking of the new century. I say the "best" thinking, because my own comfortable cynicism sees the world bent in the most determined way on deepening, everywhere, the influence of every benighted vision imaginable; at the same time the planet is being utterly used up. So the "best" thinking is desperately needed. The larger venture is one of producing a conceptual vision (or any number of such visions) of our place in the world, coherent and humane at the same time it discards, one by one, every last trace of the (grand, pretended) invariances – the perennial truths – of ultimate reality, knowledge, thought, rationality, virtue and value, logic, science, intelligibility, and the rest that have falsely reassured us all the while we disorder the planet. So many candidate theories of these sorts have had to be abandoned that I dare suggest that they probably all have to be given up. At any rate, *no* such genuinely powerful doctrines seem likely to convince their better critics for long, which is hardly to deny that they will stand their turn against all comers. What we need are radically new options.

The other thought is this. Someone was kind or unkind enough to tell me some time ago of a choice epithet he had heard applied to my work: "baroque analysis" or "analytic baroque" was the appraisal. I take it as a compliment: because it signifies (to me) an honest effort to depart from the ingrained habits of analytic philosophy without abandoning its genuine sense of rigor; because it signifies a determined effort to range over the philosophical landscape without a sense of oddity or betrayal in bringing together materials that the natural snobbery of the analytic tradition treats as beyond the pale; and because it signifies an admission that, in our own time, an adequate philosophy (like an adequate science or poetry or religion) must be moved by a planetary spirit if it is to survive at all, even where it expresses itself in a local idiom. In any case, the cheerfulness of my own cynicism has quite transmuted the epithet's sense for me. I hope its self-serving function will not disturb you, but will yield instead a fair suggestion of where the best philosophical energies lie.

I must thank Adele Harrison for putting the manuscript in initial good order. I must also thank my good friends for remarks of all sorts that have helped me shape the argument in its final form: in particular, Tom Rockmore, Eugene Lashchyk, and Michael Krausz, who have stayed with the manuscript or with the gathering argument – and with me, of course – for a good long while. And I must "thank" the goddess Fortuna, who infects every sort of order and has deigned to make it possible in the most banal of senses for me to measure Protagoras as I have. But I see that I must not delay any longer over these niceties.

J. M.

Philadelphia
October 1990

Foreword

The family of views that has come to be known as relativism has, since ancient times, inspired a suspiciously hot reaction of scorn and fear. Relativism conjures up an image of weak or wild intelligence that neither understands nor cares about the nature of the stable invariances of life and thought that govern the human condition and make it whole and humane. One sees this already in Plato's and Aristotle's reaction to Protagoras' teaching. One feels the contempt and the sense of danger. The startling thing is that the elemental quality of their language runs like a continuous stream from the Greek world to our own and has hardly abated. More than that, many of the same arguments that Plato and Aristotle collected (or invented) and poised like battering rams against a barbarian mind are still in use and hardly improved. It's hard to believe, but it's true.

There is a deep conservatism in the heart of Western philosophy that one begins to surmise is meant to serve an even deeper conservatism, a conservatism fearful of the very nature of change – or, better, of changeableness, of radical flux, of the absence of fixed structures. The unreasoned charge – we need not say, irrational – apparently does believe, believes with almost desperate conviction, that genuine stability in anything either is, or depends upon, an unchanging underlying order of reality, and that any threat to it is quite mad and beyond the pale of reason. Protagoras was the first bold spirit who seized upon that claim – call it *archism* – and said, quite simply ... Nonsense. He has been reviled for that, charged as the most stupid and dangerous of thinkers, a man pathologically incapable of a coherent argument. That we attack him again and again, that we never tire of doing so, that he springs back with the same primitive undeveloped tale through which, unfortunately, his teaching has been passed down to us (since, of course, his entire thesis is largely lost) suggests a kind of perseveration that defeats the very possibility of strengthening his argument and (equally) of improving the counterarguments mounted against him.

Protagoras is the patron saint of relativism – no more than that. We cannot really return to his theorizing subtleties, no matter what they were. They are lost. We have only the word of those who present his thesis in order to attack it. We begin to see its lineaments, of course, by a kind of reverse English. But the truth is that *our* world has its own need for a ramified relativism that cannot be content with mere archeology. The contemporary world has the distinction of believing (or, at least of harboring many who do believe) in the most unforced way possible, that the world *is* a flux.

Doubtless there have been other ages that have been drawn to the same theme. But ours is surely distinctive in this regard because it has combined (quite unintentionally) all the conceptual and inspirational sources for sustaining that conviction. It has done so in a way that may well be the most complete and most infectious possible. This is due, perhaps, to two particular developments: one, to the emergence of the peculiar modernity of having radicalized history, so that the very nature of human understanding and human existence is taken to be inherently historicized, denied any necessary fixity of structure; the other, to the development and concentration of the equally modern sense of technology and technologized science that regards the "world" of the physical and biological *sciences – a fortiori*, the world of human culture – as indefinitely plastic and ultimately somewhat artifactual. We are the Fausts of radical history and radical artifice, ourselves socially constructed Demiourgoi who have replaced Plato's divine artisan – drawn to working only with the remembered images of invariant Forms, now that there are none to be had.

Relativism, therefore, is a deep thesis about man's self-understanding. It is contestable, to be sure. What claim is not? But there is a civilizing necessity in pursuing it. We must understand whether it *can* take a coherent form, and what, if it can, that form might be. We must understand what is risked or lost among our dearest convictions if relativism can be sustained; and, of course, we must sustain it (if we mean to) in some way that catches up the puzzle usually assigned it: the puzzle at the heart of its claiming to have found a way of reconciling what appears to be flatly self-contradictory or incoherent, namely, that the same assertion may be both true and false or may be so construed that that inconsistency is avoided without favoring a merely disjunctive adherence to the one or the other option. Ultimately, as we may already realize, the conviction of essential invariance to which we all cling most is simply this: that man's nature remains unchanged through all the currents of changing history; and, because of that, that there must be a fixed order hidden in change itself, an order adequate for saving the norms and the very meaning of human existence, for grounding our science, for giving our active interventions an intelligible and real space in which to move rationally.

One sees at once what is so risky about relativism. It threatens chaos and the sheer contingency of everything we cling to. Of course, in both the East and the West, something like its message is also said to be the beginning of wisdom. But if it were only that, it would be gained at the price of deliberately losing the entire world. Relativism is meant to be the intellectual means for a sanguine recovery *of* the world – not a betrayal or renunciation of it – under the condition of a deepening sense of ubiquitous change and impermanence. It does have a bit of the spiritual journey about it. But it is also an eminently practical exertion. Wherever it gains a foothold, it relieves us of the forms of intellectual inertia that are attached, like barnacles, to the distributed stabilities of conception that keep us from a more daring – because a freer, a less encumbered – understanding of ourselves and our place in the world. The notion of the flux is simply the postulated context of all contexts in which *every* fixity may be subverted or tamed.

The essential insight is this: order does not require or entail unconditional invariance, not at the level of the real structures of the world, and not at the level of the conditions of our understanding and intervening in the world. Can that insight be fleshed out in every corner of human interest? Can it recommend itself as neither anarchical nor destructively skeptical nor ultimately irrational? We shall have to see. But more than that, we cannot afford to fail to search out the answer – seriously now – in a world that is itself increasingly consecrated (though it hardly knows it) to the reality of the flux and to the viability of a relativist's understanding of it. The fears that warn us are fair enough. More than that, they are human enough. No one, for instance, will not want to know, say, whether relativism can hold on to adequate critical resources against Nazism. That's a crude way of putting the point of resisting relativism, but it also makes the point. It makes it in a way that must be seen to extend to science and art as well as to morality and politics and law.

The verso of the serious charge implied has it that we have been whistling in the dark these many years, pretending to draw our strength from an invariant order of norms and natures that we cannot confirm. So, to continue the rude example, it's not that relativism relieves Nazism of its universal condemnation; it's rather that it exposes the pretense, the paper objection, for what it is, and insists that if we mean to oppose Nazism (a mere specimen, of course, of what we do mean to oppose) we must proceed by more than benign blackmail. The argument of the relativist is, quite simply, that the master tradition of Western philosophy *is*, in large measure, a compendium of blackmail arguments, of arguments that trade on the subliminal fears of all those thinkers who cannot believe that the denial of essentialism, universalism, strict nomologicality, all invariance – and their discernibility by man – can possibly yield a human-enough niche in which, metonymically, the Nazis won't run wild and free. The canny opponents of relativism – Plato and Aristotle as much as ourselves – have been very careful to pick and choose just those decent invariances that make the world a little safer for our own dear prejudices. One quite influential contemporary philosopher, for example, who may remain nameless for the moment, fearful of just what Nazism did mean in our own (and his) yesterday, insists that, through the flux of human history (he does concede that history has no permanent structure and that man has a history rather than a nature), we actually do discover and continually reconfirm that man is Hellenic in ultimate inspiration and endeavor, forever committed to the humane vision of classical Greece! Apparently, this is as true for the Asian, African, native American worlds as it is for his own Eurocentric vision. Well, it's a nice thought, but, as Protagoras might have said, it's nonsense. Also, if it *is* nonsense, it is also nonsense on stilts for our vision of science and philosophy as well as for the eternal verities of the good life.

Relativism is a theme of courage, therefore, an exercise of conceptual rigor (to be sure), but an exercise pursued against the grain. Anyone not familiar with the hidden brutalities of professional confrontation cannot imagine all the unlovely forces that will be instantly gathered to protect the order of things against the least sign of attack by the barbarian relativist. It's a little purple to insist on placing what, after all, is nothing but a philosopher's discussion in a setting that smells of the presence of thugs. But of all the conceptual options that have ever crossed the mind of the philosophical tribe, none has attracted quite the scorn and ridicule of the relativist. Certainly, the skeptic and the solipsist are respectable, however odd. Even the anarchist has his decent inning. But the relativist is profoundly suspect in a different way. He means to reclaim the seemingly safe, the entire housebroken world in a way that preserves its best achievement – the discipline and intelligibility of its science and logic and mathematics, for instance – but in a way that utterly subverts the assurance that any such achievement requires that we be in touch with a strictly invariant, timelessly fixed order of things. That, apparently, is what is so discomfiting about the relativist, what was so troubling about Protagoras originally. Apparently, Protagoras cannot be forgiven

– though, of course, the denial of invariance is not yet the relativist's thesis.

The remarkable thing is that we have hardly moved very far from the first condemnations of relativism. Our leading theorists still condemn it, and condemn it in nearly the same words as were used at the beginning of Western philosophy. But there is a difference. Our world has now put in easy and customary doubt the old assurance that there is an inflexible order of reality. It has actually made that doubt quotidian. It has arrived at the offending suspicion in a natural way – almost inattentively, in fact – through the very processes of modern history. The notion that there *is* no inflexible order is hardly a merely brilliant or crazy speculation penned in an attic. It is more nearly the normal medium that grows stronger and more convincing as we approach our own day, incarnate in all that we do and think in the practices of actual life. The relativist's thesis is an abstraction now drawn without the boldness of its ancient vision. It still needs the resources of good argument, but it is no longer an outlaw theory.

All this has been set in motion in a local way by the technologized science of the Renaissance and by the structural slippages of history that began to dawn on us after the French Revolution. That is at least the short chronicle of what we have left behind and what we have now come to. Protagoras seems to have grasped the point without the advantage of being modern. It is just what sets him apart as an opponent of Parmenides and, more tellingly, of Heraclitus. But our own intellectual totems, given the picture just sketched, must surely include Francis Bacon and Vico and Hegel standing on the edge of their as yet somewhat unfathomed worlds. In our own time, the original protagorean themes are being recovered through a reinterpretation of Marx and Nietzsche at least, thinkers who have only recently been themselves released from certain preposterous readings – a commitment to excessive fixities of structure (Marx) and an excessive taste for sheer incoherence (Nietzsche). They are now more or less recovered for respectable readings: two somewhat ailing gentlemen, rather mild patrons of the ultimate flux. There are others that could be mentioned, of course. But the slim array of figures now in place does manage to yield a light summary of the drift of two thousand years of philosophical work that brings us a bit more hospitably to the doctrine we are here recommending.

It is, frankly, a prejudice we are recommending: a prejudice in the old sense, in the sense of (discerning) the deep preformative themes of our operative judgment horizonally formed by the very practice of historical life. On the relativist's own thesis, it could not be more than that. But that's not to say that argument is lost in persuasion and influence, only that the forms of argument are relatively reliable abstractions drawn in a setting that is always subject to unexpected subterranean changes. That itself, as we shall see, is the key to answering the original indictments of Plato and Aristotle against Protagoras and to answering their contemporary progeny (whether innocent or not).

Relativism sees itself, therefore, as breaking a temple or two. Nothing too grand, perhaps, but a way of letting some fresh air into those closed buildings of the mind. Its conviction is that we have and can have no way of returning to the fixities we were once persuaded "must be there," and that we must still find a conceptually satisfactory way of holding on to what we think we *have* achieved without the pretense of the old securities. They may be gone forever; and we may still have to face a genuine chaos if we cannot construct a coherent account of how it is possible to have achieved a language, a culture, a science, a critical understanding of having done all that, on the premiss of the flux. In a larger sense, relativism presents itself as a philosophy of the free spirit, of all those unwilling to let *any* premiss count as privileged or fixed, of all those unwilling to divide the world between the revealed and the debatable. There are no such divisions, says the relativist. That is also Protagoras' implicit reading of Socrates' teaching: "Man is the measure" is the meaning of "Know thyself."

There's the denouement intended. So let the play begin.

Prologue

I

The most persistent myth about relativism is this: it is impossible to formulate the thesis – the philosophical thesis – consistently or coherently. Extraordinary!

Philosophy is of course notorious for its inability to make its most exemplary claims stick. No sooner does it proclaim some nontrivial truth than the jousters of the field enter the lists and eventually bring down the champion's standard, often by very modest means: by identifying a lacuna in the argument, by charging a *reductio* or an *ignoratio elenchi*, or simply by constructing a limiting case in which the sweeping charge is set aside. Curiously, relativism does not seem to have attracted even that much interest. First of all, there are remarkably few stalwarts who have ever defended relativism in a sustained way; second, there are even fewer who believe the adverse charge will not hold; third, even curiouser, hardly anyone bothers to fix the essential doctrine or to speculate on relativism's genuine options; and finally, there is a casual but persistent impression abroad that the fatal blow must have already been delivered in ancient times, even though the ancient claims are no longer found compelling in the way they once were. It is hard to think of another thesis of comparable importance that has been treated so shabbily.

When it first appeared in what must have been a reasonably strenuous form, in the work of Protagoras at least, relativism was systematically dismembered and ridiculed by both Plato and Aristotle. In fact, we know of Protagoras' view principally through the seeming distortions and special pleading of those two worthies. All of Protagoras' texts have been lost; we know him only as the somewhat foolish, however daring, sophist who could not keep himself from self-contradiction. The general diagnosis declares that what Protagoras maintained, would hold only if truth-claims could, at once, be both true and false in the same respect. Of course, they cannot. Hence, it was thought to follow – it has somehow been supposed, by a sort of conceptual inertia, to have been demonstrated across the twenty-five hundred years that separate us from Plato and Aristotle – that relativism could never recover from that original and decisive defeat. But the truth is, *pace* classical philosophy, that Protagoras has never been effectively shown to have supported the fatal view attributed to him in ancient times, or that his relativism could not be coherently and plausibly reinterpreted (against Plato's and Aristotle's foxiness), or that modern versions of relativism could not coherently redeem the main lines of Protagoras' argument *and* escape the fatal blow directed against it – or, *a fortiori*, that there were no other possible grounds on which a viable relativism could be constructed, bearing at least a family resemblance to the ancient model.

The issue at stake is not primarily an antiquarian one, not, for instance, one of righting an ancient wrong. The marvel is, rather, that the whole history of Western thought has been arrested on this single pivot for at least twenty-five hundred years and that, although it cannot be supposed to be the single most important conceptual dispute confronting the human race, it is a most strategic issue implicated very centrally in nearly every question that *is* thought to be philosophically essential. Vindicated, relativism has the force of deepening in the most profound way every incipient doubt regarding the presumptions of cognitive fixity, certainty, unconditional truth, irrelevance of context and history and personal and societal perspective in both theoretical and practical matters – hence, of course, regarding the timeless reliability of specialist pronouncements on the grand Truth of anything – once and for all. You can see, therefore, its subversive possibilities, particularly *if* there were a chance of recovering the thesis as a fair contestant against the canon that has remained informally in place through all that time. Once we concede that we cannot rule out relativism unconditionally, a workmanlike inquiry must strengthen our resolve to see whether its enabling conditions may be more favorable than are usually reported; and once we discover that they are a good deal more than merely reasonable conjectures, we must go on to explore the benefits of relativism as well as its plausibility in the company of its opponents.

One version of the canon takes the following form: that it is possible, under real-world conditions, to discern what, *tout court*, is true or false about things. But what is true, it is said, is timelessly true, even if it addresses what is transient; hence, truth cannot be restricted merely to what appears or seems to be the case, and seeming incompatibilities regarding truth can only be relativized (benignly) to our contingent beliefs at this or that moment of inquiry. Any stronger claim (relativism) must (so the argument goes) be incoherent or self-contradictory *at some point* in successful inquiry. Relativism is an *alethic* theory (a theory about the nature of truth) under favorable *epistemic* conditions (under conditions that assume that the truth about the world can be humanly grasped); or, even more strenuously, it is a peculiar alethic theory embedded in the optimistic epistemic constraint just mentioned, which is itself embedded in an even more strenuous *ontic* constraint (namely, that reality is inherently changeless). Hence, *if* we may count on collecting the truth about the world, and *if*, in addition, the real world that we collect the truth about is itself invariant, than it *is* conceptually preposterous to hold that *"true"* simply means "true relative to this perspective" and "true relative to that perspective" and so on (for all actual or possible perspectives); or, "true in L_1" and "true in L_2" and so on (where "L," suitably subscripted, signifies that "true" is restricted in use to the space of the sentences of this and that language or to the cognate counters of this and that practice, habit of mind, convention, or whatnot). There is, here, a potential equivocation that we shall need to examine more closely later. For, although we acknowledge (here) the *alethic* option of construing "true" as meaning "true in L" or the like, we must consider that *that* sort of relativization is *not* equivalent to relativizing the *epistemic* treatment of truth-*claims* (employing "true" and "false" *sans phrase*) to the cognitive resources of a community of inquirers working with L or some contingent cultural tradition embedded in L. Whatever the logical difficulties confronting "true in L," the fate of the truth-claims of this or that society, confined (in a sense that is obviously trivially necessary, because ineluctable) to whatever its historical resources happen to be, does not at all entail treating "true" as "true in L". In fact, it does not as such or as yet entail any interesting form of relativism.

The pretty thing is that the embedding notion that locates the pertinent alethic option within the terms of a strong epistemic thesis within a strong ontic thesis *is* the shorthand summary of the classical philosophical canon ranging, in rather different ways, through Parmenides, Plato, and Aristotle (and, of course, Heraclitus and Democritus as well). Call it the *archic* canon. On the assumptions of the archic canon, particularly in Plato's and Aristotle's separate treatments of Protagoras, it *does* follow at once that *anything* like Protagoras' (alethic) notion of "man the measure" (the ancient locus of relativism) is conceptually preposterous.

Now, the entire history of Western philosophy has very slowly, but

also very steadily, moved from Aristotle's time to our own in eliminating the ontic leg of the ancient conceptual tripod. There are vestiges, to
be sure, of the ancient doctrine: all philosophies die reluctantly. But
there is certainly no general consensus *now* that it is either incoherent or
wildly unreasonable to suppose that the real world has no fixed structure. So part at least of what Protagoras had maintained, which was
thought conceptually contemptible in the ancient world – namely, the
denial of the ontic thesis, that we could count on the fixity of reality,
and (or), epistemically, that we could count on that or such a fixity's
being cognitively accessible to man – has at long last been sustained. The
modern quarrel has moved on to contest the strong epistemic thesis,
once separated from the notion of an invariant reality. After all, if the
world has no fixed structure, and if human knowledge is itself an
achievement of some kind within that same world, then what could
possibly provide the basis for supposing that, under real-world conditions, human truth-claims *can* be adequately managed, distributively and
once and for all, in terms of the uniquely strong bivalent values "true"
and "false" that are supposed to obtain? What reason do we ever have
for supposing that there *are* discernible criteria – timelessly suitable,
under the terms of the argument – *for* matching truth-claims to truth
and falsity *tout court*, or for reliably approximating to them?

This second issue is hardly settled, let it be frankly said. But it is at
least in dispute. It is in fact one of the principal foci of philosophical
and scientific quarrel at the end of the twentieth century, at the end of
our own century and on the threshold of the next. We cannot say, just
like that, that relativism is now vindicated. That would be too much to
claim, on the evidence. But it is now in the debater's park: two of the
three legs of the ancient tripod have been broken without the complete collapse of the entire philosophical stool. That much is just what
Protagoras had originally supposed, though certainly not for the reasons
we might now be prepared to tender.

The truth is we really don't know *what* Protagoras' view of the
alethic issue was. We have only Plato's and Aristotle's say-so; and *their*
judgment is hopelessly colored by their having supposed that none
of the legs is really at risk and that the least damage to the ontic and
epistemic claim would disable altogether any coherent talk of the alethic
option. Well, that has proved to be quite untrue. But if that is so, then
it is surely premature to suppose that the fatal refutation of relativism
was ever given in the ancient world. We don't know what Protagoras'
reading of the alethic thesis amounted to. We are clearest about his
epistemic thesis: possibly, then, not (pointedly) about the ontic thesis
either, though perhaps at least about its irrelevance in real-world episte-

mic terms. Ultimately, it doesn't matter, for we ourselves are entirely free to redeem the argument under the terms of the prevailing philosophical winds, and they are now blowing more and more favorably in relativism's direction than was ever true in ancient Greece.

There you have the penny argument for reviving relativism. It's actually quite a stunning argument, because it collects in a handful of words the greatest run of philosophical thinking the West has produced, and shows it to have been completely indecisive on what has so casually been supposed to be one of its exemplary refutations. It also confirms, of course, that relativism is not entirely an independent issue. It becomes an interesting and viable option only when the "archic" presumptions are rejected or forced into an open contest with contrary claims that attract their own measure of respect. It had once been thought that *any* deviation from those strong presumptions (the "archic" ones) could not be conceptually tolerated at all. But that has proved false, unless we are prepared to say that the whole of late twentieth-century thought is hopelessly incoherent in challenging that part of the ancient tradition. Well, you may test the possibility if you care, but you will find it hard to draw support from the considered views of any of the leading minds of our time. Saying that, of course, is not meant to be a proper argument, only a reminder that a provisional stalemate is really all we need. And we have it now. To put the point in an absurdly obvious way: if relativism is conceivable as an alternative to the archic doctrine, then it surely ain't incoherent. QED.

II

It would be flat-footed to say that the philosophical tradition has actually conspired to keep relativism from receiving the same sustained attention and sanguine interest that every other comparable doctrine has attracted – skepticism and solipsism, indubitability and apodictic certitude, for instance. But the fact remains that the arguments against relativism are peculiarly inert: they have hardly changed at all since ancient times. Also, if vindicated, relativism would have the most profound effect on matters of practical and public policy, especially regarding the authoritative direction of human affairs and the conceptual standing of every supposed invariant truth on which such direction rests.

All that is changed now. For reasons not narrowly tied to the fate of relativism, our own contemporary world has been ineluctably drawn in directions distinctly hospitable to relativistic options. The principal

attractions are these: a strengthened adherence to the cognitive intransparency of the world; an increasingly radicalized sense of the historical
nature and conditions of human existence; an insistence on the horizoned, preformed, fragmentary, biased cognitive and affective orientation of human life; the impossibility of extricating reason, inquiry,
the reflexive critique of any judgment or commitment from any of the
above conditions; the recognition of divergent and moderately incommensurable conceptual schemes compatible with the survival of the race;
the likelihood that our perceptual and critical acquaintance with the
world has been and continues to be heavily overdetermined in theorizing and conceptualizing respects; the realization that we cannot in
principle distinguish between the constructed nature of our intelligible
world and the "independent" structure of the brute world; and the
admission of the real-world impossibility of ever judging, except under
endogenous constraints, whether we are actually approaching closer
to an understanding of all possible conceptual schemes or, using this
scheme or that, closer to the fixed Truth about the world.

These are the salient philosophical themes of the age. They are none
of them forms of relativism; furthermore, relativism is entailed by none
of them. That is just the fresh advantage relativism claims: an unforced
change of conceptual scenery, developed over centuries and coming to
rest in a variety of visions that could not be more hospitable to its own
fortunes. It is very odd, therefore, that, observing the general march of
philosophical events leading to the present climate of opinion, opponents of relativism have never bothered to mount a fresh defense against
the inevitable reversal of the ancient line of defeat. But the fact remains
that there are no really new arguments to consider. Our own strong
critics have chosen to echo the ancients; they have allowed themselves to
be overtaken, therefore, by the sheer drift of the philosophical currents.

The salient themes mentioned constitute, then, a new playing field
on which to test the reasonableness and validity of relativism and the
doctrines that oppose it. What we may conclude is this: the adverse
conceptual conditions under which Protagoras was originally obliged to
compete against the archic canon have now been either removed or
attenuated, neutralized, nonplussed, even stalemated without its having
been true that any large part of the continuing philosophical tradition
was ever preoccupied solely or chiefly by an interest in vindicating
relativism. That is what is so important about conceding, or insisting,
that relativism is not an altogether independent issue. Its fate has always
depended on the fate of larger philosophical currents.

But the needed themes are now in place, inestimably stronger than
any that could have been available to Protagoras himself, though

certainly not inimical to whatever he seems to have believed. On the contrary, the thesis "man is the measure" is now entrenched in a remarkably powerful way in all our thinking, except of course that the prevailing contingencies under which we might care to rely on any of our findings have now been made to yield much more radical demurrers (against the canon) than were ever formulated in Protagoras' world. These surely have to do with our having historicized and artifactualized human nature under the condition of intransparency and the open possibility of conceptual inventions we cannot even imagine as yet.

In a word, if relativism may be defended, it is probably best defended in our own time; and if Protagoras was right, he was right for reasons that include many he could not possibly have imagined. These favorable changes have deepened the complexity of the question; but they have never, in doing that, brought relativism closer to skepticism or anarchism or nihilism or irrationalism, as many have supposed. Relativism is an affirmative doctrine, a positive claim about the conditions for successful truth-claims. It is, in a sense, a *strong theory* that favors *logically weak truth-claims* by which skepticism may be offset.

At this point, someone will raise the nagging question: Is relativism true then? For, if it is, it will be said, it has defeated itself out of its own mouth; and if truth is abandoned, then relativism is no competitor at all. Well, it is fair enough to say that that is a puzzle that will need looking into. But there is no reason to think that it will be any more decisive against relativism than the original canon. Why, after all, couldn't the force of relativism (against the claims of its opponents) be an instance of its own sort of claim? Why couldn't it invoke its own alethic doctrine? And why couldn't certain claims be treated nonrelativistically (at least in principle) while others are construed relativistically? These are purely formal options, of course: there's no point in pursuing them in this idle way. But think for a moment about what the new question means: it effectively concedes that its own query is a thinner one than the original charge of incoherence or that it is merely the same charge in a new guise. In any case, it is hard to see that it moves the debate on to a sterner test.

III

There is a sense in which relativism is a formal thesis, a thesis about the nature of truth or about constraints on the use of the values "true" and "false" or similar truth-like values – an alethic thesis, as we were saying. But the *use* of "true" is inseparable from our theories about what we mean by knowledge and the apprehension of particular truths; and our notion of that connection is similarly inseparable from our theories about the nature of the knowable world. So, although it is helpful to treat relativism as an alethic doctrine, there is no way of disjoining the alethic and the epistemic, or the epistemic and the ontic; *a fortiori*, there is no way of giving conceptual priority to alethic questions over epistemic and ontic ones. This is why the celebrated analysis of knowledge as "justified true belief" is so utterly vacuous: first, because "truth" is not, in that formula, able (as required) to be, or to be satisfied as, an independent and co-equal condition, if the formula is to function as a criterion; and second, because it is impossible to say or specify in the abstract whether there is a conceptual link, or what is the conceptual link, between "believing that *p*" and "knowing that *q*," or between being "justified" in "believing that *p*" and (because of that) being "justified" in "knowing that *q*." There is the decisive clue affecting the famous (that is, insoluble) formal puzzles regarding the nature of knowledge: for *knowledge has no purely formal nature*. One may reasonably conclude, then, that neither logic nor epistemology is an autonomous discipline, though modern analytic philosophy has always mistakenly supposed they were. We need not press the advantage, although it is worth bearing in mind. Our purpose in raising the issue is, rather, to ensure our *caveat* regarding treating relativism as an alethic issue.

Once we view matters this way, it is extraordinarily convenient to distinguish between two sorts of alethic readings of relativism: in one, truth-values or truth-like values are themselves relativized or, better, *relationalized*, so that (for instance) "true" is systematically replaced by "true in L_k" (for some particular language, perspective, habit of mind, social practice, convention or the like, selected from among a set of relevant alternatives ["k"] that might well yield otherwise inconsistent, incompatible, contradictory values when judged in accord with the usual canonical bivalent values ("true" and "false"), themselves taken to range over all such k's. In the other, "true" is *not* thus relationalized at all, but, rather, the bivalent values are systematically *replaced* in a formal way by a logically weaker set of many-valued truth-values or truth-like values; so that, where, on the bivalent model, logical inconsistency or contradiction obtains, now, on the replacement model and in accord with appropriate relevance constraints, such *logical incongruences* (as we may call them) need no longer be treated as full *logical inconsistencies, incompatibilities, contradictions*, or the like. On the first model, certain well-known fatal paradoxes of self-reference inevitably arise; on the second, they do not. On the first model, *when* joined to the archic canon or not, Protagoras would certainly be defeated at a stroke; on the second, *whether* disjoined from the archic canon or considered without regard to it, not only could Protagoras be redeemed, but he could be redeemed in a way close to his original intention (which we can only guess at), and, in any case, *we* could defend a relativism that might bear a fair resemblance to the original Protagorean position. In fact, as we shall see, there are really two distinct versions of the attack on relationalism: one is the ancient version (developed in somewhat different ways by Plato and Aristotle) that depends decisively on assuming the truth of the archic thesis; the other is the contemporary version (developed in a very clear way by Hilary Putnam for one), that abandons archism, addresses the self-referential paradoxes in a more formal way, and yet still manages to link the attack to the notion of a "fit" between word and world that continues the realist objection of the ancients.

There are, therefore, two quite different sorts of relativisms to be examined: one, *relationalism*, is admittedly prone to insoluble paradox, incoherence, self-contradiction when taken to range over genuine truth-claims; the other, which we may label in an obviously tendentious way, *robust relativism*, suffers no such logical embarrassment. Both may be drawn from the historical record. But strangely, *no* critic of relativism has ever addressed the second option or shown it to be fatally defective. Defenders of "relationalism" are best advised to weaken their version of relativism so that it no longer concerns truth-claims directly, or no longer does so at any point at which its well-known self-defeating maneuvers surface. It is, for that reason, either irretrievably flawed or not terribly interesting. The defense of "robust relativism" insists on addressing truth-claims or truth-like claims without first partitioning (in the "relationalist's" way) the scope of limited plural sets of would-be truth-values.

The robust relativist's thesis is that there is no purely formal reason why many-valued truth-values should function inconsistently or incoherently; or why such values cannot be distributively applied in an advantageous way in this or that particular sector of inquiry. In fact, the relativist claims there is no reason for supposing that bivalent and many-valued truth-values cannot be systematically used together (with due care) without risking conceptual disaster.

The critical maneuver is simply this: that, where many-valued truth-values ("robustly") *replace* the usual bivalent values, they are offered as an alethic option, not as a mere epistemic concession (as, for example, in introducing probabilistic truth-values that remain, in principle, tethered to overriding bivalent values).

The adjustment required is a remarkably small one, but it has the most surprising consequences. In any case, robust relativism differs from relationalism in that the latter, but not the former, *defines* truth-values *in* epistemically restricted ways; whereas the former, but not the latter, construes truth-values, whether bivalent or many-valued, alethically only, even where it *theorizes* about the epistemic and ontic conditions under which the replacing values it favors are able to be *used*. The relationalist *introduces* relativistic truth-claims by assigning all claims a set of possible truth-values that make no initial sense except in terms of the relationalist's own theory of *epistemically* relativized values. The robust relativist, by contrast, *shares* with the opponents of relativism the ordinary *alethic* options of bivalent and many-valued truth-values: his distinction rests, rather, in theorizing that, in this or that sector of inquiry, the intelligible world can coherently support truth-claims that, on a bivalent model, would yield inconsistency and self-contradiction (just where we have reason to resist such results). He urges, therefore, the replacement (in alethic terms) of bivalence (and *tertium non datur*): in the interpretation of artworks and human history, for example, or in the appraisal of high-order theories in physics and metaphysics. The relationalist would restrict epistemically the formal meaning of all our *truth-values*, whereas the robust relativist only restricts (where needed) the epistemic power of our *truth-claims*.

The relationalist, then, imposes a more strenuous constraint on truth-values than does the robust relativist; and, as it happens, the condition he imposes cannot fail to produce certain self-defeating paradoxes. The robust relativist merely makes a formal selection among possible truth-values; his own epistemic considerations concern the actual use of those values in servicing particular truth-claims: they do not qualify the values themselves. No contradiction is entailed alethically, therefore, unless (what no one believes) the mere advocacy of many-valued truth-values is already self-contradictory. This has the interesting consequence that the relationalist may be defeated on formal grounds, but the robust relativist cannot be: an opponent of the latter must attack his substantive arguments regarding the nature of the world or regarding our knowledge of the world. Hence, it is preposterous to suppose that relativism must be generically self-contradictory or self-defeating. Even Plato and Aristotle maintain that Protagoras defended an untenable position because of his epistemic and ontic views (in effect, opposing the archic claim). Certainly, if he had held that one and the same proposition or statement could be at once true and false in the same respect, his obvious defeat would have nothing to do with relativism as such; and if he merely abandoned or restricted excluded middle in order to service the kind of claims the ancients attributed to him, then, on a fair argument, his position was not self-contradictory at all; or, if it was, its defect must somehow depend on grounds that do not presuppose the validity of the archic claim – since most contemporary theorists would not concede that that was true or necessarily true, and yet they typically still regard relativism as untenable.

Furthermore, the absurdly simple key to the self-referential paradoxes of the relationalist's option is this: *if* the relationalist supposes that a given proposition may be "true in L_1" but "false in L_2" (or even "true in L_2") and *if* no further nonrelationalized sense of "true" is available to him in his own discourse, then the relationalist cannot even express what he assumes to be the case: namely, that "true" *is* relationalized. It would then be otiose for him to suppose that *his* use of "true" was relationalized, and he could not make sense of independent alternative practices regarding the alethic use of "true."

Finally, in this regard, the relativist cannot be supposed to have introduced an option like the probabilist's. For the probabilist relativizes truth-*claims* in evidential and cognitive terms *under* the constraint of *non*relativistic truth-*values*; whereas the robust relativist does not relativize truth-*claims* at all (or the epistemic meaning of the would-be truth-values they implicate). He argues only from the limited epistemic power with which we may *assign* truth-values to our various claims, and his argument may easily take a nonrelativistic as well as a (robust) relativistic form.

Now, the stunning fact is this: *every* known defeat of relativism is committed, explicitly or not, to the first, the "relationalized" interpretation of the doctrine; either it never considers the second interpretation at all or, when confronted with it, it insists, of course, that that is "just not relativism." ("If you *mean* by relativism nothing *but* the second interpretation," one can almost hear them saying, "then of course *that is* a possible position to take, but *it's not relativism*.") This also explains just why the opponents of relativism have been so casual over twenty-five hundred years. From their point of view, it hardly matters whether the archic doctrine of Plato and Aristotle withstands scrutiny; it is already quite enough that the logical constraints on the use of "true" are (and are forever) so much in accord with the ultimate invariances of human thought that relativism can never recover from its ancient defeat.

But that's all changed: it is true, now, that relativism can be shown to be coherent as well as plausible when applied in favorably selected sectors of inquiry *and* that its recovery provides a reasonable interpretation of Protagoras' original thesis. So it is quite remarkable that recent discussions of relativism should have proved so primitive – in being so insouciantly prepared to risk everything on its never being necessary to go any distance beyond the ancient *reductio*. Or, alternatively, wherever the more recent themes of philosophy have seemed to threaten to recover some form of relativism or other, opponents have been quick to insist (too quick by half) that such newfangled notions – notably, conceptual incommensurabilism, historicism, puzzles of interpretation in intentional contexts – merely reinforce, possibly even deepen, the disastrous consequences of the first reading of relativism.

We may now offer an explicit challenge on the field of philosophical honor: *there are* (we claim) *no formal or plausible substantive grounds for rejecting relativism in terms of the alethic "replacement" reading; the "relationalized" reading is admittedly indefensible; the "robust" reading is not; the two are entirely independent of one another; and there are no other generic forms of relativism that address the alethic question.* There you have the structure of the argument that follows. It is not, of course, the argument itself, and it does not actually formulate any particular relativistic thesis. It is, we may say, the template of the argument but not the argument.

IV

Since so much nonsense has been written about relativism, a responsible champion must ensure his bona fides. It is not enough to sketch the template of the argument, but it is too much to expect to condense it into a few compelling lines. We need a sense of where its new force lies.

We have segregated two sorts of alethic distinctions subtending different families of would-be relativisms: one, manifest in its most developed form in relationalism, which relativizes "truth" and "falsity" by relationalizing their meaning epistemically *and* by confining the resulting truth-values within suitably compartmentalized spaces of application; the other, manifest in its most developed form in robust relativism, which does not relativize or relationalize "truth" and "falsity" at all but, rather, replaces, distributively, the usual bivalent pair with some set of many-valued truth-values or truth-like values, and then claims, on pertinent epistemic and ontic grounds, that different sectors of inquiry may be able to support only claims that take these logically weaker truth-values and do so in such a way as to validate "incongruent" claims.

In either case, merely alethic proposals are not yet relativisms in any interesting sense. Certainly, nonrelativists and opponents of relativism are fully entitled to favor the use of many-valued logics without the stigma of being relativists for that reason alone. Relativism emerges, in the sense of the second family of views, only with the supposed *coherence of incongruent claims.* Remember that, by incongruent claims, we mean truth- or truth-like claims that, on the bivalent model but not now, would be inconsistent, incompatible, or contradictory: on the argument, incongruent claims never devolve into such logically defective claims, because the usual bivalent values are, now, *systematically replaced*, alethically, not merely approximated in any logically dependent evidential or related sense; also, the boldness of the relativist position may be readily assessed by measuring the theoretical range of application of the values in question in inquiries addressed to the real or actual world. The greater the range, the bolder the claim.

So relativisms (of the second sort) do not behave logically in the same way that probabilizing strategies do in the sciences or in inquiries similarly modeled. For, where one supposes that p is probably true (true with a probability of P) and p is probably false (false with a probability of Q), the truth-like values "probably true" and "probably false" are not meant as such to be synonyms for the bivalent values "true" and "false"; they are, rather, members of a set of many-valued truth-like predicates, they are relationalized (for instance, to different or even the same evidence, E_1, E_2 ... E_k, from which, importantly, they are not formally detachable), *and* they are such that their application in truth-claims is normally construed as an evidential approximation to the logical force of bivalent values, that, in principle, still apply to the same claims, take precedence over probabilized truth-values, and, ideally, may always be invoked with respect to them. It is the last consideration that precludes incongruent judgments and also explains why an *alethic probabilism* is *not* interpretable as a version of the first sort of relativism.

Having said that, we must hasten to add that the admission of incongruent claims is not intended to eliminate considerations of inconsistency or contradiction or anything of the sort. Even in probabilized discourse, it is normally not thought to be contradictory to maintain that, say, "Nixon [probably] knew about Watergate in advance" and "Nixon [probably] did not know about Watergate in advance"; although it would normally be thought self-contradictory to maintain that "Nixon knew about Watergate in advance and Nixon did not know about Watergate in advance." Relevance considerations are pertinent here, but it may well be impossible to provide these reliably in advance of particular cases or on purely formal grounds.

These homely distinctions permit us to refine our sense of the first sort of relativism as well. Remember that, on an argument still to be supplied, we mean to treat relationalism as logically incoherent. We are conceding in this regard the ancient verdict that was rendered on Protagoras – not, however, the force of the reasons Plato and Aristotle adduce as far as Protagoras' own view is concerned, and not the correctness of their interpretation of Protagoras' position. That is, it *is* true that relationalism cannot be recovered, but to say that is neither to vindicate Plato or Aristotle nor to condemn Protagoras.

Nevertheless, theorists attracted to something like relationalism are normally attracted to two quite different conceptual options: on one, they favor *cultural relativity* (or perceptual or affective relativity or something of the sort); on the other, they favor some form of *noncognitivism*. Neither option is of any strategic interest as far as relativism is concerned, though they are interesting in themselves and do have a role to play. They have had their adherents.

Cultural relativity and its analogues simply affirm some state of affairs with respect to plural practices, conceptions, values, norms, perceptions, interests and the like: in particular, that different percipients see things differently from this or that perspective, or that different societies are committed to different values, or that different groups of scientists hold different beliefs and apply different conceptual schemes in addressing closely related matters. *Nothing* follows from this regarding the fate of relativism, and *nothing* regarding the fate of relativism depends on affirming or denying any putative facts of these sorts. A fair way of putting the point is this: cultural relativity concerns only *first-order* factual questions about the beliefs, feelings, interests, conceptual distinctions of some human society or aggregate; but it never, as such, addresses *second-order* or legitimative questions. On the other hand, under real-world conditions, the resolution of alethic questions – questions regarding the use of these or those truth-values – are always, or always entail, legitimative questions. The choice of truth-values always implicates epistemic and ontic considerations. Hence, there is no logical connection between cultural relativity and either of the two sorts of relativism sketched. Cultural relativity, therefore, is not a philosophical thesis at all. (There is, of course, the fashionable question to consider of whether there *is* a second-order legitimative issue implicated in merely making or recognizing truth-claims. The notion that there is not is the current darling of the so-called postmodernists. We can only go on record, here, as an opponent of the postmodernists. But the question deserves an inning.)

You might suppose that the claims collected as evidence of cultural relativity could be made to constitute an actual relativism; but it is not so easy to do. The reason is obvious. If we set aside the alethic predicates, "true" and "false," all probabilized truth-values, and all many-valued truth-values (as well as those like "knows" or "is rational," that may entail the alethic predicates), then *all* the predicates whose use confirms cultural relativity or the like are not only completely neutral to the fate of relativism but they are also analogues of the very predicates

Plato and Aristotle first theorized about as a way of defeating Protagoras' relativism: that is, they include predicates like "looks red to S
seen from here" as distinct from "looks blue to P seen from there" and
similar distinctions. This suggests what is fatally wrong with the ancient
condemnation of Protagoras; also, what is fatally decisive about relationalism. Now, relationalism may be construed as that form of relativism that moves directly and illicitly from the admission of relationalized
nonalethic predicates to the admissibility or necessity of relationalized alethic predicates. There is, of course, no evidence whatsoever that
Protagoras ever favored such a move, or ever had to; and it is just such a
move that entails the self-referential paradoxes *with respect to the use of
alethic predicates.*

Now the ancient lesson has not fallen on deaf ears. Hence, *anyone* who
wishes to recover cultural relativity as *something* like a relativism of the
relationalist sort will have to opt for a form of *noncognitivism.* Here, by
noncognitivism, we mean only that what, in the context of relativism,
would have been a claim or judgment – an utterance invoking or
implicating the use of alethic predicates – now no longer is one. For
instance, if he tried to analyze an apparent judgment such as "This painting
by Jackson Pollock is one of the great paintings of the twentieth century,"
the relationalist might say that it was (perhaps) "true relative to Clement
Greenberg's conceptual scheme" but "false relative to E. H. Gombrich's
conceptual scheme" *and* that "that's all there is to it." A noncognitivist
might say, rather, that "Greenberg *judges* it to be great" and "Gombrich
judges that it is not" *and* that "that's all there is to it." The relationalist, as
we have said, is committed to relationalized truth-values. The noncognitivist, on the other hand, abandons truth-values altogether, though without
(apparently) abandoning the sense in which people do "judge," do
"claim," do "reach verdicts" and the like; the noncognitivist therefore
construes such predicates as "claims" and "judges" as *not* entailing the
actual *use* of any alethic predicates. Very prudent.

So the noncognitivist very likely supports relationalized nonalethic
predicates but demurs wherever relationalized alethic predicates are invoked. He therefore holds a philosophical position, but he is no relativist. He wins his case, of course, at the small cost of making his position
utterly irrelevant to the fate of relativism. It is not surprising that this
sort of noncognitivist view has an attractive inning wherever moral,
aesthetic, religious, and similar forms of social and political tolerance are
favored. But then, noncognitivism is merely the formal analogue of a
sort of political *pluralism*, where pluralism is no form of relativism at all.
(Needless to say, we are merely recommending certain terms of art. Call
noncognitivism relativism, if you wish; it will change nothing.)

There is one other peculiarly strenuous way of escaping the trap of relationalism without subscribing to robust relativism, all the while one nudges the busy facts of cultural relativity in the direction of one relativism or another: that is, by introducing, wherever incongruent judgments are likely to prove embarrassing, some convenient barrier or other, usually both epistemic and ontic (in the sense supplied), a zone of relevant matters on which we must commit ourselves but, regarding which, "there is no fact of the matter," or regarding which the fact is that the truth-values that do apply are strictly segregated and bound to "worlds" or "world versions" *without being relationalized to such spaces.*

It is easy enough to recognize that these two versions of the same solution are the ones famously favored, respectively, by W. V. Quine and Nelson Goodman – who, of course, for just such reasons, uneasily straddle the relativist and nonrelativist alternatives. There are difficulties with their respective views that it would be inappropriate to consider here. (We are concerned, after all, merely to map the conceptual possibilities.) Quine and Goodman are, however, not relationalists because they are obviously clever enough to avoid the self-referential paradoxes; and they are not robust relativists either, because they never really abandon the principle of excluded middle or *tertium non datur.* On the other hand, we really don't know *what* their position is because they never quite explain the difference, or how they legitimate the difference, between advocating many-valued truth-values yielding incongruent judgments and "merely" advocating truth-value gaps for bivalent values in ways that are not to be construed as abandoning excluded middle. The option, frankly, is a serious one only because of the importance of its advocates. But it raises no serious difficulties as far as mapping the principal options are concerned. Technically, it favors a sort of noncognitivism just at the point that a relativism threatens. Hence, in a way, ironically to be sure, it actually confirms the force of our original claim that all relativisms are of one or the other of the two alethic sorts we first introduced. For the sake of convenience, we may dub all views of the sort just sketched, versions of some sort of *holism.* The thesis then amounts to this: that wherever would-be distributed claims entail a knowledge of the whole universe of discourse, indeterminacies of truth-value assignment arise (and so relativism is obviated). The question remains, of course, whether *that* demarcation can be coherently sustained or manageably restricted so as to admit truth-claims at all.

Given these considerations, we may find it helpful to introduce the deliberately elastic notion of *cultural relativism* – as opposed to the nonrelativistic notion of *cultural relativity.* By the first, we may now understand (purely for verbal convenience, remember) any would-be relativism that (rejecting the archic canon) posits pertinent alethic distinctions (either relationalist or robust) on the strength of an interpretation of the supposed facts of cultural relativity; or, even (more loosely), a philosophical thesis that, once again, builds on the facts of cultural relativity as before, but is specifically intended to obviate or oppose either of the alethic alternatives favored by relationalism and robust relativism. Hence, what we are now calling noncognitivism and holism may, if we wish, be treated as versions of "cultural relativism" though they will have nothing in common in a positive way with the central relativist options we mean to examine. The fact remains, as we shall see in the account that follows, that it is quite usual to draw attention to the "cultural relativist" tendencies in Quine and Goodman and many others, who actually oppose the alethic options we regard as central to relativism. We shall allow the usage for convenience of reference, but we shall have to be careful to keep what is said in its name from coloring our findings about relativism proper. We shall not rely on the notion in any strong sense.

V

Seen in the terms we have been laboring to put in good order, the argument that follows is committed to demonstrating the viability and force of various forms of robust relativism. Here, we begin to intrude on what will require the most careful attention. But we may at least venture the barest sketch of the alternatives to be considered in order to round out our map of the philosophical terrain. Let us, first of all, introduce the notion of the "least form of relativism" (LF): Any doctrine counts as a form of relativism if it abandons the principle of excluded middle or bivalence (and tertium non datur), or restricts its use, so that, in particular sectors of inquiry, incongruent claims may be validated. LF is the least common denominator of all viable relativisms. It is also formulated in the thinnest alethic sense and, for that very reason, it is not an "interesting" theory at all beyond the bare consideration that it is not incoherent as it stands. Every "interesting" form of relativism must embrace LF at least; but what makes a relativism interesting is just what it says about the epistemic and ontic features of the real world, in virtue of which bolder and more and more ramified relativisms can be sustained.

Once we concede that much, we should be prepared to agree that a generic sort of relativism going beyond LF and constituting a fair interpretation of Protagoras' dictum, "man the measure," may be

formulated as well. What this involves is recovering the oldest form of
relativism (or a relativism adjusted to the oldest dispute we have any
record of) that moves beyond the merely alethic considerations of *LF*.
Call it *protagoreanism*. It simply amounts to this: integrating *LF* with a
rejection of the "archic" thesis drawn from the ancient Greek tradition;
that is, (a) rejecting the necessary invariance of what is real, and (b)
denying that knowledge addresses such and only such invariance.
Wherever, in the spirit of Protagoras' account, knowledge or justified
belief is so constrained by conditions affecting the sense of "man the
measure" that the legitimation of validating incongruent claims may
then be provided in its name, we have achieved some form of protagoreanism. We may then claim that every viable relativism entails both
LF and protagoreanism. The argument is entirely straightforward.

Now, the modern world, particularly the contemporary world, has
introduced a variety of more daring theories on epistemic and ontic
matters than were ever available in Protagoras' time. There is no reason
at all, therefore, why there should not be more and more radical forms
of relativism that could be vindicated in terms of the newer conceptual
options of our age. Remember that protagoreanism is really no more
than a blunderbuss thesis: it is entirely reasonable to suppose that all
recent forms of (a viable) relativism simply introduce alternative ways
of giving determinate form to the epistemic and ontic details of protagoreanism itself. So seen, there are at least two principal lines of
contemporary thought that deepen relativism's challenge: one emphasizes epistemic considerations – *incommensurabilism*; the other, ontic
considerations – *ontic relativism* (let us say).

VI

We cannot, of course, hope to give an entirely satisfactory characterization here of these last two options: the conceptual ground has not yet
been properly laid. But, by incommensurabilism, we may understand at
least any relativism committed to *LF* and protagoreanism that, in addition, acknowledges moderately incommensurable conceptual schemes,
both diachronically and synchronically specified, both intra- and inter-
societally functional, not construed along relationalist lines, and not in
principle able to be conceptually overtaken (in real-world terms) in
ways known to escape such incommensurabilities.

The key notion in incommensurabilism is not merely that moderate
incommensurabilities obtain among different conceptual schemes – notably among those entrenched in natural-language practices that support

strong claims of cultural relativity – but also that there is no reason to believe that such incommensurabilities can be overcome as far as the epistemic use of truth-values is concerned. That the phenomenon is not taken to disable effective communication and understanding within and between societies confirms that it would be a *non sequitur* to conclude that if a relativism of the incommensurabilist sort were admitted, it would have to be relationalist as well, although that indeed is the favored verdict on incommensurabilism. On the contrary, the incommensurabilist holds that his thesis is indifferent to the difference between the alethic options posited, that it affects the *use* of bivalent values in the same way it affects the use of many-valued truth-values. Nevertheless, many critics of incommensurabilism suppose that the thesis leads directly to the self-referential paradoxes of the relationalist. What they really mean, of course, is that incommensurabilism is either ultimately incoherent or inconceivable (as in Donald Davidson's well-known opinion) or never actually insuperable (as implied, for instance, in the otherwise opposed views of Jürgen Habermas and Hans-Georg Gadamer). Unfortunately, conceptual incommensurabilism has not been developed very thoroughly in analytic terms. Its current prominence is undoubtedly due to the comparatively undeveloped but intriguing suggestions of T. S. Kuhn and Paul Feyerabend. It is probably true, however, that it will in the long run owe more to the strongly historicized poststructuralism of such thinkers as Michel Foucault than to the analysis of discernibly discontinuous paradigm shifts. That is, the strength of incommensurabilism lies in its not being possible to demonstrate that, on the admission of widespread cultural relativity, it is regularly, or it can in principle be knowingly, overtaken. Since the philosophical temper of the times favors such themes as cognitive intransparency, the tacit preformation of conceptual behavior, the social construction of human subjects, the impossibility of conceptual totalizing, the absence of fully systematic rules of synonymy, and the historicizing of "forms of life," something like incommensurabilism seems inescapable. At any rate, our account may content itself with demonstrating this connection and leave it at that.

On the other hand, what we are calling ontic relativism is the least well-known of the contemporary candidate forms of (robust) relativism. Roughly speaking, it maintains that there is a run of phenomena – events and particulars – that "have natures" that intrinsically include complex *intentional* properties, such that those natures or features are vague or indeterminate enough to invite incongruent judgments regarding what they are, or such that their natures and properties are so alterable by interpretation alone that incongruent judgments cannot be avoided in specifying them. The principal site of such phenomena is, of course, the world of human culture – artworks, actions, histories, the psychological nature of persons, institutions, theories, practices, and whatever is similarly affected when colored by cultural interests (even the schemes for individuating natural phenomena, for instance). Charles Sanders Peirce's semiotics may well be the most ambitious version of both lines of argument.

In a narrower sense, it is clear enough that a robust relativism of the "ontic" sort is likely to be favored in literary and art criticism, in the interpretation of history, in moral, legal, and prudential matters, and wherever explanatory theories are thought to be radically underdetermined in principle. It may be helpful to add here, that where, given intentionally complex properties, the conceptual boundaries of particular referents and the determinacy with which their properties or natures may be judged to be present are distinctly vague, relativism proves to be closely linked with certain *modernist* tendencies; and where the very natures and properties of such referents are directly altered by interpretation, relativism is equally closely linked with certain *poststructuralist* tendencies. Needless to say, the fortunes of these sorts of relativism depend on the fortunes of treating intentional properties as real properties. Once again, the salient tendencies of analytic philosophy are known to be opposed to such an admission. So it is worth taking note of the fact that two of the most controversial issues of the day, *conceptual incommensurability* and *intentionality*, actually harbor radical possibilities for relativism.

Although it is admittedly controversial, ontic relativism, we may observe, does afford intuitively perspicuous examples of the fruitfulness of a relativistic conception of truth-like claims. Once we see the way it plays, we cannot fail to see how its less – or at least its differently – contentious cousins would function. Grant, for instance, that, in the remarkable history of *Hamlet* interpretation, there are many valid, confirmable, or reasonably supportable interpretations of the play that are not fully compatible with one another, such that, acknowledging the defensibility of any one, we are still strongly disinclined to reject antecedently all others that, on a bivalent model, would be inadmissible merely because they were incompatible with it.

Here, let us suppose, we are *not* inclined to treat such interpretations in the relationalist's way: that, say, this interpretation strikes *me* (but not you) as valid, that that one strikes *you* (but not me) similarly, and that that's all there is to it. (In the relationalist's sense, one might express this as not merely a matter of a difference of taste, but a matter in which the very meaning and criteria of "true" or "right" logically incorporate the epistemic import of the differentiated taste of each of us.) We *might* be tempted, but we are resisting that move here. The "robust" and "relationalist" alternatives are utterly unlike one another, but they *are* options open in the same circumstances.

The "ontic relativist" offers us a fresh gambit: on his view, the *actual* intentional structure of the play legitimates an open-ended tolerance for "incongruent" interpretations of the play's meaning. It is now seen to be reasonable to hold – on "robust" grounds – that the interpretation of *Hamlet* supports (in some sense, rigorously or objectively) incongruent readings. It's in the nature of dramatic literature, we say, that that option may be preferred.

Once we see how that possibility arises, we also see how, under altogether different circumstances (for instance, how, denying that there are any intentional structures in physical nature), even a strong sense of realism might, granting the cognitive intransparency of the natural world (say, along Quine's or Kuhn's lines of reasoning at least, certainly along the more radical lines now fashionably favored, in the philosophy of science, by Bas van Fraassen, Nancy Cartwright, Ian Hacking, Arthur Fine), be reconciled to the view that "incongruent" claims may be the best we can expect, and *that*, *not* because of contingent limitations of evidence but because of deeper conceptual limitations affecting every form of objective claim.

Mind you, we needn't show that that must be the way things are (though we may believe it): we need only show that it is a coherent, a not unreasonable view to hold. For instance, suppose we held that the analysis of the most fundamental structures of physical reality was symbiotically infected, even overdetermined, by contingently shifting conceptual schemes and theories: that no single theory could rightly claim to take into account all pertinent considerations with equal felicity, that competing theories were always somewhat inflexible when extended to whatever was salient in opposed accounts, that appraisals of the comparative force of given views were always tacitly hostage to the substantive views in question, that the measure of the "fit" between theory and world was rarely decisive in an exclusionary or disjunctive way. None of this would make our science a chaos, but it would entitle us to fall back to the robust relativist's position. The standing of relativism, then, depends (as does that of all nonrelativisms) on the power of our theories of knowledge and reality; and those theories themselves tend to behave in a relativistic way.

We must also add here, that incommensurabilism and ontic relativism may be defended in ways that are reasonably independent of one another, though there are likely to be sectors of inquiry in which the peculiarities each addresses are wedded to those of the other. The possibility of an encompassing relativism begins to loom here. But we shall not pursue these options systematically or in great detail.

Finally, the options we have collected seem to exhaust all the eligible candidate theories likely to be broached at this point, close to the end of the century. Incommensurabilism is, in a fair sense, the dominant option of the last half of the twentieth century. But the picture grows distinctly muddy as we begin to entertain the more radical philosophical options of the last few decades. It is entirely possible that even more adventurous versions of relativism than those we mean to consider may yet surface. There are certainly wilder theories that have already drifted into our ken. In fact, the defense of relativism is, now, sometimes thought to be no more than the last citadel of the archic thesis itself. Perhaps it is. But at this very moment it cannot be said that such a countermove does adequate justice to the constraints on reference and predication that, at the very start of our discussion, we conceded could not be abandoned without abandoning altogether those enunciative acts by which questions concerning the ascription of truth-values first arise.

Since we have construed relativism in certain favorable alethic terms, in order to oppose reduction to skepticism or anarchism or the like, we cannot very well now abandon the point of our inquiry. Whether and in what sense we should do so is both a very odd question and a puzzle for another time. In any case, the avoidability or unavoidability of relativism depends entirely on whether first-order truth-claims and inquiries can or cannot be disciplined in ways that invite an assessment of their comparative success (their perceived success) without implicating second-order legitimative questions. Those who regard relativism as a vestige of a hankering after arguments of transcendental necessity (notably Richard Rorty) will be ready to dismiss all claims in favor of relativism; but those who believe that, although legitimation cannot be "Kantian" in that regard, it cannot be avoided either, will be glad to pursue the question in our company. Here again, another salient (a third) philosophical issue – *legitimation* – proves to be decisive for the prospects of relativism.

If one now reflects on the program sketched, it will be clear at once that we have systematically retreated from the *use* of "true" *tout court* to the assignment of truth-values and the appraisal of truth-claims. We do mean to treat relativism as an alethic doctrine, it is true; but we shall treat it as a doctrine of that sort in such a way that the prior timeless truths of the archic canon are put in the most profound doubt, that the cognitive intransparency of the world is fully conceded, that Protagoras' "man is the measure" restricts us to speculating about the choice of truth-values and the critique of truth-claims only within the constraints of intransparency. It would take us too far afield to develop a full analysis of this extraordinary change in conceptual orientation. But there can be no doubt that it is one of the most decisive themes of the late twentieth century, on which nearly all influential philosophers agree, both within the Anglo-American and the Continental European currents.

At the risk of reviving a misunderstanding that has dogged a good deal of its history, we may not unfairly term this treatment of truth in terms only of the assignment of truth-values and the appraisal of truth-claims from a cognitive stance entirely internal to a global intransparency, a *pragmatist* theory of truth (a repudiation, at least, of all correspondentist presumptions). Once again, we do not mean to claim that pragmatism *is* a form of relativism, only that its admitted coherence and plausibility ensure a very strong inning for relativism, only that its variant forms and philosophical cousins – for instance, as may be found in Quine and Heidegger, in Putnam and Gadamer, in Goodman and Derrida, to offer a number of provocative pairs – *cannot* possibly be made so unyielding as to preclude, without a mere *fiat*, the viability of robust relativism.

A last bit of instruction may be advisable. The order of the argument that follows is not the same as the order of this prologue. Here we have isolated the formal coherence and alternative options of relativism; in what follows, we shall emphasize primarily the substantive conceptual conditions under which relativism may be expected to flourish. The two threads must be intertwined to be effective: the argument that follows must be read through the template of this prologue; and the fortunes of the options here assembled must be assessed in terms of the strongest objections and the most favorable theories the philosophical tradition has managed to mobilize. That is to say: our argument is binocular. So the distinctions here introduced will not be reintroduced, but largely presupposed, in what follows; just as the tacit strategy of having fashioned these particular distinctions lies in having anticipated their dialectical prospects in the context of the dominant philosophical disputes of the day.

1

The Worst Scenario

I

A rather well-known American commentator on contemporary social issues, Michael Novak, says the following almost in passing in a spirited defense of capitalism:

> It simply is not true that all right-thinking persons, in all conscience and with all goodwill, hold the same vision of the good and judge moral acts similarly. Pluralism in moral vision is real. To recognize this is not to surrender to moral relativism. It does not follow from the fact that persons (and groups) stand in radical moral disagreement that "anything goes," "to each his own," etc. It may well be that when persons or groups stand in radical moral disagreement, only one is correct. The problem for a free society is to discern which.[1]

There is no entry for "relativism" in Novak's ample index of concepts. The obvious implication is that relativism is indisputably defined by the anarchism of "anything goes," that that fact is well known to all reasonably informed readers, and that, as a result, relativism is beyond defense, unrecoverable, and generally known to be such.

There is no need to badger Novak about his passing remark. What is instructive about it is that it is, effectively, the view of a surprisingly large number of philosophers who ought to know better. There are, for instance, any number of casually distributed remarks in Karl Popper's extensive writings – by no means casually tendered – that afford a more pointed sense of the drift of what Novak has picked up in the usual attacks on relativism. We shall sample a few of these here, to get something of the flavor of the adverse literature. They will serve us well later on when we attempt to mount a favorable defense of relativism.

II

Popper is clearly concerned to distinguish his own view, the famous principle and program of falsifiability, from a whole family of views that either include, or are tantamount to, relativism. He remarks, for instance, that, for many years since 1935, when he had been taken for the first time to a meeting of the Aristotelian Society, at which Bertrand Russell read a paper – one year after the publication of his own book, *The Logic of Scientific Discovery*: "It never occurred to me that my own approach, my own framework, might be more liable to misunderstandings than others – that it might clash more seriously with certain widely held and unconsciously accepted views – and that as a consequence people might misinterpret my approach by identifying it with some form of irrationalism, scepticism, or relativism."[2]

This is a very typical remark of Popper's. It also introduces a distinctly influential phrasing that many seem to have borrowed, to the effect that a certain view, which for the moment we may suppose Popper and Novak and countless others support, may be misread as a version of just the sort of stand on truth and knowledge that it (relativism) actually opposes; and that that stand may be fairly catalogued as "some form of irrationalism, skepticism, or relativism."

The sense conveyed is that these three notions are either essentially the same or, at any rate, sufficiently overlapping in an essential respect that they may be trippingly collected as a set of doctrinal postures that are really beyond defense or beneath contempt. It may well be that both Novak and Popper, for somewhat but not entirely different reasons, want to make it clear that a certain sort of pluralism is *not* to be construed as eliminating the quest for truth or the logical exclusiveness of truth. That certainly is an important part of Popper's program of falsifiability, which is explicitly hospitable to encouraging the pluralistic play of contending, potentially incompatible theories and hypotheses. It is for that reason that Popper hastens to add that, "although I hold that more often than not we fail to find the truth, and do not know even when we have found it, I retain the classical idea of absolute or objective truth as a *regulative idea*; that is to say, *as a standard* of which we may fall short."[3]

The ulterior reason for mentioning Popper's view here, without adequate preparation, is to draw attention to the conceptual connection between disjoining pluralism and relativism and advocating constructive programs like Popper's falsifiability program that distinguish between paper claims and claims suitably prepared *for* effective falsifiability or the like. For Popper is, as we have seen, somewhat concerned that his own encouragement of the robust play of irreconcilable theories might lead readers to suppose that he meant thereby to encourage some form of irrationalism or anarchy (relativism, in short).

He hardly meant to do that, of course. And so, he expresses his sympathy for abandoning the principle of excluded middle at a *first* stage of debate, only to reinstate it at a *second* – in accord, that is, with being able to show that a particular truth-claim is rightly a "scientific" claim just in that it is recognizably "falsifiable."

Here we find ourselves facing a substantive matter of the greatest importance. We shall postpone its discussion for the time being. Mentioning it, nevertheless, does help in explaining a very deep-rooted conviction in Western accounts of science, truth, knowledge, logic, rationality – hence, relativism – in virtue of which relativism is treated as akin to irrationalism, skepticism, anarchism, and nihilism. One cannot say that there is no basis at all for reading things this way. But the fact remains that doing so obscures some extremely important and strategic philosophical options that cannot be recovered unless relativism is prised apart from the pejoratively labeled "stands" just identified.

III

What we can at least anticipate is that the defense of relativism is likely to center on what is lost or gained in abandoning excluded middle and, in particular, in abandoning excluded middle at a "first" or "second" stage of processing claims (in a sense rather like the one Popper has in mind in urging falsifiability). For example, it explains Popper's enormous respect for the work of the Dutch mathematician and mathematical intuitionist, L. E. J. Brouwer. As Popper himself puts the point (of Brouwer's position):

> Thus to assert a theorem was to assert the existence of a proof for it, and to deny it was to assert the existence of a refutation; that is, a proof of its absurdity. This leads immediately to Brouwer's rejection of the law of excluded middle, to his rejection of indirect proofs, and to the demand that existence can be proved only by the actual construction – the making visible as it were – of the mathematical object in question.[4]

The intuitionistic thesis that Popper favors (to this extent) is just that to claim in a scientifically serious sense that this or that is true *is*, effectively, to claim that its truth or falsity can be decided in some finitely manageable way. That was actually the point of Popper's well-known charge that Freudian psychoanalysis and Marxian socioeconomics are simply not sciences at all.[5] For our own purposes, we must not allow ourselves to be drawn in more deeply than we need into the merits of Popper's own program of falsifiability or of progress in science, by way of having raised the issue about excluded middle. The issue of exluded middle bears in an absolutely essential way on the logic of relativism: but Popper's falsifiability program is simply one option regarding the relationship between scientific claims and the principle of excluded middle; and excluded middle can (as we shall see) be championed in a variety of ways. Just how limited Popper's own use of excluded middle is meant to be may be judged by his advocacy of Alfred Tarski's theory of truth; for Popper clearly means to reconcile a relaxation of excluded middle, favoring some form of the decidability (or falsifiability) condition, together with a strict adherence immediately thereafter to the regulative function of truth (as remarked earlier).[6] We shall return shortly to the generic strategy that Popper's maneuver illustrates.

IV

We may perhaps collect a few more specimen views, therefore, before we attempt a full analysis of what the prospects are of defending some form of relativism.

A very famous view, possibly the best-known in the entire literature concerning relativism – that is, the point of Aristotle's attack, in *Metaphysics*, on Protagoras' reported version of relativism – is very much alive in our own day. It is clearly connected with the advocacy of "the classical idea of absolute or objective truth" that we observed Popper to have championed in the same context in which he favored some relaxation of the principle of excluded middle. The view we now need to illustrate makes no such concession. The two views may be packaged together, in spite of appearances, simply because the one we now mean to illustrate refuses to abandon excluded middle at the "first" stage of entertaining a would-be rational or scientific claim, whereas Popper's position (somewhat favoring the intuitionist) refuses to abandon excluded middle at the "second" stage (that is, once some form of assessing the decidability of a would-be claim has been itself decided). The informality of sorting instances of these "first" and "second" stages need not adversely affect our issue at this preliminary point in the argument.

At any rate, in a perfectly standard way, a knowledgeable contemporary philosopher of science, William Newton-Smith, has refurbished Aristotle's attack on Protagoras (without reference to either) in a fashionably current idiom:

> The central relativist idea [he says] is that what is true for one tribe, social group or age might not be true for another tribe, social group or age. If that were so, it would appear to license one to talk about the different tribes, social groups or ages as inhabiting different world[s], as relativists have been notoriously prone to do. Schematically expressed the relativist thesis is: Something, s, is true for ψ and s is false for ϕ. But what is that "something"? The trick is to find some one thing the truth of which can vary giving us an interesting version of relativism without lapsing into incoherence. Clearly it is just boring to take the something as a sentence.... Alternatively one might say in the interest of avoiding triviality that it is propositions and not sentences that vary in truth-value. But this is to take the short road to incoherence. For propositions are individuated in terms of truth-conditions. It is just incoherent to suppose that the same proposition could be true in ψ and false in ϕ.... It is a necessary (but not sufficient) condition of two sentences having the same meaning that they have the same truth-conditions.... If we cannot be relativists about truth could we none the less be relativists about reason? ... it is hard to see how there could be variation in patterns of valid reasoning if there cannot be variation in truth ... if truth cannot vary, neither can deductive logic.[7]

This is a pleasantly straightforward pronouncement. It is particularly useful to cite, because it is not tempted in the least by any doubts about excluded middle, because it takes the manly no-nonsense view of reason and science, because it hints rather broadly at the weakness of those who are attracted to some form of the "different worlds" concession, and because it squarely exposes the essential *incoherence* of what is "central" to relativism. Nothing could be neater. It fleshes out at least the plausible line of reasoning according to which Popper's easy linkage of "irrationalism, skepticism, or relativism" would be found compelling.

V

In fact, Newton-Smith explicitly brings his argument to bear on Thomas Kuhn's well-known worries about the continuity of scientific progress across apparently discontinuous shifts from one so-called paradigm to another, all the while the scientists who work with one or another paradigm are said to inhabit "different worlds."[8] In a rather genial way, Newton-Smith relieves Kuhn of the explicit charge of incoherence, in view of Kuhn's equally genial backsliding from the strong incommensurability of discontinuous paradigm shifts – that is, in the direction of treating the divergence of scientific theories as a relatively superficial *sociological* rather than a deep *logical* thesis about the supposed realism and progress of science.

It is in this sense that Newton-Smith characterizes Kuhn as "a temperate non-rationalist" (meaning, by that, that Kuhn is not altogether consistent about the sort of strictures we have just seen Newton-Smith impose on what would be a coherent use of sentences, meanings, propositions, and reasoning).[9] So Kuhn comes dangerously close to being Newton-Smith's sort of relativist, and indeed is more than tempted by relativism's theme, although he himself counters its effect (to Newton-Smith's relief) by insisting on certain (in fact, five) "characteristics of a good scientific theory" that hold across *all* paradigm shift, though they cannot be applied "algorithmically" and cannot be made precise across scientific "worlds."[10] The five values include "accuracy, consistency, scope, simplicity, and fruitfulness" and are said to be "all standard criteria for evaluating the adequacy of a theory"[11] – that is, *standard* in a way that is (unaccountably) unaffected by the vagaries of historical science and historicized human life.

VI

We shall return to the issue Kuhn's seemingly stronger thesis raises. But for the moment, we are interested only in the fact that Newton-Smith (and Kuhn somewhat, by way of his obvious philosophical uneasiness) adheres to a very strong thesis in favor of giving no quarter to any retreat from something like Popper's insistence on the "regulative" function of the notion of "absolute or objective" truth. Kuhn himself is clearly unhappy about the possible charge of incoherence affecting his incipient relativism: he pulls back in a way that blunts the force of his original thesis, without yet supplying an adequate account of his altered view (if, that is, it is to count as a responsible relativism).[12] And Newton-Smith goes on to exhibit the apparent incoherence of – the effectiveness of a *reductio ad absurdum* argument against – Paul Feyerabend's cognate conception. For, on Newton-Smith's view,

Feyerabend (but not quite Kuhn) treats all philosophy as ideological in the sense that no one can "provide a reason for believing his philosophical case which is a reason for anyone no matter what his ideological perspective"; and yet, also on Newton-Smith's view, Feyerabend does appear to concede (inconsistently) that "inconsistency provides an objective (i.e. non-ideologically based) reason for rejecting an ideology, even if a philosophical position is an ideological position."[13]

Certainly, the appeal to the ineliminability of consistency *is* an important part of the more than plausible force of Popper's original claim. We shall have to contend with it in defending any form of relativism. Nevertheless, it is true as well that Feyerabend *correctly* observes that "contradictions in science are not handled according to the naive rules of formal logic [or not handled according to those rules alone] – which is a criticism of logic, not of science."[14] He means, of course, that relevance constraints and scientific fruitfulness (in a sense not altogether different from Kuhn's and not altogether captured by *any* formal rule) encourage a manageable accommodation of apparent or provisional contradiction. Here, we begin to see possibilities – logical possibilities – for avoiding the full force of Newton-Smith's (and Popper's) "absolute" requirements.

In fact, Feyerabend does favor a measure of relativized or ideology-relative "coherence" or "rational acceptability." Newton-Smith acknowledges the point and concedes, for his own part, a certain sympathy for it (though he formulates his view quite differently from Feyerabend's). He does say, for instance, speaking as a "rationalist" about science (adhering to some general principles or methodology for ranging over the whole of science relative to evidence),[15] that, though in a sense Feyerabend is right, "No rationalist need be committed to (and few have taken it that they are) a conception of method as a system of binding, unchanging, exceptionless algorithmic rules."[16] This is an extraordinary – actually, an ineluctable – admission, given the energy that has been spent in contesting the so-called anarchist version of relativism that Feyerabend frankly espouses, just the one, in fact, that champions the motto that so worried Novak, "anything goes." Presumably, its import cannot be confined to that of a merely benign form of cultural relativity.

For the moment, we may acknowledge that the *formal* rule of consistency may have no exceptions; but then, it is only interesting when *applied* under relevance constraints, under what would otherwise be exceptions – for instance, bearing on the ongoing history of science itself. *There*, the formal rule may be overridden or provisionally muted; or else, particular contradictions may indeed be acceptable, but only when circumscribed by relevance constraints of a suitable sort. In either case, a stalemate must be admitted, apart from rhetorical extravagances on both sides. "Absolute or objective truth" will no longer seem as unbreachable as it was originally presented as being. This is not to say that the defense of relativism depends essentially, primarily, or exclusively on a tolerance for contradiction or inconsistency *tout court*. But relativists may, if they wish (so may nonrelativists), provisionally accommodate inconsistency in restricted contexts, without falling at once into incoherence or irrationality; and the pretense that the defense of relativism cannot do that is now seen to be just that, a pretense. Newton-Smith gives up what he seems to regard as inviolable, and Feyerabend nowhere favors sheer or total incoherence, particularly not where he is prepared to tolerate a measure of inconsistency. Since, as already remarked, Newton-Smith's argument amounts to a recovery of Aristotle's argument against Protagoras, we shall have occasion to return to the matter when we attempt to redeem Protagoras. In any event, the piecemeal accommodation of inconsistencies is not a distinctly relativist maneuver.

Both Newton-Smith and Popper probably mean, here, to join two rather different considerations. On the one hand, they mean to hold a very firm line on an inviolable bivalent logic under the constraint of an "absolute" regulative ideal; on the other, as reasonable men, they recognize the profound informality, divergence, and dialectical nature of fruitful scientific discovery, and would not wish to discourage it. Of course, it is entirely possible to combine them in a single program; but, in doing so, it is not in the least necessary to construe the second limb as affecting *any* alethic restriction originally belonging to the first. Perhaps, then, Newton-Smith (as distinct from Popper) has not represented his own view entirely perspicuously (through no fault of his own). For his seeming tolerance of an element of what, in Feyerabend, would be rightly regarded as "anarchist," is, in Newton-Smith, merely a practical accommodation regarding scientific discovery, not an adjustment affecting the formal features of truth itself. The matter is of some importance because many critics of Feyerabend have supposed that he must be committed to some form of relationalism – by way of a strong cultural relativism – whereas the truth is that he need not be so committed at all (as the recovery of Newton-Smith's concession makes clear). If this were not conceded, then, for that very reason, Newton-Smith (and the other strong critics of relativism) would be guilty of their own charge. Hence, we too must be careful to distinguish Newton-Smith's alethic thesis and his practical advice on the provisional management of truth-claims.

VII

Let us add a final specimen for our initial collection. There are bound to be others of the same sort as our discussion widens, but we need to have before us a candid sense of the kind of prejudice and strong feeling that the mention of relativism seems to uncover. It looks very much as if the advocacy of relativism is taken to threaten certain "eternal verities," the universal truths of mankind, "absolute and objective truth" (as Popper seems to believe), possibly the very underpinnings of a humane world. This is, in fact, very much the view popularly and widely circulated by Richard Bernstein, although Bernstein's attitude regarding the "eternal verities" is hardly simple or straightforward.

The title of the recent book in which Bernstein presents his attack on relativism makes this quite clear: *Beyond Objectivism and Relativism*. We may understand by that title that Bernstein intends to offer a third way between the thesis of the "absolute and objective truth" we have provisionally reviewed through Popper, Kuhn, and Newton-Smith and the disreputable versions of what we have broadly called relativism that (we may take it) the partisans of Truth would have us unconditionally repudiate.

Up to this point it may have seemed that there was only a disjunctive option before us; although, as we have already noticed, Newton-Smith clearly yields in the direction of a no man's land that he shares (inexplicitly) with the likes of Feyerabend and Kuhn at least. Now, Bernstein comes forward to advise us that there is indeed a third option, one that, though it yields against the stiff-backed presumption of "objectivism," also does not (for that reason alone) need to yield in the direction of the sort of relativism the older objectivism (Popper's "absolute and objective truth," functioning as a "regulative" principle, say) had correctly exposed. Between Novak and Bernstein, then, we begin to get a fair sense of the philosophical horror that relativism inspires.

Bernstein never wavers from the view that relativism is incoherent. He sees relativism, however, as initially excusable at least as a reaction (however intemperate) against an overweening – may we say "sinful"? – presumption regarding the finality or certitude or absoluteness or unconditionality of what may be claimed in the name of science or knowledge in general. For example, he says: "Relativism ultimately makes sense (and gains its plausibility) as the dialectical antithesis to objectivism. If we see through objectivism, if we expose what is wrong with this way of thinking, then we are at the same time questioning the very intelligibility of relativism."[17]

"Questioning the very intelligibility of relativism!" Bernstein means what he says, of course. The conceptual puzzle that he wishes to resolve rests with that habit of mind, that "underlying belief," that holds "that in the final analysis the only viable alternatives open to us are *either* some form of objectivism, foundationalism, ultimate grounding of knowledge, science, philosophy, and language *or* that we are ineluctably led to relativism, skepticism, historicism, and nihilism."[18] Elsewhere, Bernstein makes it clear that *he* would include – as versions *of* relativism – irrationalism and anarchism as well, except that he finds the line of demarcation between Kuhn and Feyerabend not quite as sharp as Newton-Smith does and except that he is a little more favorably disposed to Feyerabend.[19]

Be that as it may, it is plain enough that Bernstein redeems the use of Popper's epithets in a context that attempts to reserve a middle ground between the very strong so-called "rationalist" view of science (that Newton-Smith favors) and the entirely indefensible option that relativism seems to afford. Bernstein's rationale, however, has it that relativism is always "not only the dialectical antithesis of objectivism, it is itself parasitic upon objectivism."[20] In this, Bernstein explicitly follows the view of Hans-Georg Gadamer, who insists, in an entirely reasonable way, that human reason can never overcome its historical setting or horizon. In this sense, it can never achieve what *objectivism* requires (for instance, in accord with Popper's or Newton-Smith's arguments). The relativist sees this and (on Bernstein's view) inappropriately draws the altogether negative conclusion that the dire epithets already collected are meant to identify and repudiate.[21] The point is that the contemporary champion of objectivity sees that historicizing science and human reason precludes the simple confidence of the "objectivist." In this, Bernstein means to reconcile Kuhn and Gadamer.

VIII

It is not necessary, we may suppose, that the relativist consciously respond to some form of what Bernstein identifies as "objectivism." He is said to be reacting nevertheless, because, otherwise, *we* are left with a stand that (on Bernstein's view) is patently "unintelligible" or worse. It *is* unintelligible or of doubtful intelligibility or worse. But its initial plausibility – all that it ever has – is apparently exhausted by its reacting (fairly enough) against the presumptions of objectivism. The trouble is that it goes too far.

Now there is clearly something missing here. Bernstein never actually offers a distinctive charge (like Newton-Smith's, for instance) to the effect that the relativist simply commits himself to the old, self-contradictory, self-defeating position of Protagoras. Bernstein has no doubt that protagoreanism is untenable. But his own characteristic diagnosis is not that the relativist is *stupid* (as, on Newton-Smith's account, he must be). He finds, rather, that the relativist is excessively *discouraged, depressed,* or *perverse,* in turning to what in effect is a self-destructive stand, a stand that gives up all pretense of reason, rationale, rigor, objectivity, justification, method or the like; or else (he finds) the relativist seeks to *confine* any and all such considerations entirely *within* the segregating boundaries of different social practices, within the boundaries of "different worlds." Finding those to be the relativist's options (not the supposed stupidity) apparently justifies Bernstein's severe condemnation: that relativism just is skepticism, nihilism, and the rest.

Of course, if we were to agree with Bernstein's characterization, there would be nothing for it but to label whatever we thought we could recover *of* a would-be relativism as being something other than such a relativism. That, however, is a terminological extravagance we need hardly be bound by. We may, therefore, admit something of Bernstein's reading of the history of philosophy without refusing to defend the position he scants.

There is, in fact, in Bernstein's more recent criticism of Richard Rorty's thesis – what, in effect, on Bernstein's view, *is* a throwback to the form of relativism he opposes – a straightforward clue as to what he really objects to:

There is [he says] something askew in Rorty's emphasis. Throughout he argues as if we were confronted with two alternatives: *Either* all justification, whether in matters of knowledge or morals, appeals to social practices or to illusory foundations....
To tell us, as Rorty does over and over again, that "to say the True and Right are matters of social practice" or that "justification is a matter of social practice" or that "objectivity should be seen as conformity to norms of justification we find about us" will not do. We want to know how we are to understand "social practices," how they are generated, sustained, and pass away."

What this means is, first, that Rorty *is* a relativist of the sort Bernstein wishes to oppose; and secondly, that, because of that, Rorty may be said to fall back to the dichotomous option (or some ambiguous variation of it) that Bernstein wishes to replace by introducing his own third option, an option that he (Bernstein) thinks he shares with Kuhn, with

Gadamer, with Jürgen Habermas, with Hannah Arendt, and to some extent with such figures as Popper, Alasdair MacIntyre, and Charles Taylor.

IX

The ultimate charge that Bernstein now brings against the relativist is the modern alternative, *incommensurabilism*, viewed more or less as the up-to-date replacement of the ancient doctrine, *protagoreanism* (that Aristotle unmasks). We may leave the full analysis of these doctrines for a later occasion. But it becomes increasingly clear that what, on Bernstein's view, accounts for the doubtful intelligibility of relativism is its advocacy of a certain extreme form of incommensurability. For instance, in reviewing Kuhn's position in the favorable way he does, Bernstein observes:

> if we are to sort out what is and what is not problematic in the incommensurability of paradigm theories, we must carefully distinguish among *incompatibility*, *incommensurability*, and *incomparability*. Frequently these three notions have been treated as synonyms by Kuhn's critics, and even by his defenders. For example, Kuhn's (and Feyerabend's) remarks about incommensurability have been taken to mean that we cannot *compare* rival paradigms or theories. But such a claim, I will argue, is not only mistaken but perverse.[23]

It is true that *some* theorists have subscribed to the view Bernstein attacks as perverse. But surely there are many fewer than he supposes. For example, he apparently believes (as many others have – also quite wrongly) that Peter Winch was committed to such a view, in his *The Idea of a Social Science*. Winch *was* straining to defend a certain sort of relativism – a sort of relativism that *did* take seriously the threat of conceptual incommensurabilities – but it is surely clear from the text itself that Winch was *always* occupied with the conditions under which we *do* understand an alien society (the Azande, for instance). We may object to the inadequacy of Winch's defense; but, contrary to what Bernstein suggests, it is extremely difficult to find a mainstream relativist who denies cross-cultural, cross-paradigmatic, cross-linguistic, cross-theoretical intelligibility or comparability.[24] *It is also difficult to show that the defense of incommensurability is equivalent to the denial of cross-cultural comparability.*

In any case, that charge is certainly *part* of what Bernstein understands by the "nihilism" of the relativistic stance. The other part seems
to have been supplied most perspicuously by Rorty, in *Philosophy and
the Mirror of Nature*, in holding (*on* Bernstein's account, doubtfully)
that relativism (or at least something very much akin to relativism) is
committed, by cultural incommensurability, to confining the "justification" or legitimation of our practices (cognitive or ethical) to their bare
conformity with our particular, our segregated "social practices," whatever they happen to be and without regard to the practices of any other
society. That is, Bernstein's charge – nihilism or skepticism – rests on
the complaint that our social practices do not (when construed relativistically) permit us to examine *their* justification or legitimation as part of
the unified effort to find *those objective grounds that all mankind could
be expected to support*. So, by a somewhat circuitous route, Bernstein's
objection to relativism converges rather nicely with what we have
already seen to be common ground as between Popper, Kuhn, and
Newton-Smith. Newton-Smith favors the charge that the relativist is
incoherent (stupid); Bernstein favors the charge that he is a nihilist or a
skeptic (discouraged and unimaginative). But they do effectively agree
(not altogether explicitly) on *what*, logically, a relativist must claim.
And, in that, they are simply shortsighted.

X

The story, then, is this. Bernstein rejects "objectivism," the presumption
of "some permanent, ahistorical matrix or framework to which we can
ultimately appeal in determining the nature of rationality, knowledge,
truth, reality, goodness, or rightness." But he also rejects the fear the
objectivist voices, namely, that, if we cannot have that assurance, then
"we cannot avoid skepticism."[25] The relativist agrees with the objectivist
but draws the unintelligible and perverse conclusion that, therefore, we
have no basis for claiming knowledge or ethical direction at all, or
that we are at best confined to the mere appearance of things within our
own cultural ethos. There is, *for the relativist*, no third way between the
two. That's the trouble, and that's the source of anarchism, nihilism,
skepticism, and the rest.

Let it be said, by way of a promissory note, that Bernstein does not
supply a workable account of what that third way must be like. He only
announces *that there must be one*. For our own purposes, it is enough
to have before us the principal hopes and fears surrounding the question of relativism. Beyond all that, there is clearly supposed to be some

very deep conviction about an objective order that every human society may (and must) appeal to, relative to which relativism may be safely repudiated.

The trouble is that wherever objecti*vity* is secured by "objecti*vist*" means, the contemporary champion of objectivity is persuaded the price is much too high and neither necessary nor worth paying; and wherever the false option is rejected but meant to be replaced, we find ourselves left with little more than a lively but completely unsecured hope. Furthermore, wherever universal constraints of reason are said to be advanced against relativism – for instance, regarding consistency and coherence – they simply crumble: they invariably yield in the direction of context, relevance, application, exception, interpretation. Among those prominently said to oppose all such constraints utterly and wantonly (anarchists and relativists, say), we are likely to find only a handful of undistinguished souls who insist on examining piecemeal the application of any would-be universal rules and accommodating, wherever plausible, seeming violations of those same rules.

So we have the empty charge before us, but not its argument, and not, of course, its refutation.

Notes

1 Michael Novak, *The Spirit of Democratic Capitalism* (New York: Simon and Schuster, 1982), p. 63.

2 Karl R. Popper, *Realism and the Aim of Science* (from *The Postscript to the Logic of Scientific Discovery*), ed. W. W. Bartley, III (Totowa, NJ: Rowman and Littlefield, 1983), p. 18.

3 Ibid., p. 26. Popper goes on to explain that "The change [his account has] made is not with respect to the idea of truth but with respect to any claims to *know* the truth; that is to say, to have at our disposal arguments or reasons which suffice or even very nearly suffice, to establish the truth of any theory in question" (p. 26). This distinction he thinks has been helpfully supplied by W. W. Bartley, III, "Rationality versus the Theory of Rationality," in Mario Bunge (ed.), *The Critical Approach to Science and Philosophy* (New York: Free Press, 1964). This distinction is essential to Popper's doctrine of verisimilitude (cf. particularly p. 20), which Popper himself has had increasing misgivings about and which is suspiciously open to the charge of incoherence. But that is not our concern here.

4 Karl R. Popper, "Epistemology without a Knowing Subject," in *Objective Knowledge: An Evolutionary Approach* (Oxford: Clarendon Press, 1972), pp. 133–4.

5 See Karl R. Popper, "Reply to My Critics," in Paul Arthur Schilpp (ed.), *The Philosophy of Karl Popper*, book 2 (La Salle, Ill.: Open Court, 1974).

6   See Karl R. Popper, "Philosophical Comments on Tarski's Theory of Truth," in *Objective Knowledge*, pp. 319–40.

7   W. Newton-Smith, "Relativism and the Possibility of Interpretation," in Martin Hollis and Steven Lukes (eds.), *Rationality and Relativism* (Cambridge: MIT Press, 1982), pp. 107–8. Essentially the same position is more briefly sketched in W. H. Newton-Smith, *The Rationality of Science* (London: Routledge and Kegan Paul, 1981), chapter 2. In some recent lectures (1989) at Swarthmore College, Swarthmore, Pennylvania, Newton-Smith clearly indicated his intention of departing from the severe terms of *The Rationality of Science*; but he did not appear to have relented regarding relativism.

8   See Newton-Smith, *The Rationality of Science*, chapter 5; also, chapter 6, which is much less hospitable about the related views of Paul Feyerabend. See also, T. S. Kuhn, *The Structure of Scientific Revolutions*, 2nd ed. enl. (Chicago: University of Chicago Press, 1962), p. 17.

9   *The Rationality of Science*, p. 121.

10 Thomas S. Kuhn, "Objectivity, Value Judgment, and Theory Choice," in *The Essential Tension: Selected Studies in Scientific Tradition and Change* (Chicago: University of Chicago Press, 1977), pp. 321–2.

11 Ibid.

12 See, for instance, ibid., preface, particularly pp. xxii–xxiii. In his as yet unpublished Shearman Memorial Lectures, delivered at University College London (November 1987) and provisionally titled "The Presence of Past Science," Kuhn effectively softens his radical view even further by presenting the issue in terms of the continuities and discontinuities of historical narrative. All the essential issues – of incommensurability, untranslatability, reference, different worlds – are permitted to arise only in a way internal to that narrative and without fully implicating the seemingly strong relativism of the original *Structure of Scientific Revolutions*.

13 Newton-Smith, *The Rationality of Science*, p. 127, in the context of the whole of chapter 6.

14 Paul Feyerabend, *Science in a Free Society* (London: NLB, 1978), p. 211. Cf. the rest of chapter 5.

15 Newton-Smith, *The Rationality of Science*, p. 4.

16 Ibid., p. 146. See also, Paul Feyerabend, *Against Method* (London: Verso, 1975), pp. 284–5.

17 Richard J. Bernstein, *Beyond Objectivism and Relativism; Science, Hermeneutics, and Praxis* (Philadelphia: University of Pennsylvania Press, 1983), pp. 166–7.

18 Ibid., pp. 2–3.

19 Ibid., Part Two.

20 Ibid., p. 37.

21 See Hans-Georg Gadamer, "The Problem of Historical Consciousness," trans. Jeff L. Close, in Paul Rabinow and William M. Sullivan (eds), *Interpretive Social Science; A Reader* (Berkeley: University of California Press, 1979).

22   Richard J. Bernstein, "Philosophy in the Conversation of Mankind,"
     Review of Metaphysics; reprinted in Robert Hollinger (ed.), *Hermeneutics
     and Praxis* (Notre Dame: Notre Dame University Press, 1985), pp. 82–3.
     Bernstein is criticizing Richard Rorty, *Philosophy and the Mirror of
     Nature* (Princeton: Princeton University Press, 1979).
23   Bernstein, *Beyond Objectivism and Relativism*, p. 82.
24   Cf. Bernstein, ibid., pp. 24–30. See, also, Peter Winch, *The Idea of a Social
     Science* (London: Routledge and Kegan Paul, 1958).
25   *Beyond Objectivism and Relativism*, p. 8.

2

Bipolar Truth-values

I

We have been collecting gossip, of course, important perhaps, but gossip none the less. What we need now is a fresh beginning, a point of logic buried in the deep prejudice of logicians.

There is a marvellous confession worn on the sleeve of an excellent recent discussion of propositions that should serve us well. "*A proposition*," Robert Stalnaker offers, "*is a function from possible worlds into truth-values*." Stalnaker means to defend this thesis in the account that follows, but he stops to say something about truth-values themselves:

> There are just two truth-values [he says] – true and false. What are they: mysterious Fregean objects, properties, relations of correspondence and noncorrespondence? The answer is that it does not matter what they are: there is nothing essential to them except that there are exactly two of them. We could formulate the definition of proposition in a way that did not mention truth-values at all without changing its essential character: a proposition may be thought of as a rule for selecting a subset from a set of possible worlds. The role of the values *true* and *false* is simply to distinguish the possible worlds that are members of the selected subset from those that are not. But is there not more to truth than this? Should not an adequate theory of truth include some explanation of why curious people seek it, honest speakers aim at it, and good arguments preserve it? Shouldn't it help us to understand and solve metaphysical problems, such as disputes between realists and idealists? Somewhere in a theory of propositions and propositional attitudes such explanations must be given, but according to the account to be developed here, these questions are concerned less

with truth itself than with belief, assertion, and argument, and with the relation between the actual world and other possible worlds.[1]

Why should this be so? Why should there be only two truth-values? Suppose there were a third: *Indeterminate*, say, not merely undecided or undecided for insufficient evidence? Would there be some mistake or blunder or contradiction or even falsity in so supposing? Well, you might answer that the world's not like that, that everything is crisply what it is and not another thing. But if you did, you would, however reasonably, have violated what Stalnaker says about his rule for truth-values. You would have consulted the world in some sense, in order to decide how many values were needed, or how many values we needed for this or that purpose. Stalnaker may have given us his rule for a private game; but there is no reason at all why, considering what we might wish to say about the actual world – or possible worlds, for that matter – there need be only two truth-values. In fact, *if* we follow Stalnaker in favoring belief rather than truth, it becomes more rather than less plausible that we may need to admit some scheme of many-valued truth-values.

The truth is that Stalnaker's requirement answers to his purpose. He does not intend to feature "disputes between realists and idealists," for instance, or the "relation between the actual world and other possible worlds," or "belief, assertion, and argument"; but he does mean to feature a certain way "of solving the problem of intentionality – the problem of explaining the nature of intentional or representational mental states."[2]

It may be that his strategy works. The important thing is that it is a selected, a limited device meant to serve a limited purpose. It's not the case – and Stalnaker nowhere attempts to mislead us that it is – that we are unconditionally bound to acknowledge that "There are just two truth-values – true and false." That is, it's not the case that we are bound to concede that there are just two truth-values, *no matter what our interest in the world may be*.

Another way of putting the same point is simply to admit that it is open to us to be governed in an exceptionless way by the principle of excluded middle, or to restrict its range of use, or to waive its application in certain sectors of inquiry or discourse, without violating any rule of reason, without contradicting ourselves in so doing, without producing nonsense or incoherence merely in so doing. It comes as a breath of fresh air to realize that excluded middle is not an inviolable rule of any kind, regardless of whatever we may suppose needs to be said about consistency and noncontradiction. Admitting that much, we cannot help reminding ourselves of a number of the quarrels we touched on in the preceding chapter. For there we noticed that a good many of the differences among such theorists as Popper, Kuhn, Newton-Smith, and Feyerabend depended on the fortunes of the principle of excluded middle. The essential trick is this: decisions about the logic of any inquiry are not unconditionally *a priori* to that inquiry, totally unaffected by what we may find to be the structure of a given domain. They are instead internal to and part of the cognitively pertinent characterization of the domain itself. At any rate, such a policy is internally coherent and viable. It can be disallowed at the start only by pure fiat – which effectively, of course, amounts to precluding any inning for relativism at all.

II

Consider, now, that, in a complex account of the ontology of artworks, but going very far beyond the world of art itself – in fact, going on to "everything" – Nicholas Wolterstorff offers the following principle, which he calls "ontological" and which he says "seems to me to be true":

> *Principle of Exemplification*: Everything x is such that for every property P and every time t, x has P at t only if x exists at t.[3]

Wolterstorff has clearly gone very far beyond Stalnaker's sort of proposal. He thinks the Principle of Exemplification is true – ontologically. He draws the immediate conclusion that "we cannot refer to what does not exist."[4] Of course, *if* we hold that we *can* refer to what does not exist, then we should hold, correspondingly, that the Principle is false, or simply not wanted; but in so saying, we should not need to say also that reference to what does not exist is something that is "ontologically" possible. We might simply fall back to the sort of guarded proposal Stalnaker makes.

Wolterstorff will have none of this, however. He goes on almost at once to advance another principle:

> *Principle of Completeness*: For everything x and every property P, x either has P or lacks P.

"This [again, he says,] seems to me a true principle, and accordingly one that we ought to respect in our construction of theories."[5] Wolterstorff does not mention anything like Popper's concession to Brouwer's intuitionism, to the possibility that a proposition or an assertion might be well-formed in a formal sense without being known or shown or believed to be decidable in some finitely manageable way. Recalling what we suggested earlier on regarding this matter, we can now say that Wolterstorff insists on adhering to the principle of excluded middle in a very strong exceptionless way, in a way that is explicitly ontological, in a way independent of determining the truth-values of what is said or asserted, in a way that applies at the "first" stage of admitting all well-formed truth-bearing entities (propositions, say) quite apart from our (irrelevantly or intrusively) admitting them to be such – in short, in a way that applies to whatever God might timelessly entertain about reality. (We should perhaps recall the old archic melody.)

Thus read, it is of course Wolterstorff who tells us (in effect) what is true of God's mind, of what God would say of all that is possible or real. For "x" and "P" clearly stand for any of an indefinitely extended set of determinate entities and properties; and yet Wolterstorff does not bring himself to explain how it is that we can be certain that the Principle of Completeness applies to all of that. Surely we might balk, as the intuitionists do; again, we might suppose (being perverse) that reality harbors some *indeterminate* things such that Completeness is just false or unhelpful. Why not? The decision really rests with the sort of consideration Stalnaker had indicated was (for him) of secondary importance.

If, for instance, Bernstein was right to reject what he calls objectivism, then *anything* like Wolterstorff's optimism would be more than premature – it would be inadmissible. We should never be able to combine Exemplification and Completeness – that is, we should never be able to apply Completeness *to* the actual world – with Wolterstorff's confidence. The preformation of our conceptual bias, the intransparency of the world, the contingency of our historicized sense of cognitive puzzles would never (on Bernstein's view) allow it. We should never be able to apply the two at what we informally have termed the "first" stage of reviewing the scope of the principle of excluded middle. We might demur for intuitionistic reasons, or we might demur for reasons of a looser, more informal sort, for instance, because of incommensurabilist considerations of the kind Kuhn and Feyerabend have put forward. There may be other reasons as well. There is no way of telling in advance what good reasons may persuade us to entertain applying excluded middle only at some postponed "second" stage of reflecting on what appear to be reasonably well-formed propositions. But it would then obtain only distributively, only on the strength of sufficient evidence, only regarding selected beliefs, and never with the antecedent assurance that it must obtain everywhere.

III

In the pertinent literature, speculation of the "first" stage sort (Wolterstorff's for instance, even Stalnaker's in an attenuated sense) is said, usually, to be "realist" talk; and speculation of the "second" stage sort (Popper's, say, or Brouwer's, even Kuhn's implicitly or Bernstein's, though the last two do not address the matter explicitly) is said to be "anti-realist" (or "idealist") talk. The distinction, "anti-realist," which is obviously idiosyncratic and at times misleading, is due to the coinage of Michael Dummett.[6] It is or could be misleading, because (on Dummett's view), the anti-realist is not really opposed to realism (in a more natural sense), not really opposed to taking it that restricting excluded middle to a range of finitely decidable statements *is* still intended to serve our understanding *of* what is true about the real world.[7]

Dummett develops his point in the context of the metaphysics of mathematics:

> If one believes, with the platonists, that we have conferred on our mathematical statements meanings such as to render them all determinately either true or false independently of our knowledge, then one will find it natural to adopt the picture of a mathematical reality existing, fully determinate, independently of us. If, on the other hand, one believes, with the intuitionists, that the content of a mathematical statement resides entirely in our ability to recognize what constitutes a proof of it and a disproof, so that, when we lack an effective means of arriving at a proof or a disproof, we have no right to declare it either true or false, one will prefer a picture according to which mathematical reality is constructed by us, or, at least, comes into existence only as we become aware of it. But, on this understanding of the matter, these are only pictures, however irresistible.[8]

The concession has its obvious charm and a certain plausibility. But it is a concession controlled (not at all unreasonably) by an intuitionistic bent. It is notorious, it must be said, that when Dummett extends his bias to the empirical sciences and practical life, he offers no reason at all for thinking that the constructivist perspective of the mathematical intuitionist will function as well to ensure the adequacy of those famous bipolar values, True and False. The point is not merely one *of* their adequacy in this or that sector of the world. It is a question rather of *deciding* the adequacy of the intuitionistic proposal *with regard to* this or that particular sector of the world. That is, the very question of decidability, the question the intuitionist raises against the "realist" (Wolterstorff, say), comes back to haunt the intuitionistically minded theorist who has so hastily generalized that constructive conditions for deciding truth invariably then ensure *the adequacy of those two values, True and False, for the domain in question.* There is an obvious lacuna in the argument.

There is no difference in this respect between Stalnaker's and Dummett's conviction: the first thinks the matter can be resolved without at all attending to what the world requires or would reasonably support; the other thinks that there are only two values all right, but they can be invoked only (and always) after answering the decidability question for distributed claims.

As it happens, Dummett's own efforts at illustrating decidability among empirical questions are plainly inadequate. For example, he never tells us – he cannot, no one can – what the precise time factor is for indexing decidability with regard to given empirical matters. Does the speed of light, say, have a truth-value? Could one have (in principle) truly or falsely said, at the time Clerk Maxwell first puzzled over the matter, that light travelled at this or that particular velocity? Say: by merely guessing? Maxwell thought the question undecidable in real-time terms, and hence, that the velocity of the ether was also undecidable. But shortly thereafter Michelson invented a procedure for observing a signal of light on the earth by which to study its motion, and he did indeed calculate its velocity. Now, did light *have* a determinate velocity at the very moment Maxwell thought the question undecidable? It seems difficult to deny that it did, or at least it seems impossible to deny that it did on intuitionistic grounds alone.

What, after all, is the rule regarding decidability that fixes the interval in which *that* question can itself be decided? To blur the intended contrast is to retreat from the contest between the "realist" and the "anti-realist" (or "idealist"), between the "first" stage and the "second" stage theorist regarding the use of the principle of excluded middle. The intuitionist has a clear advantage over the unthinking realist; but the realist has a corresponding advantage over the unthinking intuitionist. And *we* may claim an advantage over both, merely by insinuating the possibility that, with respect to the views of both the realist and the (intuitionistic) anti-realist, it may well be that, *in this or that sector of the world, the bipolar pair, True and False, may not be adequate at all for what we need.*

IV

There is no inviolable logical objection against the piecemeal waiving of excluded middle, just as there is no objection to postponing the use of excluded middle from the "first" stage introduction of seemingly well-formed claims to the "second" stage review of given claims in accord with the constraint of decidability.

Did Sherlock Holmes, for example, have a mole on his back? Conan Doyle's stories do not *say*? And they do not say enough to enable us to infer what the truth may be. It's hardly a question of insufficient evidence. There is no further evidence to be supplied. So, *if* we resist Wolterstorff's obviously canny objection to our referring to what does not exist, we are bound to say that the answer to the question is neither true nor false; it is objectively *Indeterminate*. There you have a defense, by illustration at least, not merely of the plausibility of introducing a third truth-value (under constraints of relevance, to be sure) but also of the plausibility of deciding *whether* to introduce a third truth-value on the basis of inspecting the different sectors of the actual world or of possible or imagined worlds, and on the basis of determining what constraints they may be taken to impose on reference and the like. (Of course, the actual world is not an imagined world.)

What needs to be added at once is that we cannot say *a priori* that the actual world (whatever we may suppose that to be) would *never* similarly support the introduction of a third truth-value or of a many-valued scheme of truth-like values. The irony is that Dummett, who, for broadly intuitionistic reasons, takes the most strenuous stand against the simplicity of the "realist," never bothers to ask himself whether, for comparable reasons applied to a different question, there might not be intuitionistic grounds (but perhaps they can no longer be called intuitionistic) for thinking that the empirical or effective decidability of an empirical question (in this or that sector of inquiry) cannot be settled in accord with a bipolar logic.

Dummett asks us to abandon what he calls "the semantic principle" of *bivalence*, namely, that "every statement is true or false" in accord with the would-be "logical law" schematized as "*A* or not *A*." He himself favors construing excluded middle in accord with another would-be law, schematized as "It is not the case that neither A nor not A," but he admits that the first usage has its following.

It is important to observe both that Dummett invokes the "semantic" principle wherever we are confronted with statements and not mere sentences or propositions – which suggests a good part of the justification for his constructivist or intuitionistic conviction. In any case, Dummett wishes to disallow *bivalence* because of the priority of raising questions of decidability with regard to determinate *statements*. Realists like Wolterstorff simply never explain how it is that we are justified in taking it that a seemingly well-formed sentence can be counted on to have (within bipolar options) a determinate truth-value anywhere in God's good world.

Nevertheless, once having decided that a statement is decidable, Dummett hurries on to declare, in accord with a semantic principle he is unwilling to abandon, that *any statement* thereupon addressed *cannot* violate excluded middle. The second semantic principle he calls "the principle of *tertium non datur*," that is, the principle that "no statement is neither true nor false" once decidability is favorably settled.[9] It is certainly possible that Dummett believes that there *is* no way of answering the decidability question except in accord with *tertium non datur*, but he never explains why this is so. We may well wonder whether he does not implicitly share a prejudice with Stalnaker, though with less justification, since Stalnaker (but not he) believes the matter to be settled in a way that does not require any inspection of how the world would support our efforts at decidability.

V

It is almost a joke to say that Dummett is something of a victim of his own anti-realist suspicions: because, after all, on something like those suspicions – possibly not canonically intuitionistic suspicions – the question arises as to whether, once bivalence fails, it must invariably be the case that *tertium non datur* succeeds. "To give up the principle of bivalence," Dummett urges, "does not mean going back on the principle of *tertium non datur*, the principle that, for no statement, can we ever rule out both the possibility of its being true and that of its being false, in other words, the principle that there can be no circumstances in which a statement can be recognized as being, irrevocably, neither true nor false."[10] But we have already seen that the question regarding Sherlock Holmes's mole may well be, "irrevocably," neither true nor false. And, though we have still to make the case, it *may* well be that, with regard *to the actual world*, under conditions of decidability – in fact, under conditions of abandoning a straightforwardly transparent world, determinately "there" in some sense independent of inquiry, and cognizable as such by human investigators (recalling such concessions as Popper's, Kuhn's, Bernstein's) – *tertium non datur* will, for quite contingent reasons, fail.

It may be, in short, that there *is* no determinate sense in which we may suppose that *tertium non datur* is irrevocable. What could that seriously mean? And what could Dummett possibly mean by *saying that*, once he has conceded (as he has) that the realist must give way to the "idealist?"

Two remarks of Dummett's may serve to give us a correct impression of his own view and to secure the one we are now advancing. For one thing, Dummett clearly says: "it is possible to hold that the intuitionist substitution of an account of the *use* of a statement for an account of its truth-conditions as the general form of explanation of meaning should be applied to all realms of discourse without thinking that we create the world; we can abandon realism without falling into subjective idealism."[11] And for another, in responding to his own critics, Dummett concedes that he

> did not suppose that the abstract structure of all these disputes [metaphysical disputes, for instance] would be precisely the same; indeed, I am prepared to assert positively [he says] that no two of them agree exactly in their abstract structure. There was therefore never any presumption that there would be any sound argument establishing, *for all the cases simultaneously*, the correctness of a realist or of an anti-realist view. The only presumption was that a uniform approach to these disparate metaphysical problems would be *fruitful*.[12]

Dummett, however, says these things, having in mind only the question of whether he would have to yield in the direction of bivalence; he does not consider that he may have to give up *tertium non datur* as well. But he opens the way to considering the possibility.

As already remarked, that last concession would be an essential one for the defensibility of any genuinely interesting form of relativism. But we must proceed slowly here.

We are considering a precondition for an important set of philosophical options. *If* excluded middle – whether as bivalence or as *tertium non datur* – were "inviolate," then a great many of the well-known charges against relativism would be at once secured, completely vindicated. For example, it would no longer be unreasonable to package relativism together with nihilism, irrationalism, anarchism, skepticism, and the like. The curious thing is that, having examined the issue of excluded middle, no knockdown argument suggests itself why the principle should be supposed to be unconditionally and invariantly required. On the contrary, Stalnaker is satisfied with some arbitrary fiat about bipolar values. Wolterstorff seems to affirm his adherence theologically, without any further need for argumentative support. Dummett concedes that it is not in the least required – indeed, is definitely faulty – in the received sense in which it masquerades as bivalence; he goes on to concede that his own insistence on another interpretation (*tertium non datur*) is essentially one of a rather pragmatic sort, in the face of a general ignorance about how the relevant question might actually and ultimately oblige us to proceed. Furthermore, he simply never addresses the question we have posed. So why should we bind ourselves by such implausible and dubiously indecisive prejudices? And how could the enemies of relativism have hoped to disarm any serious audience by merely announcing that relativism was obviously some sort of affront to reason? There seems to be no basis for the charge at all. Certainly, we are entitled to proceed as if the various forms of relativism were entirely rational, for all we know – at least on the fair condition that no one seems to have been able or willing to show that an adherence to relativism in accord with abandoning excluded middle (either piecemeal or wholesale) constitutes an affront to reason.

Of course, many would say that this is not the most important, or the only, or the essential objection. But we have gained some ground nonetheless. We shall have to look into the question of whether relativists are really irrational or incoherent, in a deeper and more serious sense. For example, perhaps they regularly contradict themselves in saying what they do. Or perhaps they regularly offer a doctrine that cannot be intelligibly formulated. As it happens, the first of these charges, self-contradiction, *is* regularly laid against Protagoras or the *protagoreans*; and, as it happens, the second charge, unintelligibility, *is* laid against the so-called *incommensurabilists*, Kuhn and particularly Feyerabend. So it would be both unfair and decidedly premature to trumpet the bona fides of relativism at this early stage of the argument. We shall have to see. Nevertheless, we are hardly exceeding the bounds of fair play if we take notice here of the paper tiger of intellectual scandal generated by the barest hint that a maverick theory, making its way against mainstream philosophy, must have hopelessly compromised itself by having opposed one of the guardian rules of reason itself. Relativism *does* oppose excluded middle. But the evidence is that doing so affords no grounds at all for running it out of the logicians' club. It may be a practice frowned on by the old guard; but, in itself, it hardly shows that the relativist has taken leave of his senses. Also, of course, opposition to excluded middle is not as such advocacy of relativism. *That* is most important.

VI

We need to adjust our account a little more favorably. For one thing, Dummett's attack on bivalence is merely intuitionistic, focused on the quasi-formal matter of constructing finite proofs for particular claims. It says nothing about the supposed nature of the world itself, in virtue of which, say, the fortunes of intuitionism (extended beyond mathematics) are themselves placed at considerable risk. And so, Dummett quite reasonably recovers *tertium non datur*, precisely *by* taking the constructivist requirement seriously.

But what if the world, or the world made intelligible by the preconditions of human inquiry, were such that something like the construction of arguments and proofs and reasonings and the weighing of evidence was affected and infected by a certain ineluctable informality? Let us not pretend that such arguments would be strictly acceptable to the intuitionist, or that the intuitionist has actually earned the right to judge their admissibility, or that a closed and comprehensive canon could be worked out in principle for all such processes, or that seeming exceptions with respect to any provisional canon could convincingly count as evidence of incoherence or unreasonableness or illegitimacy or failure of any sort. Merely entertaining the question confirms the possibility of waiving excluded middle on grounds more fundamental than the intuitionist's. For the intuitionist proceeds methodologically or epistemologically, even though the very point of casting doubt on the "realist's" simple faith rests with some recognition of the indissoluble symbiosis of realist and idealist elements in what we posit *as* the real world. After all, that *is* the upshot of Dummett's concessions.

Speculating in this way also suggests that it may not even be necessary to regard excluded middle as *false*, formulated only abstractly; it may only need to be construed as inapt, inapplicable, inert without an interpretation by which it is applied to a given sector of the world. It is in fact in this sense that logic and mathematics are normally construed as empirically constrained formal systems. In fact, some theorists, some philosophers of science, regard it as a mistake to treat these "formal" disciplines as autonomous, separable from the empirical sciences they service. They are, they say, integral parts of those sciences, bound and affected therefore in precisely the same sense in which the more "empirical" sciences are said to be. The paradoxical findings of recent physics are said to confirm at least that much.[13]

So we may leave the more controversial issue benignly unresolved at this point in the argument. Nothing more radical is being claimed by "bracketing" or "waiving" excluded middle than that, *for particular sectors of inquiry*, probably as a consequence of the indissoluble linkage between "realist" and "idealist" elements, but without at all yielding to a denial of objectivity or to an affirmation that the world is nothing but a "subjective" construct of some sort, excluded middle does not adequately serve the requirements of inquiry, does not suitably there match what we take to be the lineaments of reality.

At least this much, then, is clear: change one's theory of the nature of the real world, and the prospects of excluded middle are affected one way or another. So Stalnaker must have been wrong to have been so insouciant; Wolterstorff must have been premature in seeing no other option; Dummett must have been too partisan to have stopped so abruptly after unseating bivalence. Still, we must be honest enough to admit, abandoning or waiving or delimiting the application of excluded middle *is not*, as such, equivalent to advocating relativism.

VII

That remarkable American original, Charles Sanders Peirce, considers the question of excluded middle from a point of view utterly unlike Dummett's. That is, Peirce really absorbs Dummett's question in the context of the larger metaphysical question of what the world is like and of how deciding the truth or falsity of particular claims is affected by the world's nature. Peirce begins a pertinent discussion of the matter by remarking

> that anything is *general* in so far as the principle of excluded middle does not apply to it and is *vague* in so far as the principle of contradiction does not apply to it. Thus, although it is true that "Any proposition you please, once you have determined its *identity*, is either true or false"; yet *so long as it remains indeterminate and so without identity*, it need neither be true that any proposition you please is true, nor that any proposition you please is false. So likewise, while it is false that "A proposition *whose identity I have determined* is both true and false," yet until it is determinate, it may be true that a proposition is true and that a proposition is false.[14]

We cannot afford to become enmeshed in Peirce's extraordinarily complex system. Nevertheless, Peirce's warning here is quite straightforward. First of all, terms, predicates, possess a certain inherent generality; insofar as they do, they set a provisional limit on the applicability of excluded middle. Secondly, the avoidance of that sort of generality cannot be achieved by a restriction of *terms*: in Peirce's semiotic idiom, "everything indeterminate is of the nature of a sign"; *and* "the entire universe – not merely the universe of existents, but all that wider universe, embracing the universe of existents as a part, the universe which we are all accustomed to refer to as 'the truth' – that all this universe is perfused with signs, if it is not composed exclusively of signs."[15] So *the intelligible world*, the world symbiotically rendered intelligible by the conditions of human existence, cannot, because it is thus semiotically prepared, because it is "perfused" with signs or predicates or the like, altogether eliminate generality (the reverse of absolutely singular identity, in Peirce's usage) *by* the precision of additional terms. Terms remain "definite" and relatively "precise" *for* the purposes for which they are introduced;[16] but they do not accommodate excluded middle unconditionally.

Peirce's remarkably helpful notion here depends on his conceding that *where* "formal knowledge is absolutely universal, exact, and necessary" (if we are prepared to concede the point), it is such only relative to "ideal constructions" (systems of idealized propositions, say, fitted for deductive argument); but *there*, we cannot assume that such constructions appropriately fit the actual world. "Their applicability to the real world," he says, "is at the best doubtful and, as I think, false; while in their ideal purity they are not synthetical."[17] Peirce's argument is at least coherent.

Hence, when excluded middle is applied to experience, to the experienced world, rather than to mere idealized terms, we *cannot* ensure its applicability except relative to our distinctions, provisionally with regard to their acceptance, and conditionally on the inherent inexhaustibility of experience or the experienced world.

On Peirce's very bold view: "A *state of things* is an abstract constituent part of reality, of such a nature that a proposition is needed to represent it. There is but one *individual*, or completely determinate, state of things, namely, the all of reality. A *fact* is so highly a prescissively abstract state of things, that it can be wholly represented in a simple proposition, and the term 'simple,' here, has no absolute meaning, but is merely a comparative expression."[18] Furthermore, Peirce adds, "man is so completely hemmed in by the bounds of his possible practical experience, his mind is so restricted to being the instrument of his needs, that he cannot, in the least, *mean* anything that transcends those limits."[19]

On an argument of this kind, an argument more metaphysically focused than Dummett's – one, in fact, that accommodates the sort of constraint of intransparency that, as we noted in the preceding chapter, is generally now admitted (recall Bernstein's thesis) – there *is* no once-and-for-all argument to vindicate the inviolability of excluded middle. There cannot be. Furthermore, wherever it is invoked, it is invoked conditionally, on grounds that it cannot itself ensure. From that point of view, if the rejection or restriction of excluded middle is a concession to relativism, then relativism cannot, in some good sense, be obviated altogether.

The lesson is plain enough.

Notes

1   Robert C. Stalnaker, *Inquiry* (Cambridge: MIT Press, 1984), p. 2.
2   Ibid.
3   Nicholas Wolterstorff, *Works and Worlds of Art* (Oxford: Clarendon Press, 1980), p. 137.
4   Ibid.
5   Ibid., p. 140.
6   See Michael Dummett, *Truth and Other Enigmas* (Cambridge: Harvard University Press, 1978).
7   Ibid., pp. xxviii–xxix.
8   Ibid.
9   Ibid., p. xix.
10 Ibid., p. xxx.
11 Michael Dummett, "Truth," *Truth and Other Enigmas*, pp. 18–19.
12 *Truth and Other Enigmas*, preface, pp. xxx–xxxi; italics added.
13 See, for instance, John Stachel, "Comments on 'Some Logical Problems Suggested by Emergent Theories' by Professor Dalla Chiara," in Robert S. Cohen and Marx W. Wartofsky (eds), *Language, Logic, and Method* (Dordrecht: D. Reidel, 1983), p. 92.
14 *Collected Papers of Charles Sanders Peirce*, vols 5–6 ed. Charles Hartshorne and Paul Weiss (Cambridge: Harvard University Press, 1960), vol. 5 par. 448.
15 Ibid., vol. 5 par. 448 n. 1.
16 Ibid., vol. 5 par. 449.
17 Ibid., vol. 6 par. 595. Peirce's argument here depends on what he himself terms his "Scotistic mind" (par. 401).
18 Ibid., vol. 5 par. 549.
19 Ibid., vol. 5 par. 535. The remark appears in a dialogue and is assigned to the Pragmaticist. Cf. also vol. 6 pars. 95, 34.

3

Classification Run Riot

I

The carelessness, the arbitrariness, the spleen, the sheer cussedness and idiosyncrasy with which accusations and claims of relativism have been tossed about over a considerable part of recent history pretty well scuttle the possibility of providing a neat diagnostic classification of its true variety. But then, by the same token, it would be preposterous to grant anyone the authority to specify its "genuine" forms, which, quite frankly, on the evidence of the opportunism of the professional world, usually signifies an intention to gain a public relations advantage by declaring relativism to be little more than stupid, incoherent, or base. The record speaks for itself. We took notice of something of this spirit, for instance, in Newton-Smith's characterization of "the central relativist idea" which proved, on Newton-Smith's analysis (hardly unreasonably), to be incoherent. How comfortable it is to summarize an entire range of possibilities by declaring them all null and void.

For his part, Alasdair MacIntyre, in a recent professional address, makes the rather nice observation that "relativism, like skepticism, is one of those doctrines that have by now been refuted a number of times too often. Nothing is perhaps a surer sign that a doctrine embodies some not-to-be-neglected truth than that in the course of the history of philosophy it should have been refuted again and again. Genuinely refutable doctrines only need to be refuted once."[1] But MacIntyre neglects to supply the telling "doctrine."

II

Still, it pays to take the measure of the running discussion; and, as we shall see, whether we care to dwell on the details or not, the more recent the discussion, the more entangled and opaque it seems to become.

Richard Rorty, for instance, has certainly set off a good many hares by the popularity that predictably follows his every pronouncement. It was not to be, therefore, that relativism would escape a certain confident dismissal benefiting from his endorsement, even if Rorty would himself have wished that it were otherwise. So Rorty says, in an American Philosophical Association Presidential Address preceding MacIntyre's by some five years: "'Relativism' is the view that every belief on a certain topic, or perhaps about *any* topic, is as good as every other. No one holds this view. . . . [But] if there *were* any relativists, they would, of course, be easy to refute. One would merely use some variant of the self-referential arguments Socrates used against Protagoras."[2] Rorty retracts the easy label a little. "Perhaps 'relativism' is *not*," he very kindly remarks, "the right name for what so many philosophers find so offensive in pragmatism. . . . For my purposes, [he adds,] it is the issue [the one he really means to explore] about whether we [philosophers and more] can be pragmatists without betraying Socrates, without falling into irrationalism."[3]

Rorty obviously characterizes relativism as simplistically as Newton-Smith. He relents only by way of an afterthought; and, even in offering that qualification, he reminds us of the ancient charge against Protagoras and the evident incoherence of the Protagorean position. So it hardly matters whether he has the right label after all.

We may also observe, shifting somewhat abruptly here, that, for *his* part, Hilary Putnam affirms that "there is a deep irrationalism to cultural relativism, a denial of the possibility of *thinking* (as opposed to making noises in counterpoint or in chorus)."[4] It may be that *his* account is also simplistic, almost in a sense indistinguishable from Rorty's; but one has the feeling at least, reading Putnam, that he is reacting primarily *against* Rorty's extravagance. In any case, he is bent on attacking that particular form of relativism that he labels (and that many label) "cultural relativism." The irony is that Rorty's view is his chief specimen of that failed category.

The cultural relativist says (think, here, of Rorty or of Michel Foucault, according to Putnam):

> "When I [that is, the relativist] say something is *true*, I mean that it is correct according to the norms of *my* culture." If he adds [says Putnam], "When a member of a different culture says something is true, what he means (whether he knows it or not) is that it is in conformity with the norms of *his* culture," then he is in exactly the same plight as the methodological solipsist.[5]

What the relativist says is incoherent and "irrational" because it is "inconsistent" in the peculiar way it is: "his two stances." Putnam explains, like those of the methodological solipsist, "are ludicrously incompatible."[6] (Clearly, Putnam's cultural relativist is our relationalist.)

Of course, it may not have been entirely just for Putnam to have charged Rorty with such inconsistency, since Rorty, as we may remember, had himself posed much the same objection against the relativist. Rorty uses the term more inclusively than Putnam, but then he relents. Putnam confines his fire to the "cultural relativist"; but he turns it against Rorty, even though he does not quite demonstrate that Rorty *is* actually in the position he attacks or *is* in a position akin to that of the methodological solipsist. There's a bit of a mess here.

III

The best way of reading Putnam seems to be as follows. The cultural relativist comes in two sizes: in one, the smaller and simpler, he is merely irrational, though perhaps not developed enough to be finely inconsistent. He merely denies "the possibility of *thinking* [*philosophically*]"; he claims – this is, now, Putnam's one-line book review of Rorty's *Philosophy and the Mirror of Nature* – that "philosophy, as traditionally understood, is a *silly* enterprise."[7] It seems entirely reasonable to attack *this* thesis; but it does not strike the mind as very closely connected at all with the larger, more developed relativist position that Putnam shows to be inconsistent in the way he does. Though we may allow his choice of epithets – labeling the simpler view the central version of cultural relativism – Putnam has confused the issue by his extraneous association. Certainly, it neither entails nor is entailed by the more developed view that he says is tantamount, or is at least parallel, to the thesis of methodological skepticism. It's the latter notion (however mislabeled) that deserves our attention.

The upshot is that Rorty, on his own account – and now, on a reading of Putnam's – is *not* a champion of the more developed, inherently inconsistent, version of relativism; he is a champion of the "irrational" version and a critic of the other. We would have to walk a very long mile with Putnam to make the case that the "simpler" view *was* interesting *as* a form of relativism.

One elementary way of showing that Putnam must be wrong or at least spendthrift in his choice of labels is that relativism is normally viewed as an honest, quite "traditional" *philosophical* thesis that entertains the possibility that other opposed but pertinent options may actually be able to settle a certain bona fide question more perspicuously than it itself can. Philosophical debate, therefore, is not "silly" *for the relativist*. (That is also Rorty's view.) Rorty's own program, by contrast, *is*, precisely, *meant to do philosophy in, as it is "traditionally" practiced.* It is, therefore, meant to be "deeper" than relativism just as it is deeper than philosophy.

It may be true that Rorty espouses a distinct philosophical thesis *in* repudiating transcendental or legitimative second-order questions about the nature of science, knowledge, truth, and the like.[8] If so, then Rorty may be inconsistent in a further important regard that should be exposed; but not, for that reason, because his view harbors doctrines of a relativistic bent – unless, of course, taken in that utterly wild sense in which (as we have seen) relativism is amusingly, perhaps a little maliciously, lumped together with anarchism, irrationalism, skepticism, and the like. In a word, Rorty is *not* a relativist in the respect Putnam isolates, though he may be a nihilist or an anarchist or a skeptic – or just a good-old-boy liberal of the *laissez-faire* school – because, on Rorty's reading, the relativist simply wishes to contend as a philosophical equal among other "traditional" players and because Rorty himself wishes to dismiss them all as 'silly." If that is relativism, it's certainly a very deviant form of relativism.

IV

No, the important complaint of Putnam's is directed against the inconsistency of the more developed "cultural relativist" who behaves as Putnam says he does – the same theorist we ourselves have labeled, in the prologue, a *relationalist* regarding truth. That particular fellow is just the one Rorty also condemns. We have, in fact, quite a managerie of specimen theories now. Rorty says the relativist – we may suppose he means the "cultural relativist" or the methodological solipsist functioning as a relativist – is one who maintains that any belief on "any topic" or on "a certain topic" *is* "as good as every other." *That* doctrine Rorty takes to be refutable. It seems to be very close to the view Putnam also believes can be refuted, except that he, Putnam, believes (quite wrongly) that Rorty actually subscribes to it. (It is also not clear whether *this* too often defeated doctrine is the one MacIntyre believes harbors a "truth" that needs to be secured.) Furthermore, Rorty, Putnam, and MacIntyre are all rather coy about their own relativistic inclinations, since the first two formulate what relativism means, as a doctrine, in a way that is entirely indefensible, while professing some sympathy for relativism; and the latter never quite says what we are supposed to salvage, as the philosophical gem it is, from the usual muddled disputes. Again, the views of Rorty and Putnam do also seem to be very close to Newton-Smith's.

There are still two quite different doctrines mingled here, both untenable and both often attributed to the foolish relativist (notoriously, Protagoras): one says that the same proposition or statement can be at once both true and false; the other says that "true" and "false" are (alethically) relationalized to the insulated life and experience of one particular society (*or* person) or another, hence *not* merely that particular claims are (epistemically) decided in accord with whatever such life and experience may recommend (which, after all, is trivially true).

V

Actually, Newton-Smith offers the most straightforward charge: assuming that a given proposition does not change its meaning, "it is just incoherent to suppose" it could be both true and false in any relevantly partitioned respect. Surely, this is rock-bottom. If we are disposed to be philosophically fussy, regardless of Newton-Smith's own inclinations, we may take an additional moment to observe that the condition imposed on invariance of meaning obviates the need to separate talk of "propositions" and talk of "statements" (for instance, along lines congruent with Dummett's and Peirce's way of putting things). Furthermore, as just cited, Newton-Smith's formulation does not absolutely require that either propositions or statements take only bipolar truth-values, though the context confirms that Newton-Smith is indeed a strong champion of excluded middle. Newton-Smith's formulation is also so close to the original classical attack on Protagoras that we may reasonably suppose that it recalls that argument (perhaps even intends to recall it). In any case, *if* his complaint against the relativist identifies all there is to the *relativist's* position – or if Protagoras' position comes to nothing more than that – then we should be grateful to Newton-Smith for having dispatched at one stroke both relativism and (what we have already termed) protagoreanism. Also, *if* Rorty and/or Putnam took his own formulation to be equivalent to, or identical with, Newton-Smith's, then the matter would be speedily settled, except perhaps for local misunderstandings. And, of course, *if* MacIntyre thought he could salvage *that* thesis, he would be very much mistaken.

What one suspects, however, is that it's not very likely that the relativist *or* Protagoras *or* the protagorean is all that stupid. Why should anyone in his right mind support a barefaced contradiction? And why should anyone in his right mind suppose that anyone, pursuing the issue of relativism with a modicum of skill that does not utterly bore the clever philosophers of our own time, would ever have slipped into a final claim that was that stupid? It is hard to resist drawing the conclusion that it is just plain stupid (or knavish) to suppose everyone else to be so stupid.

VI

There is good evidence that Newton-Smith does more than affirm that the relativist is fatally committed to the contradiction he sets out. He also considers, putting his knockdown finding aside, whether relativism might explain – that is, function as "a successful explanatory hypothesis" (a philosophically pertinent hypothesis) of – the general phenomenon of "the variation in belief and in reasoning from age to age and from social group to social group."[9] His conclusion, as one might anticipate, is that it cannot. But that was already entailed by his original characterization of relativism: since it was known to be inconsistent, it could not possibly function in an explanatory way. To entertain the explanatory option seriously, one would really have to *set aside* Newton-Smith's first reading of relativism and then try to formulate another that was *not* patently self-defeating. This Newton-Smith does not do, but perhaps it can be done, although to say so is hardly to foreclose on the further possibility that the alternative reading might also succumb to an inherent defect. But it could not, in all fairness, be the same chestnut we have already roasted.

Here, Newton-Smith offers the formula: "The central relativist idea is that what is true for one tribe, social group or age might not be true for another tribe, social group or age."[10] But that just compromises (much too quickly) the seemingly new option. For instance, the relativist might adjust his view of meaning and truth, or of the interpretation or application of the formal principle of consistency, so that, for the variety of customs in question, *what looks like a contradiction might be none at all.* Neither Newton-Smith nor Putnam nor Rorty seriously tries to recover such a possibility; and MacIntyre hardly comes to its rescue.

One sees at once, therefore, the charm of Peirce's quite different caveat about excluded middle and the point of our having resisted Dummett's hasty conclusion regarding *tertium non datur.* It may even be that Protagoras had something of this sort in mind in appearing to proclaim the very doctrine everyone takes to be too stupid for words.

What all this means is that we need to go slow, to give the relativist as much line as he needs. There may be a way of redeeming (Putnam's) cultural relativism by *adjusting* the charge Putnam and Newton-Smith share. Perhaps *we* could adjust the sense of what we mean by "cultural relativism" so that it still pretty well serves the explanatory function Newton-Smith is prepared to entertain, without committing it explicitly or in advance (as Newton-Smith does) to the contradiction he originally set before us. It's a possibility worth looking into seriously. (For example, perhaps we could adjust its sense along the lines of what we have already labeled as "cultural relativity" at least – possibly, then, with an additional nod as well in the direction of incommensurabilism.)

VII

Let us try now to organize our options a little more simply. They have become so terribly tangled. On a certain reading (1), a reading we should not ignore, the relativist (possibly the cultural relativist) holds that a proposition or a statement can, despite its remaining constant in meaning, be both true and false (Newton-Smith's charge). *That* is surely self-contradictory and unconditionally refuted for that reason. Secondly, the relativist, or the cultural relativist, might be said to hold (2a) that the *norms* or *criteria* of truth (as distinct from the *meaning* of "truth" – an excessively fussy point at best on one reading, a *non*relativist concession on another) vary from culture to culture (Putnam's and perhaps Rorty's charge, considerably dampened along the lines of cultural relativity); or he might be said to hold (2b) that the very meaning of "true" (at least for a *certain* set of claims) varies from culture to culture, so that *what* is true will also vary from culture to culture even if the meanings of the nonalethic terms that fix what we are talking about do not vary in the same way. It is the second of these two options (2b) that Putnam and Rorty effectively undermine in their distinctive ways (that is, cultural relativism – what we have been calling relationalism, what Putnam often terms, now rather confusingly, "cultural relativity"): Putnam, arguing by way of analogy from the methodological solipsist's fatal dilemma; Rorty, by self-referential puzzles resembling Socrates' refutation of Protagoras.

Putnam's point (remember that *he* takes it that he is criticizing Rorty in all of this) is that, when the relativist judges, say, that the sentence "Snow is white" is true in accord with the norms of German culture (presumably, in accord with what makes "*Schnee ist weiss*" true), that whole affirmation is true *in accord with* American culture – in accord with which, after all, what would be true according to German culture is determined to be such. "True," therefore, cannot vary in the way scenario (2b) requires. Hence, cultural relativism is inconsistent and refuted.[11] Putnam is right, of course; and Rorty is right, if it is indeed true that *he* does not subscribe to this version of cultural relativism. That alone, however, does not quite show that the *first* option of this *second* reading (2a) is also inconsistent. As a matter of fact, it probably is not (or need not be) inconsistent, though if it is not it must be uninteresting as a distinctly relativist option. It simply concerns the cultural (factual) plurality or variability of beliefs, values, norms, and the like.

Gilbert Harman has actually formulated a version of relativism that conforms with option (2a). He does this for morality only, since he draws a rather sharp line between science and morality, along so-called noncognitivist lines. On Harman's reading, the (moral) noncognitivist holds that "moral judgments do not function to describe a moral reality but do something else – express feelings, prescribe a course of action, and so forth."[12] On this view, it looks as if a relativist reading of *science* or of truth-bearing claims could not, in principle, be mounted at all. In fact, Harman offers a further formulation that is very close to Putnam's and Rorty's, which he is unwilling to apply to morality (on pain of contradiction) but which he is quite willing to apply to science: namely, the view of one who takes a set of claims to be truth-bearing but who also (contradictorily) espouses a form of cultural relativism. For instance, in moral matters one might hold (inconsistently), Harman thinks, "both that there are no universal moral truths and also that everyone ought to follow the dictates of his or her group, where this last claim is taken to be a universal moral truth."[13] To save moral relativism, therefore, Harman favors (moral) noncognitivism.

Just so. On Harman's view, therefore, *if* relativism were formulated in terms of truth-bearing claims, it would be inconsistent in just the way Putnam and Newton-Smith suppose it is. It need not be inconsistent, however, *on* Harman's view, because, *in* the moral sphere at least, the relevant "claims" are not truth-bearing at all.

This is a very expensive solution, you will admit: particularly if (as seems reasonable) rational disputes, advice, appraisals, judgments, and the like *are possible in the moral sphere*, are possible and not merely confined to applying "external" (inappropriate) argumentative strategies to what are just arbitrary moral *values* (values that are utterly beyond dispute themselves). For, if disputes about moral values *can* have argumentative force, then it seems impossible to deny that moral claims *are* truth-bearing in some pertinent sense, even if it is the case that such claims could not be *true because* (that is, on the grounds that) they depended on discerning, or because they actually discerned, something about an independent or objective moral reality (about which truth-claims may be advanced in the standard way they are in the sciences).[14]

The issue is rather tricky. A relativism that does not succumb to the variety of arguments we have drawn from Newton-Smith, Putnam, and Rorty now begins to seem recoverable, at least if we can fiddle effectively with the price of denying that the "claims" in question are truth-bearing. As a relativist, Harman simply holds that "different agents are subject to different basic moral requirements depending on the moral conventions in which they participate."[15] That itself does not yet appear to *require* the extreme noncognitivist maneuver, which, in any case, looks implausible, certainly too slack to be interesting for our purpose. A straightforward pluralism might serve Harman's purpose. Why sacrifice truth-values altogether?

VIII

John Mackie, as a self-professed "moral skeptic," introduces a more general option than Harman's. He adopts a certain "second order view, a view about the status of moral values and the nature of moral valuing, about where and how they fit into the world." What those values are supposed to be ascribed to – behavior, say – "are indeed [says Mackie] part of the furniture of the world, and so are the natural, descriptive, differences between them; but not, perhaps their differences in value."[16] Once we see matters Mackie's way, we realize, first, that skepticism (in Mackie's sense: skepticism about moral realism) is *not* tantamount to relativism, and, second, that Harman's *relativism* rests on a disastrous equivocation. For Harman holds that "different agents *are subject* to different basic moral requirements." He cannot mean this in a *moral* sense: since, if it is *true* that such agents are "subject" *morally*, then Harman will have (self-referentially) violated his own disjunction between science and morality; and if they are not "subject" in a moral way but only in some nonmoral way, say, in a thin, morally unengaged, "sociological" sense (merely descriptively: in the sense of taking note of mere prevailing custom), then human agents are *not* really "subject" in the moral sense at all. Harman's position is at best an extremely attenuated version of (moral) relativism, one that is utterly uninteresting in the context of the dispute Putnam and Newton-Smith have drawn to our attention. One begins to see here why views like Harman's *and* Rorty's (the *laissez-faire* attitude we briefly glimpsed before) are bound to be treated as equivalent to nihilism, irrationalism, anarchism, skepticism, and the like.[17]

IX

But we *are* on to a possibility that has eluded Newton-Smith, Putnam, Rorty, and (now) Harman, that *is* (or looks to be) a version of relativism, that *saves* an essential part of what the cultural relativist wishes to hold on to, that does not abandon the difficult concession that the claims in question *are* truth-bearing (take truth-values), and that *remains* formally self-consistent for all that. We need to be a little careful here. We are hardly home free.

Suppose we hold, playing fast and loose with Harman's option, that it is just *true* that "different agents are subject to different basic moral requirements depending on the moral conventions in which they participate." Then, we should have abandoned noncognitivism and we should have saved what Newton-Smith, Putnam, and (perhaps) Rorty identify as the heart of cultural relativism, except that we should now no longer insist on changes in the very *meaning* of "true" moving among the affected societies. That would be a great simplification if it worked. All that would be needed would be the admission that moral values, moral obligations, and the like, were (somehow) drawn from and restricted to the fabric of the actual local practices and institutions of the various societies in which (as Harman puts it) "different agents are subject" in the way they are. This much conforms, as it happens, to an essential part of Hegel's effective use of the concept of *Sittlichkeit* or moral custom, by reference to which Hegel works to defeat Kant's moral program of universal but utterly abstract, unhistorical, *unsittlich* rationality.[18]

The trick is that, on the thesis being advanced, the *moral values* in question are incompatible *in a certain sense*, even though there are no inconsistencies regarding *truth-claims* about them. There would not even be an incompatibility among those values *if*, following Harman to some degree, "different agents are subject [only] to *different* basic moral requirements" in the different societies in which they live. That is, *if* moral requirements could be confined within disjoined societies, then we should neither have (we should not need to admit) inconsistent truth-claims *nor* inconsistent or incompatible moral values. And we should not have relationalism either.

You may say: well, that's not relativism at all; that's pluralism if it's anything. And you would be right. In fact, it would now be the case that, from a God's-eye view, it would be *non*relativistically true that different folks had different obligations in different societies. What's "relativistic" about that is simply that the obligations of one society could, as such, not be the obligations of another. (It saves "cultural relativity" in the purely factual sense.) This may seem an enormous labor for very little gain, but it is not a little gain. Have patience.

Consider what we've accomplished. We've pressed Putnam and Newton-Smith in order to save relativism, but we foundered on truth. Now, pressing Harman, we've saved truth but have lost relativism. Effectively, on Harman's option, we've reduced relativism to a sort of *pluralism* (3). In Harman's hands, it takes a noncognitive *and* noncognitivist form (3a). In Mackie's hands, it takes a nonrealist or nonobjectivist (or a "skeptic") form but *not* a noncognitive form (3b). It is for this reason that Mackie points out:

> There could be agreement in valuing even if valuing is just some thing people do, even if this activity is not further validated. Subjective agreement would give intersubjective values, but intersubjectivity is not objectivity. Nor is objectivity simply universalizability: someone might well be prepared to universalize his prescriptive judgments or approvals ... and yet he could recognize that such prescribing and approving were his activities, nothing more. Of course if there were objective values they would presumably belong to *kinds* of things or actions or states of affairs, so that the judgments that reported them would be universalizable; but the converse does not hold.[19]

Of course, Mackie's right. Only, *in* that guise, there's no need to speak of relativism at all. Mackie's own pronouncement on the matter is the very soul of brevity: "the well-known variation in moral codes from one society to another ... is in itself merely a truth of descriptive morality, a fact of anthropology which entails neither first order nor second order ethical views."[20] What is interesting about this way of putting matters is that it suggests entirely reasonable parallels – in fact, much more sweeping and much more suggestive parallels – in other sectors of human inquiry and intelligence, in science, for instance, just contrary to Harman's intention.

You may find it preposterous to claim a parallel formation in the sciences, but there *is* one nevertheless, one that is very much debated at the present time. For example, when Thomas Kuhn rehearses the difference between the work of Lavoisier and Priestley, he says that "Lavoisier ... saw oxygen where Priestley had seen dephlogisticated air and where others had seen nothing at all." Actually, says Kuhn, "Lavoisier saw nature differently ... Lavoisier worked in a different world."[21] In fact, in the well-known postscript to his *The Structure of Scientific Revolutions*, Kuhn goes on to declare forthrightly (a matter on which he apparently still agonizes and cannot yet settle his own mind): "There is, I think, no theory-independent way to reconstruct phrases like 'really there'; the notion of a match between the ontology of a theory and its 'real' counterpart in nature now seems to me illusive in principle."[22] Kuhn thinks it would be "wrong" to characterize this position as "relativistic"; but if it is, then he is prepared to say, "I cannot see that the relativist loses anything needed to account for the nature and development of the sciences."[23]

X

Ignore for the moment the extravagance of Kuhn's prose, the reference to Lavoisier's living in a "different world" from Priestley. Kuhn is uneasy about the phrase but he cannot bring himself to abandon it. What is important about his maneuver, however, is that it attempts to recover what is central to cultural relativism (namely, cultural relativity – the facts about different cultures) by introducing certain further complications about meaning, theory, truth, and perception that do not (or at least do not intend to) reproduce the elementary logical blunder Putnam and Newton-Smith and Harman have so readily exposed. Let us therefore give Kuhn the benefit of the doubt. His intention is not to be stupid in the way we have already flagged. We do not know, of course, whether the strategy will work, or even what in detail it is. But that itself is sufficient to disallow both the charge of stupidity and the decisiveness of the simple criterion by which the charge was made to stick. Put another way, we are back at the quarrel about the *applicability* of such formal principles as noncontradiction and excluded middle, in the spirit in which we first sided with Peirce against Dummett. Here, puzzles about *understanding* seemingly inconsistent or incompatible claims – say, Lavoisier's and Priestley's claims – are said to take precedence over considerations of mere formal logic. That priority holds simply because, otherwise, we should never be able to *apply* logic *to* those claims. We may not agree with Dummett that propositions take truth-values only to the extent that they are decidable by us here and now; but we surely do agree with Dummett to the extent at least that propositions take truth-values only if they are intelligible, and, taken pairwise, they can be compatible or contradictory only if they are also intelligible or have an intelligible form.

Kuhn is *not* saying that Lavoisier and Priestley support contradictory claims *about the same patch of air*: that would be to fall into the trap Newton-Smith and the others have prepared. He is saying rather that we do not yet know, and may be unable to determine (because of complexities affecting meaning and theory and the rest), *whether* their "disagreement" is an explicit disagreement about the same "fact of the matter" or whether it is something else. In short, Kuhn has introduced puzzles of *conceptual incommensurability* and *conceptual indeterminacy*. For the sake of neatness, we may mark this as version (4) of our tally of kinds of relativisms.

Version (4) shows at once that the strategy shared by Newton-Smith, Putnam, Rorty, and Harman is premature, that is, however locally decisive, premature when applied to relativism *tout court*. There is no such beast. That is, *on* Putnam's strong hypothesis, *we* know (*as* relativists) that and why others judge differently from ourselves. (That is just what makes the relativist's position untenable.) We are not now resisting *that* finding; we are merely considering another possibility.

Kuhn's form of relativism may well fail; but, on the face of things, the strategy Putnam and the others adopt is simply irrelevant for defeating *Kuhn's* option, or it is at least irrelevant until the matter of incommensurability can be satisfactorily resolved. Notice that version (1) of our tally does not introduce puzzles of meaning at all and versions (2a) and (2b) require that meanings (or at least criteria and norms) change in a discernibly determinate way from one social context to another. Kuhn introduces the possibility that, although we may have good reasons for believing that meanings do change from context to context, we cannot be sure that they change in such a way as to justify our supposing that *what is true in ψ is false in ϕ*, in Newton-Smith's sense, say. The difficulty is now more elusive. That's just the point of saying – purple though the language may be – that Lavoisier and Priestley lived in different worlds.

What we now see at least is that we cannot merely segregate alethic and nonalethic predicates: we cannot hold nonalethic predicates constant in meaning between two different communities of inquirers and still relativize truth-claims to each (that is, what we take to be true) regarding the application of the nonalethic predicates; nor can we hold the nonalethic predicates constant and relativize (relationalize) the meaning of "true" to each. That would just be to produce the self-defeating paradox Putnam exposes so effectively: alethic predicates ineluctably have their nonalethic side; to know what "true" means in one community is to know how that community applies "true" in claims involving nonalethic predicates, but to know that is to know something that *cannot be coherently expressed in the relationalist's way*. To insist on relationalism here is to produce self-referential paradox. We cannot possibly know that and how another community uses "true" (in a fully alethic and epistemic sense) differently from ourselves all the while we use "true" only in the relationalist's way. We cannot know that *"Schnee ist weiss"* is true in *their* "world" but not in ours, if we suppose we are confined to what is true in our world ("true in L_1") and they are confined to what is true in their world ("true in L_2"). "True" cannot coherently mean what we (then) say it means if we can make the claim we are making.

We may pause here, without yet satisfying our curiosity about the fate of Kuhn's new option. The important point is that it is, or seems in the best sense to be, a genuinely new option. It certainly suggests that we may yet save the cultural relativist's thesis – mind you, save it in the domain of science as well as morality, save it in every sector of human inquiry – without falling victim to the dilemma of methodological solipsism or the self-referential paradoxes of Socrates' attack on Protagoras. We have prolonged the cultural relativist's thesis for another inning at least. And we have done it without taking any liberties regarding noncontradiction or excluded middle or the like. We have simply taken advantage of the entirely reasonable policy of distinguishing between the merely formal nature of logical principles and further considerations of meaning and relevance on which alone such formal principles can be shown to apply to this set of claims or that.

In the meantime, however, we have begun to isolate the two most signal forms of relativism that the recent history of the matter obliges us to examine: namely, *protagoreanism* (the most recognized ancient form) and *incommensurabilism* (possibly the most prominent modern form, given the development of twentieth-century philosophy of science). They are options obscured by certain premature harangues, both ancient and modern.

Linger just a moment longer, however. The skein of the argument combines two distinct threads: along one, we collect the proliferating forms of relativism; and along the other, we separate the fatal weakness of relationalism from the strength of robust relativism. It is the second thread that we must not drop, the one that, as we saw, Putnam manages to sort in a clear and compelling way. The point of Putnam's argument (which, as we shall soon see, is already imminent in Plato's *Theaetetus*, but oddly inexplicit there) depends on "relationalism's" combining alethic and epistemic considerations in the very definition of truth; so that the *meaning* of "true" and the epistemic appraisal of truth-*claims* cannot be separated, as they are in the option favored by "robust relativism." It is this linkage that leads directly to the self-defeating paradoxes. For, wherever he admits that different societies or different cognizing agents define truth differently *and* relationally (relative to their separate epistemic worlds), the relationalist cannot make coherent sense of his own claim *on his own assumption*. Where he identifies another relationalist's operative definition of truth only relative to and in terms of his own operative definition, *he* no longer subscribes to mere relationalism: for there is then no other cognitive stance but his own. And where he does fathom the difference between his and another relationalist's operative definitions of truth, he cannot reconcile the achievement *with any merely relationalist definition of truth*.

What is difficult but essential to grasp is this: the defeat of the relationalist option is independent of the fortunes of the merely *epistemic* option of relativizing the appraisal of truth-*claims* to our experience and cognitive orientation. (Of course, the point of that is tautological.) Relativizing the ascription of truth-values to truth-claims, by appealing to our cognitive experience (whatever that may be) is simply a matter completely different from relationalizing the very meaning of "true."

Notes

1 Alasdair MacIntyre, "Relativism, Power, and Philosophy," *Proceedings and Addresses of the American Philosophical Association* XLIX (September 1985), p. 5.
2 Richard Rorty, "Pragmatism, Relativism, Irrationalism," in *Consequences of Pragmatism* (Minneapolis: University of Minnesota Press, 1982), pp. 166, 167. See also, Richard Rorty, "Relativism," The Howison Lecture, University of California at Berkeley, January 31, 1983. Here Rorty is primarily concerned to explain why pragmatism is not a relativism, and why relativism fails to grasp pragmatism's deeper objective (favoring "solidarity" over "objectivity").
3 Ibid., p. 169.
4 Hilary Putnam, "Why Reason can't be Naturalized," in *Collected Papers*, vol. 3 (Cambridge: Cambridge University Press, 1983), p. 235.
5 Ibid., p. 237. For a sense of Putnam's own distinction between "cultural relativism" and "cultural relativity" (that is, the terms as we are using them), see Hilary Putnam, *The Many Faces of Realism* (La Salle: Open Court, 1987), for instance, at pp. 16–22.
6 Ibid., pp. 235–6.
7 Ibid., pp. 235–6.
8 Of course, this is actually true. It is for just this reason that Rorty appeals

to a certain well-known argument developed by Donald Davidson, in defeating transcendental arguments. Davidson, he thinks, has "found a transcendental argument to end all transcendental arguments." But *that* is certainly *not* intended in a relativistic spirit. On the contrary, it is intended to be unconditional. See Richard Rorty, "Transcendental Arguments, Self-Reference, and Pragmatism," in Peter Bieri et al. (eds), *Transcendental Arguments and Science* (Dordrecht: D. Reidel, 1979), p. 78.

9 William Newton-Smith, "Relativism and the Possibility of Interpretation," in Martin Hollis and Steven Lukes (eds), *Rationality and Relativism* (Cambridge: MIT Press, 1983), pp. 106–7.
10 Ibid., p. 107.
11 Putnam, "Why Reason can't be Naturalized," p. 237.
12 Gilbert Harman, "Is there a Single True Morality?" reprinted in Michael Krausz (ed.), *Relativism: Interpretation and Confrontation* (Notre Dame: Notre Dame University Press, 1989), p. 363.
13 Ibid.
14 See further Gilbert Harman, *The Nature of Morality: An Introduction to Ethics* (New York: Oxford University Press, 1977) and J. L. Mackie, *Ethics: Inventing Right and Wrong* (Harmondsworth: Penguin, 1977).
15 Harman, "Is there a Single True Morality?" p. 366.
16 Mackie, *Ethics*, pp. 22–3.
17 See further, Richard Rorty, *Contingency, Irony, and Solidarity* (Cambridge: Cambridge University Press, 1989), particularly chapters 3 and 4, and "Relativism," The Howison Lecture.
18 See *Hegel's Philosophy of Right*, trans. T. M. Knox (Oxford: Clarendon Press, 1942).
19 Mackie, *Ethics*, pp. 22–3.
20 Ibid., p. 36.
21 Thomas S. Kuhn, *The Structure of Scientific Revolutions*, 2nd ed. enl. (Chicago: University of Chicago Press, 1970), p. 118.
22 Ibid., p. 206.
23 Ibid., p. 207.

4

Protagoras Redux

I

We have now rather neatly outflanked Aristotle's refutation of Protagoras. We have not done so in a way that is altogether patent, but a little care will show how the argument may be made out. Aristotle is undoubtedly entitled to read Protagoras in such a way that, on that reading, Protagoras is refuted. But his argument presupposes a very special sort of baggage: it is perhaps not so much that he has refuted Protagoras as that he has refuted any protagorean (or *that* Protagoras) who would advance Protagoras' well-known claim *and* also subscribe to certain of the general claims of *Aristotle's Metaphysics*. There is, as we shall see, a remarkable similarity between Aristotle's strategy and that of contemporary opponents of relativism. Aristotle is very up-to-date.

If Protagoras or any protagorean could, without contradiction, reject those claims of Aristotle's on which the would-be refutation rests, then the relativism usually ascribed to Protagoras would live another day. Secondly, *we* can no longer claim just those doctrines Aristotle claims are unavoidable; or, at the very least, we cannot claim them to be unavoidable in the face of the obvious fact that the rejection of Aristotle's own claims is philosophically respectable nowadays, not in the least unusual, not generally treated as obviously self-contradictory or absurd, *and* not, as such, a relativist maneuver at all.

So the countermove to Aristotle's argument is not the proof that relativism is true, but rather that the grounds on which it is said to be inconsistent or self-contradictory are not, or need not be taken to be, compelling. Since, as we have seen, it is great sport even in our own time to declare relativism incoherent or refuted, it is not in the least negligible to show that relativism is genuinely open to a consistent reading essential or close to Protagoras' original argument.

II

Aristotle begins what amounts to an attack on Protagoras with the following fairminded opening:

> The starting-point for all ... arguments is not the demand that our opponent shall say that something either is or is not (for this one might perhaps take to be a begging of the question), but that he shall say something which is *significant* both for himself and for another; for this is necessary, if he really is to say anything.[1]

The trouble, however, is that Aristotle has set the argument in the context of characterizing very straitly the science of "being as being"; he says, in the *Metaphysics*, apparently having Protagoras in mind, such things as: "If there is nothing eternal, neither can there be a process of coming to be; for there must be something that comes to be, i.e. from which something comes to be, and the ultimate term in this series cannot have come to be, since the series has a limit and since nothing can come to be out of that which is not."[2] Similar arguments are supposed to show that the doctrine attributed to Protagoras, "that sensation is knowledge," is untenable; for, if it holds, then "all things will be objects of sense, and ... nothing will be eternal or unmovable; for all perceptible things perish and are in movement."[3]

Aristotle's argument is really quite complex. Here it shows how the supposed conception of knowledge on which Protagoras rests his claim violates what he, Aristotle, regards as a necessary condition for knowledge: knowledge is of what is unchanging, even if it is of what is unchanging *in* what does change. Protagoras' thesis cannot succeed, since it makes no provision for there being anything unchanging at all – hence, it makes no provision for the very precondition of knowledge. But this argument does not show that Protagoras commits a logical blunder detectable on formal grounds alone; nor does it show what may be characterized as a blunder on grounds independent of the validity of Aristotle's own quite disputable metaphysics. We merely understand a little better the bias with which Aristotle examines Protagoras' view.

III

Of course, that's hardly the whole story or even the principal part of it. Nevertheless, what is important in Aristotle's account – the part we have yet to spell out – is that the plausibility of the still-missing argument pretty well presupposes the argument we have just sketched. That is, the seemingly *formal* argument in which Aristotle shows that Protagoras is inconsistent ultimately rests on the presumption that *formal arguments involving noncontradiction and excluded middle hold in the way they do, because that alone would accord with the conditions of knowledge.* We may even agree with Aristotle here, in that logical principles cannot be convincingly detached from the practice of actual discourse (or science). Nevertheless, saying that hardly commits us to the validity of Aristotle's specific way of construing formal principles metaphysically. Conceivably, Protagoras, precisely in rejecting the archic doctrine to which Aristotle subscribes, may have embedded logical principles more satisfactorily (than does Aristotle) in the general process of discourse. So far at least, we have a stalemate.

Put another way, *Aristotle* does not need to face the puzzle of how to apply the formal principle of noncontradiction or of whether excluded middle may be waived or not. For, to secure any sort of genuine knowledge, noncontradiction *must* (on Aristotle's view) apply in accord with the constraints of unchanging substance and essence; no exception from excluded middle can be tolerated consistently with adopting the principle that substances have essential attributes. We can begin to see, therefore, what Dummett may have had in mind in opposing bivalence but retaining *tertium non datur*; and we can see why the radically evolutionary-minded "Scotist" philosopher, Peirce, was so hospitable to an infinite delay in applying excluded middle.

The upshot is this – even before we examine his actual argument: Aristotle has not really refuted Protagoras on the sort of "internal" grounds that Newton-Smith, Putnam, Rorty, and Harman advance. In fact, of these four, only Newton-Smith explicitly subscribes to a strenuous enough realism to lead him to resist exceptions to excluded middle.[4] Nevertheless, he (Newton-Smith) professes to find, in formulating the relativist's thesis, "internal," purely formal, evidence of incoherence.

We have already dealt with that gambit. Now we may suspect that the seeming force of Newton-Smith's own argument must depend on some invariant (realist) analogue of Aristotle's strategy, which, let it be said, Newton-Smith is aware is opposed by "instrumentalist" and "relativist" theories of science prepared to give up excluded middle. Here, the tell-tale appraisal, "more promising," is predicated, by Newton-Smith, *of* realism, in contest with these other options;[5] although, if what has been said is fair, then the "untenability," the "inconsistency," of relativism *does* depend on a strong "archic" reading *of* the logical constraint said to be imposed on us by excluded middle. As Newton-Smith puts it: "For a minimal realist, theories are true or false."[6] That constraint, however, simply does not obtain if Aristotle's or Newton-Smith's brand of realism is denied. Putnam's argument opposes such a realism, and is inconclusive against the relativist for at least that reason.

IV

We are now in an excellent position to review Aristotle's famous argument. First of all, Aristotle declares: "There must, then, even so [that is, granting change, changes in things, the predication of accidental attributes, the appearances of things, and the like] be something which denotes substance. And if this is so, it has been shown that contradictories cannot be predicated at the same time." He goes on directly to link the argument to his account of Protagoras: "Again, if all contradictory statements are true of the same subject at the same time, evidently all things will be one. For the same thing will be a trireme, a wall, and a man, if of everything it is possible either to affirm or to deny anything (and this premiss *must* be accepted by those who share the views of Protagoras)."[7]

This clearly entails Protagoras' refutation. Protagoras has, apparently, rejected (and violated) the law of contradiction. One cannot, Aristotle explains, predicate "the indeterminate" (that is, what is alleged to fall between the true and the false) even of what is real in change; for if we are talking of what is real (or if we suppose that we have knowledge of what we are talking about) then "we *must* predicate of every subject the affirmation or the negation of every attribute. For it is absurd if of each subject its own negation is to be predicable, while the negation of something else which cannot be predicated of it is not to be predicable of it."[8] This shows very clearly that Aristotle's argument cannot possibly be confined to considerations of a merely formal or logically abstract sort. (Aristotle is never tempted to disjoin logic and metaphysics.) It also shows that all the other arguments we have examined, the contemporary arguments, that pretend to defeat relativism on purely internal grounds, do so by way of putting forward a very strong *interpretation* of just how relativism *must* proceed. (Imagine, for instance, an argument against relativism based on Wolterstorff's principles.) This is a strategy we were beginning to resist in the last chapter, which (we now realize) presents the relativist's view very slyly *in* self-defeating terms. The trick is that those terms were (and are) taken to be ineluctable.

There you have the reason for returning to Aristotle. Aristotle's thesis is really the daddy of all the *reductios*, unless it is Plato's argument in the *Theaetetus*.

V

Protagoras' disputed teaching is contained in the single line: "Of all things the measure is Man, of the things that are, that they are, and of the things that are not, that they are not."[9] In itself, the line strikes one almost as a subversive parody of Parmenides' teaching. In any case, the reading, the Aristotelian reading, that Protagoras was committed to construing knowledge as perception, is, most plausibly, due to regarding the perceptual as addressed solely to the apparent and inherently changeable. Hence, the point of the parodic suggestion is reasonably well taken: Parmenides' poem is, if anything, the most extreme *realist* use of noncontradiction and excluded middle that is possible (the archic thesis). Perhaps Protagoras held the view Aristotle ascribes to him. Perhaps not. What really matters is that *we* can find in his teaching the same denial that Aristotle found – *of a realism* that posits unchanging substances knowable as such. *What* Protagoras strikes the modern reader as proclaiming is: (a) that the disjunction between knower and known is derived (somehow) from what, indissolubly, is salient to man; and (b) that that salience or appearance (conceivably, what is not altogether dissimilar to what is meant by the modern post-Hegelian use of "*Erscheinungen*," in the sense in which the real and the apparent cannot be disjoined) does not in itself ensure a changeless reality or a changeless reality that is knowable as such (however we interpret Hegel's usage).

The supreme point is this: that the only way to charge Protagoras with having defeated himself by violating the law of contradiction (and, as a necessary result, *under the circumstances posited*, by violating excluded middle) is *to demonstrate that nothing but the strong realist reading of contradiction (and excluded middle) is conceptually possible*. No one has ever shown that, and contemporary philosophy is clearly committed to *its being false*. Not that the strong realism Aristotle supports (or even the doctrine Parmenides supports) is false; only that *its denial is conceptually viable*. In fact, the distinct pragmatist, anti-essentialist, symbiotized, historicist visions of Putnam, Rorty, and Harman – and, for that matter, the related doctrines of Popper, Kuhn, Feyerabend, MacIntyre, and Bernstein, whom we have already mentioned in this connection – confirm that it is now impossible to pretend to defeat Protagoras or any modern protagorean merely by invoking the strong archic *interpretation* of contradiction and/or excluded middle that (one way or another) all of these thinkers seem disposed to favor. That is, they favor such a strategy, but only by way of the irrelevant subterfuge of pretending that the relativist, much like Aristotle's Protagoras, could not "conceivably" have intended his thesis except in the barefaced contradictory sense they are prepared to expose. Aristotle, Newton-Smith, Wolterstorff, and Dummett,[10] on the other hand, do actually draw, or implicate, their own conclusions by way of the dubious form of the realism just indicated.

What we must see is that a stalemate here is a victory for Protagoras. *If* we cannot establish the required realism indisputably, then the defeat of Protagoras on so-called "internal" logical grounds fails. Because all that we require is that Protagoras (or his modern-day protagorean offspring) simply should not be as stupid as Newton-Smith and Putnam pretend he cannot fail to be.

VI

Of Protagoras, Diogenes Laertius says: "He was the first to maintain that in every experience there are two logoi in opposition to each other."[11] This, apparently, is one of the principal sources for the view that Protagoras flouted the law of contradiction. But it could just as easily mean either of two things: (a) that the law of contradiction applies only on an interpretation of a given sector of inquiry, that is, in a sense of interpretation similar to that favored by Peirce and Dummett; and that, on such a viable interpretation, what, prejudicially or abstractly, merely look like contradictories or contraries need not be such at all; and (b) that, again on a suitable interpretation, the opposed bipolar truth-values are not always, perhaps not anywhere, adequate to the range of truth-claims that may be made of human "experience" (that is, regarding the symbiotized world of knower and known); and that a many-valued logic may be more suitable.

All of this – the elaboration of options (a) and (b) – clearly needs to be examined with care. But we are here interested only in their viability. It is their viability, after all, that both the ancients and the moderns have denied. Of course, one clear consequence of reading Protagoras this way is to confirm that he is indeed the arch-opponent of Plato. For, on the Protagorean argument (at least on the viable modern-day protagorean argument), there is no opposition between knowledge (*episteme*) and belief or opinion (*doxa*) in the famous sense Plato champions, for instance, in the *Republic* (507–13). There is no such opposition, simply because there *is* no admissible disjunction between the unchanging world of Forms and the changing world of familiar experience. There *is* no world of Forms at all. Nor is it necessary to hold that knowledge is about a changeless world.

In this sense, there is no difference between Protagoras' (implicit) opposition to Aristotle and his (apparently) explicit opposition to Socrates. Indeed, Socrates actually links Protagoras with Heraclitus and Empedocles and "a whole series of philosophers" who agree in this, that

> nothing is one thing just by itself, nor can you rightly call it by some definite name, nor even say it is of any definite sort. On the contrary, if you call it "large," it will be found to be also small; if "heavy," to be also light; and so on all through, because nothing is *one* thing or *some* thing or of any definite sort. All the things we are pleased to say "are," really are in process of becoming, as a result of movement and change and of blending one with another. We are wrong to speak of them as "being," for none of them ever is; they are always becoming.[12]

In reviewing this argument, Socrates explicitly leads the discussion to Protagoras' claim that man is the measure.[13] But he transforms it so that it takes the form of an extreme subjectivism:

> If what every man believes as a result of perception is indeed true for him; if, just as no one is to be a better judge of what another experiences, so no one is better entitled to consider what another thinks is true or false, and ... every man is to have his own beliefs for himself alone and they are all right and true – then, my friend [addressing Theaetetus], wherein is the wisdom of Protagoras, to justify his setting up to teach others and to be handsomely paid for it, and where is our comparative ignorance or the need for us to go and sit at his feet, when each of us is himself the measure of his own wisdom?[14]

We cannot be quite sure whether Socrates is correctly interpreting Protagoras' remarks. It is not a question of actually misrepresenting Protagoras: what Protagoras says may indeed bear the weight of Socrates' reading – at a price. But can he have been quite as unclever as Socrates makes him out to be? (We shall pick up the thread of this argument much later in our account.) In any case, if Socrates' reading is correct, then Protagoras may well have been a fool.

Once we grant his interpretation, Socrates has no trouble turning the tables on Protagoras. Protagoras is bound to have difficulty with truth-claims shared with others, with knowledge that exceeds momentary sensory perception, with consistency among his judgments, with distinguishing superior and inferior judgment, and the like. Socrates plays on all of these considerations, producing the self-referential paradoxes Rorty and Putnam mention. Socrates' characteristic maneuver is to remind Theaetetus of Protagoras' own calling as a teacher; for, as a teacher (of wisdom), Protagoras had conceded that there was a "better and worse" and that, regarding this, "some people were superior," though (as Socrates further remarks) he also assumed all to be equal and sufficient in wisdom, which follows from the extreme doctrine Socrates ascribes to Protagoras.[15] Contradiction is bound to arise, for it is already implicit in the premisses just posited. It turns out, for instance, that on Protagoras' "absurd" theory, no one takes another to be ignorant or mistaken in his opinion.[16]

Now, the subtle point buried in all this busy talk is this: Socrates has managed to conflate two pertinent doctrines and to ascribe to Protagoras the obviously untenable one. The two are these: (a) truth is to be construed in the relationalist way; and (b) man decides what we should say exists and is real, there is no other way to proceed. (Socrates, of course, offers several other dubious interpretations of Protagoras.) It is true that (b) threatens the archic thesis. But the defeat of (b), both in the *Metaphysics* and the *Theaetetus*, depends on its being supposed that Protagoras favors a metaphysics of impermanent realities (of merely perceptible things, for instance), *which*, it is claimed, produces contradictions that ultimately implicate (a).

The clearest form of the argument is given by Aristotle. In the fourth book of the *Metaphysics*, Aristotle advances two decisive principles regarding primary substance (*ousía*): (i) necessarily, for every attribute, a substance either possesses that attribute or it does not, which is Aristotle's version of the principle of excluded middle;[17] and (ii) for any substance, if anything may be predicated of it, then, necessarily, its attributes cannot be accidents only, or only apparent properties, the violation of which Aristotle takes to entail contradiction.[18] Protagoras, apparently, violates both[19] – which shows at least that relativism was thought in the ancient world to involve a restriction on, or abandonment of, the principle of excluded middle.

Now, *if* it is not true that reality is changeless, then, of course, (ii) must be given up; and if (ii) is abandoned, then, on Aristotle's own reading of (ii), (i) must be given up also. But the ancients understood the doctrine, "man is the measure," to entail at least that reality is not changeless – also, therefore, that if man can rightly claim to have knowledge, then, on Protagoras' argument, knowledge cannot be addressed to what is changeless in reality. This much at least yields a stalemate between Aristotle and Protagoras: thus far, neither one's thesis is obviously incoherent. But even this much favors Protagoras, because Aristotle holds that the violation of (i) and (ii) yields contradiction. More would have to be said.

Aristotle does have more to say. There is another argument, a bridge argument, that is decisive for Aristotle: "if not all things are relative, but some are self-existent, not everything that appears will be true";[20] and *that*, which is tantamount to (ii), must, *somewhere*, in Protagoras' argument, yield the denial of those properties of particular substances *that are changeless*. Nothing could be more reasonable. The only trouble is that Protagoras rejects the thesis that there *is* something changeless, and Aristotle nowhere shows convincingly that *that* produces contradiction, except, trivially, *by* presupposing the truth of what must first be shown to be true. So Aristotle fails. Certainly, in our own time, nearly every prominent thinker either believes that reality is not changeless or believes that it is not demonstrably true that believing *that* cannot but be incoherent.

VII

This is the point at which Rorty rightly takes note of Socrates' invention of self-referential puzzles. He observes very tellingly: "The relativist who says that we can break ties among serious and incompatible candidates for belief *only* by 'nonrational' or 'noncognitive' considerations is just one of the Platonist or Kantian philosopher's imaginary playmates, inhabiting the same realm of fantasy as the solipsist, the skeptic, and the moral nihilist."[21] Rorty is quite right to expose the fraud (Socrates' fraud), which shows, incidentally, that Putnam must have been mistaken in treating *him* as *that* kind of relativist (the fictional Protagorean) that he (Putnam) is prepared to do in in a manner rather like Aristotle's and Plato's (except that Putnam is not an essentialist). Rorty is partly that *other* sort of protagorean, the one who, in a sense, embraces the doctrine of "becoming," except that he, Rorty, also repudiates, as we have already noted, traditional philosophy altogether.

If Protagoras' doctrine of "becoming" *is* a philosophical thesis, as it certainly seems to be, then Rorty is more a relativist *manqué*, a sort of protagorean who accepts the flux and "man the measure" but who rejects, in doing that, the very need for philosophical legitimation – hence, for relativism. Socrates defeats Protagoras by fictive parody;

Rorty rejects relativism as an unnecessary, untenable, and (Putnam's term) "silly" philosophical doctrine beyond the entirely rational first-order use of whatever it would take to disallow the (strong realist) application of such logical principles as contradiction and excluded middle:

> "Relativism" only seems to refer to a disturbing view, [says Rorty,] worthy of being refuted, if it concerns *real* theories, not just philosophical theories. Nobody really cares if there are incompatible alternative formulations of a categorical imperative, or incompatible sets of categories of the pure understanding. We *do* care about alternative, concrete, detailed cosmologies, or alternative concrete, detailed proposals for political change.[22]

In effect, Rorty means to support the "real" use of protagorean practice but not on the basis of a "realist," "anti-realist," "idealist," or other piece of philosophical nonsense. There may be reason to examine Rorty's peculiar conceptual economy more closely; but, at the moment, he comes across as a friend of Protagoras, a friend who has no need of argument except perhaps that sort of argument that is said to demonstrate how utterly unnecessary and futile philosophical argument is. Nevertheless, Rorty's own strategy may even suggest a philosophical defense *of* relativism. Our game, however, is to show the philosophical defensibility of relativism in the face of Protagoras' opponents. So Rorty cannot help us explicitly, except by the public influence of his *obiter dicta*.

VIII

The friendliest approach to Protagoras' views, in the literature of so-called analytic philosophy, is probably exhibited by Kuhn and Feyerabend. Unfortunately, Kuhn's position is inadequately developed, and Feyerabend, as a self-styled philosophical anarchist (or Dadaist), may be even less hospitable to philosophical debate than Rorty.

Yet Feyerabend is an explicit protagorean. He formulates the following dictum, which he believes Protagoras and Herodotus share, and which he himself finds congenial, as against the views of those who take relativists to be arbitrary about rules and values and comparative judgments: "R4: laws, religious beliefs and customs rule, like kings, in restricted domains. Their rule rests on a twofold authority – on their *power* and on the fact that it is *rightful* power: the rules are *valid* in their domains."[23]

R4 (so designated in a longish list of relativist alternatives) is Feyerabend's gloss on Protagoras' doctrine (R5) of man as the measure. He understands it to favor, against the interpretation of "realists" or the realist-inclined (like Plato, on Feyerabend's résumé of the *Theaetetus*, or like Popper, as the falsificationist opponent of positivism),[24] who take R5 "as a premise 'entailing' well-defined and unambiguous consequences" (that is, rule-governed consequences, consequences that depend on "the meaning of the statement [or rule] . . . established *before* it is applied"). Feyerabend construes it rather "as a rule of thumb adumbrating an outlook without giving a precise description of it."[25]

Notice that Feyerabend maintains, in R4, that custom and belief are, in some sense, "valid" in their domains, that they enjoy "rightful" power. This is meant to offset the impression *both* that the relativist or protagorean view is arbitrary and lacking in a discipline adequate for comparative judgment, legitimation, justificatory reasoning, or the like *and* that such a discipline presupposes or requires a fixed, objectivist, realist, or essentialist discovery of the principles or criteria for such a discipline. Feyerabend links the latter, the "Platonic" objection, to the familiar "distinction between being and seeming" and he finds that that objection to relativism is also advanced by Hilary Putnam (whom, needless to say, he strenuously opposes).[26]

IX

Putnam does actually say the following:

> The whole *purpose* of relativism, its very defining characteristic, is . . . to *deny* the existence of any intelligible notion of *objective* "fit". Thus the relativist cannot understand talk about truth in terms of *objective* justification-conditions. . . . The relativist must end by denying that a thought is *about* anything in either a realist or non-realist sense; for he cannot distinguish between thinking one's thought is about something and actually thinking about that thing. In short, what the relativist fails to see is that it is a presupposition of thought itself that some kind of objective "rightness" exists.[27]

This is as close as Putnam comes to Aristotle. But the charge (Putnam's) is entirely unsatisfactory. First of all, it trades on the same supposed self-referential paradoxes Socrates trots out against Protagoras: there is no reason given to suppose that the wary relativist (Protagoras himself) cannot avoid this trap. Secondly, Feyerabend (whom Putnam explicitly attacks) has already indicated, in R4 – which he construes as a favorable gloss on Protagoras' own intention – that *he does* support validity, rightness, objectivity, and the like: we need to have a clearer argument on both sides as to whether the relativist recovery of objectivity works or fails. Thirdly, in advancing his claim, Putnam actually offers, in support, the notion of (objective) "fit" sketched by Nelson Goodman in his *Ways of Worldmaking*: but Goodman's account is, notoriously, a much more radical version of relativism than Feyerabend's, one that may well be either utterly incoherent or at least incompletely worked out, one in fact that Putnam himself later criticizes in no uncertain terms.[28] And finally, Putnam himself, despite his disclaimer, is certainly attracted to relativism, for instance in his discussion of objectivity, which corresponds very closely not only with the point of W. V. Quine's relativism but also, ironically, with the view *Feyerabend* expresses: Putnam does not *show*, in the context of that discussion, how *he* would secure objective "fit" or how he would secure it in a way that would not be open to the admitted relativist. Thus, for example, in a quite recent discussion, in attempting to make a "Dedekind cut" out of a relatively continuous ranking of a "subjective"/"objective" order of preferences, Putnam openly acknowledges that, on "my own view ... the enterprise isn't worth the candle. The game is played out. We can make a rough sort of rank ordering (although even here there are disagreements), but the idea of a 'point at which' subjectivity ceases and Objectivity-with-a-capital-O begins has proved chimerical."[29]

The result is that, given his various sympathies – the attraction (despite ultimate disagreement) to Dummett's anti-realism and the opposition to (metaphysical) realism, the general acceptance of Quine's indeterminacy of translation thesis, the favorable treatment of Goodman's formulation of objectivity, the concession regarding objectivity's informality, the opposition to cognitive transparency and essentialism – Putnam cannot really be shown to subscribe to a strong distinction between an invariant reality and a range of shifting appearances (accessible to science) that fail to reveal such an invariant reality. He claims that we require – and that he *uses* – the conceptual distinction between an objective reality and subjective appearances. But Protagoras himself seems entirely hospitable to that particular notion, *so long as it does not ensure an invariant reality knowable as such to man.* That is, the notion functions only (certainly in Putnam, presumably in Protagoras) as a reasoned posit *within* the play of appearances (internalism), *not* as an

independent criterion of any sort: not, say, either as a criterion of
knowledge or as a criterion that precludes pretensions of knowledge
addressed to the mere flux of appearances. In short, realism need not
entail the invariance of reality; hence, knowledge need not be conform-
ably restricted either.

X

Ancient relativism, then, protagoreanism (perhaps Protagoras' own
thesis), is the thesis that: (1) man is the measure of reality, knowledge,
and truth; (2) there is no independent invariant reality that man can
claim obtains or that he knows, consistently with affirming (1); (3)
the conjunction of (1) and (2) is viable, not incoherent, not self-
contradictory, not self-defeating; and (4) judgments of what is true and
false, within the space of (1), disallow any disjunction between knowledge (*episteme*) and opinion or belief (*doxa*); and, given (2), they permit
the application of the law of contradiction only under interpretation (the
interpretation of a given range of appearances) and disallow in principle
the exceptionless application of excluded middle. It follows, on accept-
ing (1) to (4), that what, *on Plato's or Aristotle's views of reality and
knowledge*, would count as contraries or contradictories – therefore, as
paradoxical or incoherent – need not be such, *on the relativist's view*.
Protagoras may be construed, therefore, as having shown that relativism
is *not* an interesting thesis except on grounds that relate formal or logical
considerations to substantive considerations bearing on the nature
of reality and man's cognitive relationship to reality. His is the first
sustained attack on the inviolability of excluded middle and on the
separability of abstract logical principles and their application to the
real world. As it happens, these are notably contemporary strategies,
although it is clear that we cannot recover their full defense from
Protagoras' fragments or from their discussion in Plato and Aristotle.
Protagoras is, therefore, at least an incipient robust relativist.

Protagoras is best characterized as the philosopher of the flux (of
a profoundly changing world, not a chaos) and of the analysis of the
nature and conditions of knowledge confined to that. His is not, therefore, a relativism addressed to history or historicized knowledge. *That*
is essential to modern – really, relatively contemporary – relativisms,
particularly so-called incommensurabilisms. But modern notions of history – historicisms – presuppose the flux and add to it certain further
complications. Hence, there is a fairly legible connection between
ancient and modern versions of relativism. We are bound to move on to

topics that never appear in the ancient world, but we are not taking undue liberty with the Greek sources. We are distinguishing here between Protagoras himself, the Protagorean doctrine Plato and Aristotle attack in their respective ways, and the protagorean thesis *we* have constructed looking back sympathetically to the others from the prejudiced vantage of what will eventually prove to be our own little game. (The typographical markers should be clear enough.)

Still, we have managed to neutralize somewhat the too easy, possibly bad-faith argument of mere formal inconsistency, arbitrariness, incoherence, irrationalism, anarchy, and the like now so familiar in standard attacks on relativism. These have become so conspiratorially successful that one often hears it insinuated (if not actually said) that anyone who cannot show how the incoherent, self-defeating "Protagorean" can be made out to be a consistent "protagorean" has simply changed the subject. Now we understand the slyness of that nasty little maneuver, and how little actually depends on it. But relativism has had a very poor press, it must be admitted, and its vindication does indeed threaten to shake a few foundations and orthodoxies at least. So there should be no surprise that its opponents are often quite willing to take any short cut at all in order to disallow – as an argument beneath contempt, beyond rational dispute – a line of thought that means to instruct us regarding the serious limits of our cognitive pretensions: that means, in particular, to spell out those limits in such a way that we cannot suppose we really guide our lives by discerning the changeless structures and norms of human nature and the natural world. Protagoreanism, therefore, is a radical doctrine, self-consciously and deliberately radical. But it is not or need not be stupid, and it is not or need not be paradoxical or careless.

The essential lesson is that the fate of relativism rests with just how to relate logical principles and ontological analysis. Contemporary critics fail to win their point because they pretend to a fixity in logical principles or in their application that they nowhere demonstrate; and the ancient critics fail because they pretend to an ontological fixity that they cannot show to be unavoidable. So the ancient and the modern critics fall between the same two stools – but in opposite directions. The relativist's recovery is equally clear: simply specify another connection between logical or formal principles and ontology.

XI

Having put this much in place, it may be helpful to make as explicit as possible, before bringing these early remarks to a close, an essential confusion that runs through a good deal of the contemporary discussion of relativism – that means to recast the ancient defeat of Protagoras. It will pay to keep the theme in mind, because it dissolves so easily and because nearly all of the recent discussions are tied to it.

Thus, to offer one example to fix the point, Harvey Siegel, who may well enjoy the distinction of having mounted the most sustained recent attack on relativism, is quite frank to say that, "re-fashioned in more modern notation," Plato's arguments in the *Theaetetus* "are [are indeed!] successful" in demonstrating "relativism's incoherence, and that contemporary relativists have thus far failed to overcome the incoherence charge against their view."[30]

What we need to bear in mind, what Siegel (and many another) does not manage to sort out neatly, are the following three distinctions: (i) the analysis of the *meaning* of "true" forms the proper basis for charging relativists (Protagoras in particular) with incoherence (as by way of the self-referential paradoxes); but that is a matter entirely distinct from the analysis of the *epistemic conditions* on which *truth-values* are ascribed to *truth-claims*; (ii) it is trivial (on one obvious reading) to affirm that the *ascription* of truth-values must be relativized to the conceptual framework of whoever makes such an ascription (how else should one do it?); but *that* relativization is not tantamount to the relativization *of truth itself to that same framework* (orientation, point of view, conviction, feeling, or whatnot), it is not tantamount to what (in the prologue) we termed relationalism; and (iii) the trivial relativization of truth-claims to one's conceptual framework (among potentially many others, whether synchronically or diachronically, whether intra- or inter-societally, construed) could be taken to *define* truth in the relationalist way *only if* the framework could itself be strictly individuated among other such frameworks and *used* in that same strict way in determining truth; but if reference to one's framework is meant to be merely holistic, open-ended, committed to "one" inclusive world in which even moderately divergent "worlds," conceptual schemes, frameworks and the like are located and compared (that is, if it is meant in the trivial sense), then the relativization of truth-*claims* in that way is emphatically *not* tantamount to the fatal relationalist definition.

Siegel offers as an example of a fatally flawed proposal of "relative truth" the following formula: "*p*'s truth is relative to the world as conceived by a framework, so that if *p* corresponds to the facts as constituted in a framework F, then *p* is true relative to F, or true for a user of F."[31] But there's all the difference in the world between: (a) claiming that *p* is true if it "corresponds" to the facts *simpliciter* (which, as it happens, cannot but be trivially "relative" to the one and only framework any claimant has or can use), and (b) claiming that there *is* a particular framework among such alternative frameworks (that a claimant can use or choose alternatively) such that *p* is true if it "corresponds" to the facts as constituted by *that* framework *but not another*. So (a) is entirely benign, but (b) *is* incoherent: it leads directly to the self-referential paradoxes, it is also close to the interpretation of Protagoras favored in the ancient world. But it *is* avoidable. Siegel's argument is, of course, symptomatic of the entire unfavorable reading accorded Protagoras. (We shall inevitably be occupied in what follows with a number of variations on this theme.)

Notes

1 Aristotle, *Metaphysics*, trans. W. D. Ross; reprinted in *The Basic Works of Aristotle*, ed. Richard McKeon (New York: Random House, 1941), book iv, chapter 4 (1006a).
2 Ibid., book iii, chapter 4 (999b).
3 Ibid.
4 W. H. Newton-Smith, *The Rationality of Science* (London: Routledge and Kegan Paul, 1981), chapter 2, particularly pp. 19, 34, 39.
5 Ibid., p. 19.
6 Ibid., p. 39.
7 Aristotle, *Metaphysics*, book iv, chapter 4 (1007b); italics added.
8 Ibid.
9 Kathleen Freeman, *Ancilla to the Pre-Socratic Philosophers* (Oxford: Basil Blackwell, 1952), p. 125.
10 See Michael Dummett, "Realism," in *Truth and Other Enigmas* (Cambridge: Harvard University Press, 1978) for the clearest evidence of his strong realism. "Realism," he says, "I characterize as the belief that statements of the disputed class [that is, statements about the physical world, mental events, processes, mathematical statements, etc.] possess an objective truth-value, independently of our means of knowing it: they are true or false in virtue of a reality existing independently of us" (p. 146). The "anti-realist" need not dispute the claim that truth concerns what is independent of our knowledge; he insists *only* that "statements of the disputed class are to be understood only by reference to the sort of thing which we can count as evidence for a statement of that class" (p. 146).
11 Cited in Mario Untersteiner, *The Sophists*, trans. Kathleen Freeman (Oxford: Basil Blackwell, 1954), p. 19.
12 *Plato's Theory of Knowledge: The Theaetetus and the Sophist of Plato* translated with a running commentary by Francis Macdonald Cornford (London: Kegan Paul, Trench, Trubner, 1935), 152C–E.
13 Ibid., 160D.
14 Ibid., 161D–E.

15 Ibid., 169D.
16 Ibid.
17 Aristotle, *Metaphysics*, 1007b.
18 Ibid., 1011b.
19 Ibid., 1011a.
20 Ibid., 1005b, 1010a; italics added.
21 Richard Rorty, "Pragmatism, Relativism, Irrationalism," in *Consequences of Pragmatism (Essays: 1972–1980)* (Minneapolis: University of Minnesota Press, 1982), p. 167; italics added.
22 Ibid., p. 168.
23 Paul Feyerabend, "Notes on Relativism," in *Farewell to Reason* (London: Verso, 1987), p. 43.
24 Cf. ibid., pp. 169–79.
25 Ibid., p. 45.
26 Ibid., pp. 49, 83. See further, Hilary Putnam, *Reason, Truth and History* (Cambridge: Cambridge University Press, 1981), p. 122; cited by Feyerabend.
27 Putnam, "Two Conceptions of Rationality," in *Reason, Truth and History*, pp. 123–4.
28 Cf. Putnam, ibid., p. 123; and Nelson Goodman, *Ways of Worldmaking* (Indianapolis: Hackett Publishing Co., 1978), p. 138; cited by Putnam. See also, Hilary Putnam, "Reflections on Goodman's *Ways of Worldmaking*," in *Philosophical Papers*, vol. 3 (Cambridge: Cambridge University Press, 1983), pp. 155–69.
29 Hilary Putnam, *The Many Faces of Realism* (La Salle, Ill.: Open Court, 1977), pp. 27–8.
30 Harvey Siegel, *Relativism Refuted: A Critique of Contemporary Epistemological Relativism* (Dordrecht: D. Reidel, 1987), pp. xiii-xiv.
31 Ibid., p. 173 n. 46. Siegel draws his case from Chris Swoyer, "True For," in Jack W. Meiland and Michael Krausz (eds), *Relativism: Cognitive and Moral* (Notre Dame: University of Notre Dame Press, 1982), pp. 84–108. We shall return to the issue later, for instance, in reviewing a proposal made by J. N. Mohanty. Cf. also Lawrence Hazelrigg, *Social Science and the Challenge of Relativism*, vol. 2 (Tallahassee: Florida State University Press, 1989), chapter 6.

5

Protagoreanism and Incommensurabilism (I)

I

To appreciate just how radical Protagoras' thesis must have seemed in the ancient world, we must keep constantly before us the sense of how uniformly the pre-Socratics focused on fathoming the grand simplicity of the cosmic order and, in particular, on fathoming how man was generated from that order or came to understand it. Protagoras threatens all that: "Of all things the measure is Man, of the things that are, that they are, and of the things that are not, that they are not."[1]

For Protagoras, there *is* no cosmic order first acknowledged as the fixed envelope within which to posit, or speculate about, whatever catches our eye. The cosmos itself, if ever we could reach such a bold conjecture, is at best a conjecture that humans venture *within* the space of an impenetrably, an indissolubly complex flux of appearances or seemings. What is impenetrable or indissoluble is the flow of appearances, which are at once what appear to man and what, to man, appear spontaneously and reflexively to have the order they do.

Protagoras does not deny order. He understands cognized order to depend ineluctably on an original symbiotic limit that we cannot penetrate. There is, therefore, what *we* should be inclined to call a *subjective* element ineliminably constitutive of whatever order – even the order of the cosmos – we may posit. The notion is cast in cognizing terms: man is the measure. But that seems to be the upshot of a deeper doctrine that can only be called metaphysical or, more profoundly still, a doctrine concerned with the unanalyzable precondition of what, subsequently, appears as a theory of human knowledge as well as a theory of the cognizable world. In any event, that entire space is denied any invariant *distributed* structure of just the reassuring sort that is posited by the countering arguments of Plato and Aristotle. That is what must have seemed so shocking to the ancients.

II

Obviously, we are speculating here. We have no choice. But it seems that the same conserving imagination must have run from Anaximander through Parmenides through Heraclitus and on to Plato and Aristotle. "The Non-Limited [the *Apeiron*] is the original material of existing things [says Anaximander]; further, the source from which existing things derive their existence is also that to which they return at their destruction, *according to necessity*; for they give justice and make reparation to one another for their injustice, *according to the arrangement of Time*."[2]

The cosmic order does not require man's presence or depend on it. On the contrary, man's own existence and capacity is derived from the other. "Come, I will tell you [says Parmenides] – and you must accept my word when you have heard it – the ways of inquiry which alone are to be thought: the one that IT IS, and it is not possible for it NOT TO BE, in the way of credibility, for it follows Truth; the other, that IT IS NOT, and that IT is bound NOT TO BE; this I tell you is a path that cannot be explored; for you could neither recognize that which IS NOT, nor express it."[3] Another fragment from Parmenides catches up the explicit and essential theme common to Plato and Aristotle: "that which it is possible to think is identical with that which can Be."[4] In Parmenides, invariant reality is determinate and determinable by thought; in Anaximander, the *Apeiron* is rather like a mythic indefinable source within which all legibly determinate reality is invariantly ordered.

The same inspiration appears in Heraclitus, despite the fact that Heraclitus is regularly taken to be the philosopher of the flux.

> The law [*logos*] (*of the universe*) is as here explained; but men are always incapable of understanding it, both before they hear it, and when they have heard it for the first time. For though all things come into being in accordance with this Law, men seem as if they had never met with it, when they meet with words (*theories*) and actions (*processes*) such as I expound, separating each thing according to its nature and explaining how it is made.... Therefore one must follow (the universal Law, namely) that which is common (*to all*). But although the Law is universal, the majority live as if they had understanding peculiar to themselves.[5]

Heraclitus has two considerations in mind here: first, the fixed order of reality does not depend in any way on man's cognitive powers; and second, the incessant change or flux of the world is not structureless or incognizable. Protagoras, we may conjecture, opposes the first straight out, both because he opposes invariance and because he opposes any ultimate disjunction between the order of reality and the order of cognition. Furthermore, he construes the second, subject to the first, in such a way that to posit knowledge of what is inherently changeable is not self-contradictory. These, of course, are what we mean by claiming that Protagoras opposes the archic canon.

III

We earlier opposed Protagoras to Parmenides: and, indeed, what Protagoras says is almost a parody of what Parmenides says. But it is also true that Protagoras and Heraclitus could not be more opposed, even though they are both concerned with some version of the doctrine of the flux. The mark of the principal pre-Socratics is their insistence on an invariant cosmic order that does not depend on man but is, under favorable conditions, cognitively penetrable by man. Protagoras denies all that: whatever order is posited is posited by man, who is himself inherently changeable, not invariantly structured in any discernible way; and what he understands or knows is impenetrably constituted in a way that is also unstable as far as invariance is concerned, because the discernible world depends indissolubly on what we barely glimpse as man's contributing or constituting function – functioning perceptually and cognitively.

Protagoras clearly strikes us as peculiarly modern. One might easily be tempted to see in him an anticipation, for instance, of Nietzsche and Heidegger. But that is not the point of indulging our speculation here. Protagoras's relativism stems from his particular way of introducing the flux: it disallows invariance, *all* determinate invariance; but it does *not* disallow perceived order or the perceiving of order; hence, it concedes an order in things and a perception of order just so long as both are construed in a way that gives up the inflexibility of excluded middle and the (unconditional, uninterpreted) applicability of noncontradiction. At least that's one reasonable way of reading Protagoras.

The Greek world begins with the cosmos and makes its way to man. That is the link running from Anaximander to Aristotle. Protagoras threatens the continuity: there you have the novelty of his relativism. To go much beyond that finding is to risk a certain textual irresponsibility. Nevertheless, what we must carefully weigh is the sense in which, in the modern world, philosophy seems to move from man to the cosmos, that

is, in the opposite direction. In context, even this may be misleading; for
the way in which the (early) moderns move from man to the world *is
not* Protagoras' way. On the contrary, it is itself regularly committed to
the same invariant structure of reality. This is the theme, say, that runs
from Descartes through Kant through Hegel (disputatiously, it must be
said) through Husserl – if we allow ourselves the luxury of treating
these four thinkers as reasonably representative specimens of the discernible phases of the master tradition of Western Philosophy – up to
our own century.

There is no single way of reading these thinkers, of course. But there
is no need to insist on one. The important point at stake is that
Protagoras is, implicitly, as much opposed to the second set as he is to
the first. The first set of thinkers, the ancient ones, agree that the order
of reality is unchanging. Somehow, this is thought to be true apart from
our affirming it. Parmenides denies the reality of change. Heraclitus
affirms change but argues that it is constrained by a changeless law. The
ancients typically affirm that what IS is peculiarly apt for human knowledge, but their confidence is never centered in cognition. The moderns
reverse matters but they arrive at the same general finding. This explains, for instance, why, when he speaks of the soul's capacity for
thinking, of its capacity for intellectual knowledge, Aristotle says, in *De
Anima*, that "the thinking part of the soul must ... be, while impassible
[as opposed to bodily perception], capable of receiving the form of an
object; that is, must be potentially identical in character with its object
without being the object. Mind must be related to what is thinkable, as
sense is to what is sensible."[6]

The theory may be preposterous. Aristotle may have been driven to
it by the needs of his system. But the theory moves from reality to
knowledge, ensures that there will be no problem of knowledge, and
does that by making its object changeless and by placing its reality
beyond doubt and conjecture.

The early moderns begin, at least if we start with Descartes, with
what is internal to "mind." Hence, to secure knowledge (for instance,
witness the maneuvers of Descartes and Berkeley against skepticism)
they must secure some form of correspondence with an independent
reality, whether by causation or not (witness Descartes and Locke), and
they must construe that reality as suitably invariant.

Locke is particularly instructive in this regard, since, replacing the
cognitive primacy of Descartes's "natural light of reason" with sensory
ideas, Locke obviously risks every form of skepticism and disconnection
from reality. But, by an ingenious economy, he lands on his feet and
restores empiricism (which the new science requires) to certain fixities

sufficiently like those favored in the ancient philosophical tradition that investigators from the end of the seventeenth century on may be assured that their attention to the world of change and appearance need not entail the loss of a changeless reality. "*Knowledge* [says Locke] seems to me to be nothing but *the perception of the connection of and agreement, or disagreement and repugnancy of any of our ideas*." He adds at once that "the mind clearly and infallibly perceives each idea to agree with itself and to be what it is; and all distinct ideas to disagree, i.e., the one not to be the other." None of this, he is careful to explain, depends on language – names or propositions – which would risk admitting a deep and disturbing contingency; also, what (he believes) amounts to exact science incorporates the agreement (that is, the correspondence) of our ideas with "*actual real existence*."[7] As is well known, on Locke's account, "the ideas of primary qualities of bodies are resemblances of them, and their patterns do really exist in the bodies themselves" – that is, just those ideas that physics requires.[8] So the lawlike invariances of Newtonian physics are made accessible through the indubitability of our internalized ideas of primary qualities, in spite of the apparent transience of sensory experience. The fatal impossibility of "resemblance" between ideas and bodies that Berkeley spotted points only to the philosophical creakiness of Locke's actual argument. It does not challenge in the least Locke's entirely conservative intention (which Berkeley and Descartes share) regarding the real invariances that modern science has discovered. It is in this sense that the moderns, beginning with the immediacies of sense perception or of reflexive thought (for Descartes includes in "thinking" an entire hamper of everything we are said to be immediately conscious of),[9] lead us back from knowledge and experience to an invariant order of reality, in much the same sense the ancients favored.

Nothing in the later development of Kant's, Hegel's, and Husserl's philosophies alters the primacy of invariance, however complex or changed the center of invariance becomes and however impossible, in the modern world, it may prove to be to disjoin metaphysical and epistemological inquiry. In Hegel, for instance, the essential invariance is found in the career of an ideal World-Spirit that, in time, discovers the directional ordering of that horizonal world that first appears to be discerned by man, himself a creature of that same flux. In Husserl, invariance is found not in the discernible objective world but in some originary transcendental (that is, universally instantiated) Subject's generation of the constituting concepts by which the seemingly intelligible world is first constituted *as* meaningful (not as real) for all. And, in Kant, the invariant structure of the accessible world of objective science is indissolubly first constituted by the invariant structure of the natural human mind, to which the flux of externally produced sensation (the source of our passive access to an otherwise unknown world) yields and must yield for the sake of intelligible order.

IV

The important lesson of these modern developments rests with Protagoras' radicalism once again. For, in embracing the doctrine of the flux, Protagoras is *not* a skeptic or a nihilist or an anarchist. *He* means, in making man the measure "of all things," to preserve knowledge or defensible belief. In doing that, however, he is taken by the ancients themselves – by Plato and Aristotle, notably – to be opposed to their own metaphysics of invariance. He implicitly opposes, in that same spirit, anachronistically, the metaphysics of the moderns; for they, too, subscribe to a form of invariance, a form in which the invariances of the cognizable world are essentially due to, or first known to be captured by, the invariances of the cognizing mind.

The ancients read Protagoras as internally inconsistent and incoherent, because *they* construed the logic of noncontradiction and excluded middle as presupposing and depending upon a realist metaphysics that either prioritizes the analysis of reality over the analysis of knowledge of reality (which sounds paradoxical to the modern ear) or else maintains that, to be knowable, reality must be invariant, unchanging in its universal structure. The moderns read Protagoras as inconsistent and incoherent, because *they* construe knowledge as *of* the universally unchanging and invariant. And the "modern" moderns, that is, the contemporary philosophers we have discussed earlier (thinkers like Putnam and Newton-Smith and Rorty), read the relativist (the protagorean) as inconsistent and incoherent because *they* construe the self-referential paradoxes and the constraints of noncontradiction and excluded middle as binding in certain restricted ways that cannot be overcome, whether or not one subscribes to a *metaphysics* of invariance.

The characteristically contemporary version of this opposition tends to attack incommensurabilism rather more pointedly than protagoreanism, because some version of the doctrine of the flux and the denial of naturalistic essentialism are generally supported in our own time (against Parmenides and Plato and Aristotle as well as the early moderns); and yet, it is maintained, whatever are the conditions of intelligibility and truth, those conditions impose limits on the nature of the flux and rule out, as incoherent (still), strategies like Protagoras' or like those of his "protagorean" descendants, for reasons having to do more with the requirements of thinking and logic and knowledge than with the presumed structures of reality. Incommensurabilisms of various sorts are thought to be akin to Protagoras' ancient claim but to require, for defeat, considerations much slimmer than the ancients had insisted on. Nothing less could explain the ease with which Putnam and Rorty, say, support the rejection of Protagoras' strategy, despite the fact that *they* also reject Aristotle's essentialism and theory of knowledge.

V

It is true that protagoreanism and incommensurabilism are regarded as similar by their critics, in the sense that both are taken to be incapable of escaping self-referential paradoxes. But the two programs are differently focused. Protagoreanism tends to center on the logical viability of supporting the assignment of truth-values in a way that, on certain canonical views, would yield contradictions. The alleged self-referential paradoxes are regarded as the price the protagorean relativist pays for pursuing his claim. He, on the other hand, defends his program by appeal to the constraints imposed on would-be knowledge by denying ontic invariance and the admissibility of determinately real structures separated from the symbiotizing complexities of human thought and cognition. Incommensurabilism, by contrast, tends to center on the historical and cultural diversity of conceptual schemes and categories, on our internalizing divergent habits of mind in acquiring such schemata as we do as we develop into the apt members of a natural human society. It also depends on our being incompletely capable of achieving an entirely neutral stance with regard to alternative orientations of thought and action or of achieving an inclusive, systematic, or totalized grasp of any such orientation (our own, for instance) or of all or all possible such orientations. (By "natural" here, we mean merely that one acquires the language, practices, habits, and aptitudes of an actual society by growing up among the apt members of an adult cohort of that same society.)

Self-referential paradoxes are thought to affect the incommensurabilist (who is also a relativist) as well. Nevertheless, the usual evidence against the mere protagorean features the incoherence with which he is bound to assign truth-values to particular claims (witness Putnam and, more simply, Newton-Smith); whereas the evidence against the incommensurabilist usually features the paradox of anyone's claiming to understand or recognize what, *ex hypothesi*, we are unable to understand or recognize.

The matter is clearly a delicate one and requires careful sorting of the various strands of both arguments. But it is already clear that the protagorean counters *his* opponent's objection by rejecting bipolar truth-values and by repudiating the necessity of subscribing to excluded middle and *tertium non datur*. Furthermore, he insists, the flux and the rejection of ontic invariance confirm the pertinence of preferring many-valued truth-values in a world in which no disjunction between knowledge and belief (*episteme* and *doxa*) can be sustained. Responding in this way, the protagorean is not yet or not necessarily a relationalist, and may not, therefore, be a victim of the paradoxes.

The incommensurabilist, on the other hand, counters *his* opponent by demonstrating that he requires no more than a moderate plurality and divergence of conceptual schemes. He favors, even insists on, open-ended, improvisational, incompletely systematized conceptual schemes, schemes subject to the horizonal prejudice of apt agents incapable of penetrating altogether (in real-time terms) significative divergences within their own society's practices and between those of their own and of another. (This second theme is plainly a huge new topic that we shall have to examine in more detail. But, for the moment, we are merely trying to understand what makes the protagorean and incommensurabilist tick. Still, it draws attention to the similarity of the conditions of intra- and inter-societal communication and understanding, which is often ignored by the critics of incommensurabilism.) In any case, the protagorean's countermove is clearly available to the incommensurabilist as well.

What we can glimpse, at this point in the story, is that there is no reason for dismay on the relativist's part. The paradoxes and the threat of inconsistency and incoherence are real enough: the street-wise relativist had better bear them in mind. But, once tagged, those dangers are slim enough. We have already seen that there are no knockdown arguments that show that excluded middle cannot be consistently opposed or that the principle of noncontradiction can be reliably applied in any sector of inquiry without a substantive interpretation of the sector in question or of the semantically determinate vocabulary with which that sector is to be described. Similarly, the argument of the incommensurabilist has it that the very condition of man's existence entails his living (viably and with some modicum of success in inquiry) in a world in which conceptual incommensurabilities are effectively ineliminable and incompletely fathomed. There is no known compelling argument to the effect that that claim must be a false one or that it must lead to incoherence – although that is the prevailing prejudice, of course. So our provisional conclusion is not that relativism is vindicated or simply true but that the objections to both protagoreanism and incommensurabilism are rather prematurely taken to be fatal. Those objections begin to look rather thin, in fact.

VI

A very good clue to the modern, and indeed contemporary, rejection of relativism (more a rejection of incommensurabilism than of protagoreanism) is afforded by one of Husserl's early notions, a notion Husserl was bound to adjust with the adjustments of his developing phenomenology, but a notion that many feel is not restricted to any merely technically phenomenological thesis. As Husserl puts it:

> The hypothetical assumption of a Real Something outside this world is indeed a "logically" possible one, and there is clearly no formal contradiction in making it. But if we question the essential conditions of its validity, the kind of evidence (*Ausweisung*) demanded by its very meaning and the nature of the evidential generally as determined in principle through the thesis of a transcendent – however we may generalize correctly its essential nature – we perceive that the transcendent must needs be *experienceable*, and not merely by an Ego conjured into being as an empty logical possibility but by any *actual* Ego, as the demonstrable (*ausweisbare*) unity of its systematic experience. But we can see ... that what is perceivable by *one* Ego must *in principle* be conceivable by *every* Ego. And though *as a matter of fact* it is not true that everyone stands or can stand in a relation of empathy of inward understanding with every other one as we ourselves, for instance, are unable to stand with the spirits that may frequent the remotest starry worlds, yet in point of principle there exist *essential possibilities for the setting up of an understanding*, possibilities, therefore, that worlds of experience sundered in point of fact may still be united together through actual empirical connections into a single intersubjective world, the correlate of the unitary world of minds (of the universal extension of the human community). If we think this over, the logical possibility on formal grounds of realities outside the world, the *one* spatio-temporal world which is fixed through our *actual* experience is seen to be really nonsense. If there are worlds or real things at all, the empirical motivations which constitute them must *be able to* reach into my experience, and that of every single Ego in the manner which in its general

features has been described above. Things no doubt exist and worlds of things which cannot be definitely set out in any *human* experience, but that has its purely factual grounds in the factual limits of this experience.[10]

This lengthy passage is remarkable for its sanguine conceptual optimism and its grasp of a number of the central maneuvers of the contemporary opponents of relativism. We may, for instance, recall Kuhn's uneasy concession that Lavoisier and Priestley inhabited "different worlds," worlds perceived in some contingent way *by us* to be "different" (in both their nature and the conditions of their perceivability) but "worlds" whose differences *may not have been discerned in real time, say, by Lavoisier and Priestley, though they cannot be said in principle (on pain of contradiction) to be indiscernibly different.* (There's the threat of the self-referential paradox once again.) They are, on Kuhn's thesis, incommensurable though intelligible; and, contingently, undiscerned by this one or that, not known *to be known* in this or that precise way by all, or any, within those worlds who are entitled to be said to have a significant knowledge of pertinent parts of those same worlds. Furthermore, to be incommensurable though intelligible – on Kuhn's thesis – does *not* permit us *now* to formulate determinate cognitive conditions, criteria, rules of any sort *by which* their intelligibility *to us* can be shown, or can be demonstrated to be intelligible or commensurable or translatable in principle *to all*. The issue concerns *distributed* thoughts and statements: it cannot be supposed to be resolved by any speculative flimflam that claims that what is good for one Husserlean Ego is good enough for all. (There are no such Egos anyway, or there are none that are in any way distinguishable from the aggregated human beings one meets in the street.)

This is the upshot of Kuhn's remarking that, although science progresses *through* incommensurabilities, science lacks any "algorithmic" device ranging over all possible incommensurable "worlds" that somehow (nevertheless) do belong within the "one" world in which we do grasp the intelligibility of such options.[11] This begins to show the irrelevance of Husserl's position for any direct attack on relativism.

Husserl's claim *can* be no stronger than Kuhn's in this regard, even though it is incomparably more attentive to the implications of the thesis. The fact remains that the "one world" thesis (Husserl's and, implicitly, Kuhn's) can only function holistically – never distributively – in the sense that, trivially, it would always be incoherent to *claim* that a specific *determinate* proposition was known to be unintelligible to us as human beings. This is clearly a form of the self-referential paradox once again.

But this and similar admissions – Husserl's maneuver, for instance – go no distance at all toward demonstrating that conceptual incommensurabilities never obtain (on the contrary, they are obviously intelligible); or that what is intelligible to one "actual Ego" under real-world conditions is and must be intelligible to every other such "Ego" under real-world conditions (quantum physics must surely have been utterly unintelligible to the Neanderthaler); or that there must be some set of ultimately invariant conditions of intelligibility that all "Egos" share, in virtue of which, not merely ideally but in real-world terms, all discourse and judgment can be rationally and universally grounded and made effectively intelligible and commensurable (obviating all forms of relativism). (One begins to see here a certain fatal similarity between Husserl's maneuver and those of such evolutionists regarding human reason – theorists motivated therefore in an utterly different way from Husserl himself – as Peirce and Popper and Jürgen Habermas.)[12]

At any rate, nothing that Husserl says here counts as disqualifying relativism or as trapping any would-be relativist into unavoidable logical paradox or inconsistency. The fact is, the relativist is not an irrationalist. What the relativist opposes in Husserl, if he opposes anything, is Husserl's penchant for his own version of the archic doctrine.

What, precisely, Husserl failed to explicate satisfactorily was this: (a) what the relationship is between a phenomenologically apt Ego and the mere "empirical" ego or mind of culturally and historically horizoned human persons; (b) what the conditions are by which we may demonstrate, in real-world terms, that, apart from coexisting viably because they communicate, the members of a society or of different societies share the same concepts by which they first "constitute" their shared world; and (c) why we have any reason to believe that empirically contingent and occasional communication must presuppose, or support the ideal recovery of, universal conceptual invariances of alethic, epistemic, and ontic sorts, or of such sorts that would be sufficient for (ideally) precluding relativism, or for rendering it no more than a mere contingency that is superable in principle.

It is, therefore, reasonably clear that the issue at stake does not depend in any narrow sense on some special theory of "Egos" or cognizing subjects or on some special program of phenomenological analysis. If we see that, then we see at a stroke the sense in which Protagoras' general argument – or the argument of any latter-day protagoreans or incommensurabilists (or of any allied thinkers) – is

altogether unaffected by the shift from the ancient opposition to Protagoras' doctrine to the modern (or contemporary) opposition. There
are no ineluctable self-referential dilemmas or formal inconsistencies and
incoherence that Protagoras *must* fail to escape even if he is perfectly
careful (and not merely not stupid).

VII

What we have now succeeded in isolating may be put in a surprisingly
trim and instructive way. If we take plural "worlds," plural societal
horizons, plural conceptual schemes, plural solipsistic agents, and the
like seriously, so that *determinate* arrays of propositions or truth-claims
can be confined *by us* to the distributed worlds intended – as, notably,
in Harman, or incipiently in Kuhn, or quarrelsomely in Protagoras
himself – then we are indeed hoist on the self-referential dilemmas
Putnam and Newton-Smith and Rorty (and now Husserl by implication) remind us of. But all of those difficulties are avoided at a stroke if,
for one thing, we admit only the *holist* reading of their charge (which no
one need deny and which yields no distributed truths or constraints on
truth incompatible with relativism); and if, for a second, we do not
exceed our powers by actually individuating the indiscernibly disjoined
worlds within which distributed truth-claims are to be confined. *Distributed truth claims require "one" common world.*

There is undoubtedly an overweening form of relativism that would
replace "true" by "true in *L*" (where "*L*" designates disjunctively one
language or another, one world or another, or some such context of
application). This is just what we have called *relationalism*. It would not
be unfair to say that Harman is tempted by such a maneuver, as is
Kuhn, but neither quite falls for the self-referential paradox. Harman
cannily retreats to noncognitivism and distinguishes between the
sciences and morality; Kuhn worries the different "worlds" of Priestley and Lavoisier, observes that *we* can distinguish them, and makes it
quite clear that there is (in a holist sense) "one" world within which
their incommensurable "worlds" are located with respect to science's
progress.

Now, the important point is that contemporary critics like Putnam
obviously are convinced that *every* pertinent form of relativism (but
most saliently, the Kuhnian and Feyerabendian varieties) must be disposed to substitute an exclusive "true in *L*" for "true," must go on to
concede that *it* can operate with and compare what is "true in L_1" and
"true in L_2," and hence must fall victim to the self-referential paradoxes.

The reason is elementary: there must be an idiom (Putnam is right) available *to us* (and the partisans of relativism) in virtue of which distinctions *relativized* to L_1 and L_2 are, *there*, truly assigned *their* truth-values. The argument is impeccable. Nevertheless, it mistakenly holds: (1) that every relativism of the relevant sort (protagorean or incommensurabilist) must commit the blunder indicated (relationalism); and (2) that there is no relevant or viable or possible relativism that accepts a *non*relativized (or, better, *nonrelational or nonrelationalized*) conception of truth (what we have earlier called *robust relativism*). It is the general presumption of a relational conception of truth that explains the persistence of the ancient attack on the protagorean theme even into the modern period, where various incommensurabilist doctrines show the resilience of the ancient doctrine in ways that were never fully developed in the ancient world. Putnam mistakenly generalizes to the inescapability of (1) and (2) from the bare plausibility of the charge that *some* relativists certainly *have* failed to avoid the self-referential paradoxes.

The problem of defending the relativist thesis then rests with being able to show precisely how a viable relativism can be squared with the ancient protagorean tradition, the developing complexities of incommensurable schemes characteristic of modern history and modern science, and the avoidance of relationalized theories of truth. But for the moment, we must be quite clear that a tenable relativism must and will eschew mere relationalized theories of truth: either such theories generate self-referential paradoxes (as Putnam and Rorty affirm), are logically inconsistent (as Aristotle and Newton-Smith affirm), or degenerate into uninteresting versions of mere pluralism (as, by way of noncognitivism, Harman's theory pretty well does).

It is a little difficult to appreciate the subtlety of the option that was being developed at the end of the previous chapter, but it looms here as well. The nerve of the argument may be put simply enough, but it will require further reflection. It is this: *Overcoming relational conceptions of truth (a fortiori, relational conceptions of meaning and knowledge) is not equivalent to retiring or overcoming relativism.*

Notes

1   Kathleen Freeman, *Ancilla to the Pre-Socratic Philosophers: A Complete Translation of the Fragments in Diels, Fragmente der Vorsokratiker* (Oxford: Basil Blackwell, 1952), p. 125.
2   Ibid., p. 19; italics added.

3   Ibid., p. 41.

4   Ibid., p. 41. Here Freeman gives the reading favored by Eduard Zeller and John Burnet in addition to her own reading.

5   Ibid., pp. 24–5.

6   Aristotle, *De Anima*, trans. J. A. Smith, in Richard McKeon (ed.), *The Basic Works of Aristotle* (New York: Random House, 1941), book iii, chapter 4 (429a).

7   John Locke, *An Essay Concerning Human Understanding*, 2 vols, ed. Alexander Campbell Fraser (Oxford: Clarendon Press, 1894), vol. 2, book iv, chapter 1.

8   Ibid., vol. 1, book ii, chapter 8.

9   René Descartes, *Meditations*, II.

10   Edmund Husserl, *Ideas: General Introduction to Pure Phenomenology*, trans. W. R. Boyce Gibson (London: Collier Macmillan, 1962), §48. I am indebted here to Jitendra N. Mohanty, "Phenomenological Rationality and the Overcoming of Relativism," in Michael Krausz (ed.), *Relativism: Interpretation and Confrontation* (Notre Dame: University of Notre Dame Press, 1989), pp. 326–38.

11   Cf. Thomas S. Kuhn, "Objectivity, Value Judgment, and Theory Choice," in *The Essential Tension: Selected Studies in Scientific Tradition and Change* (Chicago: University of Chicago Press, 1977), pp. 321–2.

12   For Husserl's general view on the limitations of empirical thinking, see Edmund Husserl, *Phenomenology and the Crisis of Philosophy*, trans. Quentin Lauer (New York: Harper and Row, 1965). Lauer has put several essays of Husserl's together under one title.

6

Protagoreanism and Incommensurabilism (II)

I

Truth-claims are constrained by the shifting historical and conceptual contexts in which we work and live and make such claims, but they are *not*, for that reason alone – or, rather, the predicate "true," as distinct from what is claimed to be true, is not – *relativized to such contexts logically*. Incommensurabilism, failure of translation, and similar difficulties do not entail untranslat*ability*, unintellig*ibility*, insuperable divergences of conceptual organization. They simply warn us, empirically and distributively, of piecemeal failures, weaknesses, perceived difficulties of mutual understanding within the very context of apparently effective understanding. We can never *state* what is unintelligible, untranslatable, conceptually incommensurable *tout court*; but in practice we always encounter the sense in which we also cannot *state* the principled, inclusive, distributively effective grounds or criteria on which every reasonably intelligible utterance can be shown to be testable, translatable, demonstrably intelligible as such *by reference to an explicit canon*. (Witness, for instance, the utter failure of positivism.)

Relativism, in a word, inhabits the logical or conceptual space between the paradoxical limit of a cognition of what cannot in principle be cognized (because of self-referential constraints) and what cannot in principle be shown to be the comprehensive, algorithmic, extensionally exhaustive, certain criteria or grounds of translation, intelligibility, truth, knowledge, and the like. Put this way, relativism begins to sound eminently sensible, hardly irrational or skeptical or anarchistic at all. And that is as it should be.

II

We have a good deal of tidying up to do before we turn to the complexities suggested by incommensurabilism that go well beyond its special claims. It is reasonably clear that there is a close connection between replacing "true" by "true in *L*" and flirting with plural actual worlds as opposed to the "one" world we all inhabit. There is more than a reasonable suspicion that if the relativized or pluralized alternatives (alternative truth or alternative world) are not merely supplementary notions, the paradoxes of self-reference will prove unavoidable.

What we must insist on, what we have already argued for, is that if we adopt the "one-world" thesis we must construe it holistically. We cannot formulate the boundaries of the *one world* we say we share. The essential point has been effectively pressed by Edmund Husserl. "The world," he says, "does not exist as *an* entity, as an object, but exists with such uniqueness that the plural makes no sense when applied to it. Every plural, and every singular drawn from it, presupposes the world horizon."[1] Everything cognitively entertained belongs, because of that, within the "one" world (the "world horizon") of that conceptual effort. "One world" signifies its inclusion ("everything cognitively entertained") within an intentional or significative order that disallows nothing so identified from being linked or compared with whatever else is so identified. Nothing follows from this holistic truth regarding the truth of distributed claims. (It is, in fact, rather close in sense to one of Wittgenstein's famous *mots*.)

In *that* sense, there can be only one world, where "one" does not have a numerical use opposed to "many" or "plural." But, if so, then, precisely, the admission of one (such) world is an expression *of* holism, of the inclusiveness of intelligibility, without reference as such to *whatever* is distributively discerned "within it"; hence, the admission does not at all preclude (as many have wrongly supposed) the admission of "plural" worlds *within* its space – so marked for local reasons (for instance, along the lines Kuhn has favored) – without disturbing the point of the other.

Furthermore, where plural worlds (as with Kuhn) are introduced in order to regularize conceptual, perceptual, methodological, and similar divergences, as in tracing the history of the physical sciences, mention of an overriding "one world" begins to be distributively unhelpful or irrelevant. It becomes unhelpful because, on the hypothesis supposed, we lack altogether an algorithm or a completely reliable and inclusive canon for determining, *within the one world* and *at any time*, the full relationship (with regard to translation, meaning, commensurability, truth, reference, knowledge, validity) between whatever is claimed in accord with any "one" and in accord with any "other" of the "plural worlds" supposed.

There *is* a use for such devices (plural worlds, plural contexts) that need not lead to the self-referential paradoxes noted. All that is necessary is that we concede, in a sense that cannot be rendered algorithmically, that those devices do not exclude our mention of "one" (holistic) world, or *our distributed use*, within it, of the predicate *"true"* *sans phrase*, nonrelativized, nonrelationalized, without context. There is only one condition under which the range of *use* of "true" (as opposed to its meaning) could be outfitted with a completely comprehensive criterion of application: only if the ("one") world were completely transparent cognitively, only if a cogntively apt agent could discern in principle everything actual or, in discerning the actual parts of the world, could fix the place and properties of everything in such a way that that practice would never be subject to the vagaries of the horizonal plurality we have seen the protagorean and incommensurabilist insist on. Since we lack any assurance that such a condition does or could obtain – the entire thrust of contemporary philosophy being against it – there is no distributed use for the (otherwise merely) holistic mention of "one" world confining the use of truth-predicates (*sans phrase*) in processing actual distributed truth-claims. For that reason, truth-*claims* but not truth (*not* the meaning of "true") cannot fail to be relativized to the resources of one society or another. But that sort of relativization is not tantamount to relativism.

One sees this, for instance, in the ultimately vacuous (distributively vacuous) use, deliberately intended in Quine, of the notion of one world advanced in his famous doctrine of the "indeterminacy of translation" – which (the indeterminacy thesis), it must be said, *is* a version of relativism rather similar to, though thinner and more inclusive than, the incommensurabilist's account. It is thinner because it lacks (or resists offering) an account of knowledge and conceptual understanding *in* historically and culturally divergent terms, even where it considers, as in the use of the expression "Gavagai!" a communicative confrontation between alien peoples; and it is more inclusive because it is said to be ubiquitous. As Quine puts it:

> The infinite totality of sentences of any given speaker's language can be so permuted, or mapped onto itself, that (*a*) the totality of the speaker's dispositions to verbal behavior remains invariant, and yet (*b*) the mapping is no mere correlation of sentences with

equivalent sentences, in any plausible sense of equivalence however loose. Sentences without number can diverge drastically from
their respective correlates, yet the divergences can systematically
so offset one another that the overall pattern of associations of
sentences with one another and with non-verbal stimulation is
preserved.... The thesis is then this: manuals for translating one
language into another can be set up in divergent ways, all compatible with the totality of speech dispositions, yet incompatible with
one another.... Most of the semantic correlation is supported
only by analytical hypotheses [that is, the tacit presuppositions
governing the observer's translations], in their extension beyond
the zone where independent evidence for translation is possible.
That those unverifiable translations proceed without mishap must
not be taken as pragmatic evidence of good lexicography, for
mishap is impossible.[2]

Quine's argument relies at a critical point on his well-known attack
on the analytic/synthetic distinction,[3] on the impossibility (related to
that attack) of distinguishing between the puzzles of intra- and interlin-
guistic communication and intelligibility, on the cognitive intransparency of the world and one's own cognitive claims (also linked to that
attack and to the notion of "analytical hypotheses"), and on the impossibility of fixing reference distributively in "one" all-inclusive world
(though, holistically again, whatever we do does obtain in that "one"
world).[4] So Quine's "one" world actually accommodates his own relativistic tendencies; and his "analytical hypotheses" serve as analogues
of "plural worlds" within one world.

III

These considerations help to avoid the extravagances usually (but un-
necessarily) attributed to the protagorean and incommensurabilist, and
to accommodate benign references to plural worlds where there is
no intention to construe "true" as meaning "true in *L*" in ways that
entail what is objectionable in the paradoxes of self-reference. Perhaps
the best-known attack on all such accommodation appears in Donald
Davidson's well-known address, "On the Very Idea of a Conceptual
Scheme," which is pointedly focused on Kuhn's incommensurabilism as
well as on the notorious conceptual relativism of the American linguist
Benjamin Whorf. Whorf advances the bold and intriguing thesis (hardly
in the mad way usually attributed to him) that "language [that is, natural

language] does in a cruder but also in a broader and more versatile way the same thing that science does.... We are thus introduced to a new principle of relativity, which holds that all observers are not led by the same physical evidence to the same picture of the universe, unless their linguistic backgrounds are similar, or can in some way be calibrated [shown to be conceptually commensurable with those of all others]."[5] The point, crucial to Whorf's and Kuhn's thesis and generally agreed on in nearly all contemporary currents of Western philosophy, is: (a) that the habits of mind of particular societies of investigators are formed (in some significant and insuperable degree) *by* the very natural acquisition of language and sedimented theories and categories of the culture in which one develops; (b) that there is no neutral cognitive stance that one can count on or achieve within the constraints of (a); and yet (c) that evidence does arise internal to the terms of (a) that confirm that, within and between particular societies, diverging and incommensurable conceptual schemes are regularly employed in the very process of successful communication. Nothing said so far entails the relationalist formula.

Davidson misses the force of (a) to (c), because he insists, particularly in addressing the views of Kuhn and Feyerabend, that "it is essential to this idea [of incommensurability or, on Davidson's reading of Kuhn and Feyerabend, of 'failure of intertranslatability'] that there be something neutral and common that lies outside all schemes."[6] There *can*, however, be nothing cognitively neutral.

There is an important equivocation here and reportorial mistake. *Everyone* who is a realist of some sort pertinent to the achievement of the physical sciences is committed to "one" world in the holist sense we have already supplied. Perhaps that *is* the assumption of "something neutral and common." But no strong incommensurabilist and no strong theorist of Quine's stripe (whom Davidson professes to follow) – and, of course, no one committed to the world's intransparency – would hazard the thesis that, relative to the "one" world we make inquiry about and within, there *are* "neutral and common" phenomena that can be *distributively specified* independently of the conceptual schemes we learn to employ. Davidson seems to think that an important part of demonstrating the incoherence of the incommensurabilist's thesis relies on reminding us of their presumption of a "neutral and common" ground. Well, if it is there, the presumption is benignly vacuous when construed holistically; also neither necessarily nor characteristically *do* the champions of incommensurabilism claim that there *is* a neutral "something" on which the thesis of the "difference (even the incommensurability) of conceptual schemes" depends. (Kuhn explicitly opposes the idea, and it is unthinkable in Feyerabend's account.) And, of course, there *is* no known procedure *for* determining translat*ability* in principle, or for determining the correct transla*tion* for all relevant cases. Davidson is mistaken in at least two important ways: first of all, he supposes that "the failure of intertranslatability is a necessary condition for difference of conceptual schemes," whereas incommensurable schemes may be translatable, and a failure of translation need never invoke a failure of intertranslatability as such; secondly, he supposes that "it is essential to" the failure of translation "that there be something neutral and common that lies outside all schemes," whereas it is enough (if we must speak this way) that there be something "outside all schemes" – the world – that we can never show, determinately, to be neutral and common.

In fact, in the context in which he presses the incoherence of the incommensurabilist thesis, Davidson cites a salient remark of Kuhn's (answering his own critics) in which he says quite straightforwardly that "Feyerabend and I have argued at length that no such vocabulary [that is, no 'pure sense-datum language,' no 'basic vocabulary ... independent of theory,' no neutral ground] is available."[7] Davidson's notion is simply (there can be no other explanation) that the claim of incommensurable conceptual schemes must entail the self-referential paradoxes, if there were no neutral ground from the vantage of which to identify them as different schemes; that, if there were such a ground, incommensurability would have to be denied; and that, since there cannot be such a ground on the hypothesis supposed, the thesis must be incoherent. Davidson's finding, then, is that "Neither a fixed stock of meanings, nor a theory-neutral reality, can provide ... a ground for comparison of conceptual schemes" and that his argument holds both for "partial [as well as] total failure of translation."[8] But then, Kuhn *could* have availed himself of something akin to Quine's thesis – which, after all, rejects any meaningfully neutral ground and still admits divergent parsings of the world.

We can agree with Davidson that, since we must give up "dependence on the concept of an uninterpreted reality, something outside all schemes and science," and since, in doing that, we do not need to "relinquish the notion of objective truth," we must still (and may willingly) admit that "truth of sentences remains relative to language" (as well as to conceptual scheme) without fear of incoherence or of being forced to adopt incoherent versions of relativism.[9] (All one really has to do is avoid relationalism and its analogues regarding meaning.) The degree of relativism involved (if it is relativism) is then only holistic, and neither risks nor bears on the distributed difficulties the incommensurabilist wishes to confront. So far so good.

But in the same sense in which he wrongly reports what the incommensurabilist must or does commit himself to (whether in Kuhn's or Feyerabend's or Quine's or Whorf's account), Davidson is also clearly mistaken in supposing that there is and can be no way of defending *moderate* forms of incommensurabilism (or related conceptual shifts and slides) *within* the space of "one" world or in accord with the use of "true" *sans phrase*. His error is simply that he extravagantly conflates piecemeal failures of translation, detected more or less empirically in the process of pursuing science, with wholesale, global, or in principle untranslatability. His entire case is occupied solely with "complete, and partial, failures of untranslatability."[10] The trouble is that no one – Davidson included – has a working theory of *translatability*. No one seriously claims the principled untranslatability of terms or conceptual schemes, whether incommensurability is involved or not. The supporters of incommensurability make no such claim. It's true enough that they resist any all-inclusive programs of translation or of wholesale translatability offered in the spirit in which universal rules might ensure and test successful translation. But *no one* really believes that there are such rules. Translation and comparisons of commensurability are always and only matters of *degree*, and are normally quite intuitively managed. There is nothing wrong at all with the idea of the relative success of the translation of incommensurable schemes. Nothing at all. Hence, *moderate incommensurabilism is quite viable conceptually and forms an important family of relativisms*. Also, remember, conceding the incommensurabilist's thesis is hardly tantamount to adopting the relationalist's interpretation of truth. That is extremely important.

There are no arguments against incommensurabilism that are more strenuous than Davidson's. Any retreat from his severe conditions, therefore, leads away from the self-referential paradoxes usually ascribed to Whorf and Kuhn. (That is not to say that they are rightly accused.) A more accommodating vision than Davidson's might treat the discerning of moderate (but real) conceptual incommensurabilism as no more than the empirical (first-order) findings of inquirers who actually work with them (like Kuhn and Quine) or like those who deal with more alien schemes (say, Peter Winch, Hans-Georg Gadamer, and Michel Foucault).[11]

IV

We may perhaps round out our story by introducing a few more specimen views that bear on moderate incommensurability, plural worlds, and the use of "true in L." Ian Hacking, for instance, contesting the very view advanced by Davidson we allowed a moment ago – that is, the view that "truth of sentences remains relative to a language, but that is as objective as can be" – maintains that, "for part of our language, and perhaps as part of any language, being true-or-false is a property of sentences only because we reason about those sentence in certain ways.... The relativist ought to say that there might be whole other categories of truth-or-falsehood than ours."[12]

What Hacking means is that "candidacy" for "truth-or-falsity" is inseparable from ("internal" to) the practices of reasoning that obtain in a particular society, that there may be alternative such practices relative to different societies (affecting what we are prepared to assign truth and falsity and other values to – and how), and that such variable "candidacy for truth-and-falsity" is a function of the historically evolved and divergent "styles of reasoning" that have developed in one society or another. (Hacking may even be hinting at certain poststructuralist options open to the relativist: those suggested not only by Foucault but by Jean-François Lyotard, for example – that is, "styles of reasoning" that we can't even imagine as yet.) On this basis, Hacking is prepared to pronounce (against Dummett, for instance, against bivalence and *tertium non datur*) that "bivalence is not the right concept for science."[13] He mentions the famous case of Clerk Maxwell's treating certain propositions "about the relative velocity of light" as being "intrinsically incapable of determination," propositions which were (as he says) "positive" but "never bivalent" *at the time* Maxwell uttered them; that were given precise values later, in fact by Michelson, as a result of further work and an altered technology.[14]

In saying that Maxwell's claims were "positive" but "never bivalent," Hacking wishes to emphasize that Maxwell's claims *fit* the science of his time (in a sense he draws from Auguste Comte's positivism) and strongly appeared at that time to have a truth-value; that is, Maxwell's claims did fit the "style of reasoning" of the age (for truth-assignments), but, for that very reason, they were and are subject to further changes of candidacy with further changes in the prevailing "style of reasoning." That, Hacking insists, is a matter altogether different from what Davidson means by a "scheme that confronts reality."[15] One strong way of clinching the point is this: Hacking relativizes the *ascription* of truth to the conceptual schemes we use, but he does not thereby *relationalize* truth itself even where he challenges bivalence.

In fact, we now see, in comparing Quine, Kuhn, and Hacking, a variety of possible conceptual divergences that could yield viable forms of relativism not easily captured by any one form of protagorean or incommensurabilist vision. Doubtless, there are many other sources of what is usually dubbed cultural relativism that could quite easily admit moderate and empirically detectable, diachronic or even synchronic, division-of-labor relativisms more in keeping with Hacking's notion of "styles" of reasoning – or, for that matter, with Wittgensteinian forms of life, Gadamerian horizons, Foucauldian *epistemes* – than with Davidson's static notion of "conceptual schemes." We may, then, regard ourselves as entirely justified in dismissing Davidson's argument insofar as it is directed against relativism, while at the same time we admit it poses certain compelling constraints on our conjectures about the possible divergence or incommensurability of alternative conceptual schemes. Still, on Hacking's argument, it loses a good deal of force even there.

V

Interestingly, J. N. Mohanty, who favors Husserl's use of the notion of "one" world, also favors Davidson's general argument against conceptual schemes. And yet, he resists both Husserl and Davidson on the grounds that both take "a short cut," both oppose the relativist too quickly and too easily. Mohanty means to reach a conclusion congruent with theirs but by a gentler and more extended process, by going through the variety of cultural relativisms rather than by dismissing them out of hand. We may suppose, therefore, that Mohanty would accommodate thinkers like Winch, Hacking, Kuhn, Gadamer, Foucault and others (to the extent that they are really not incoherent), but he would do so with the ulterior objective of ultimately escaping all forms of relativism. He mounts his case by admitting an initial "home language and a home 'life-world'" that yield some ground in the direction of plural worlds, incommensurabilities, and the like.[16] He then lays out a strategy for overcoming the relativism that is there provisionally conceded. Here is Mohanty's summary of his strategy:

Let us view each world [each plural "life-world"] as a noematic structure [the structure of meaning in accord with which the experienced world is meaningfully ordered]. To each such structure there would correspond an entire nexus of interpretive acts on the part of the community for which such a world obtains. We may then speak of a noesis-noema correlation that is itself non-relativistic. If [Husserl's] essentialism was a shortcut and also too formalistic a step, and the typing of all meaningfulness to experienceability by *any* ego too liberal (inasmuch it permits every one to be an insider to every world), the present manner of isolating invariant noesis-noema correlation structures overcomes relativism by taking seriously the phenomena on which relativism is founded. The next step would be this: just as the identity of an object is constituted by the system of noemata through which "one and the same" object is presented, so also in the case under consideration the one world – not in the sense of the totality of all worlds, but in the sense of that whose versions they all are – may be looked upon as that regulative concept which not only orders the various quasi-uncommensurable worlds but also delineates the path that shall lead us out of a possibly hopeless chaos toward communication and understanding.[17]

Mohanty's project is a generous one. But there is an essential difficulty embedded in its generosity. *If* the initial condition *is* relativistic, as Mohanty concedes, in the sense that, although it is open to moderate incommensurabilities or divergences of "life-world," understanding, communication, translation, truth-value assignment, and the like *are already viable there, then the claim that that condition can or must yield in the direction of overcoming relativism is as yet logically unnecessary, empirically or conceptually still undefined, and not yet demonstrably accessible within the actual play of plural life-worlds.*

Several observations strengthen our finding. First of all, Mohanty takes it that, within each life-world, the "noesis-noema correlation" (the correlation of the conditions of meaningfulness of distributed experience and the active efforts to interpret experience on the part of informed agents who share a life-world) is already "nonrelativistic." This is much too strong a claim. For if we cannot, for instance, distinguish satisfactorily between what is internal and what is external to a given life-world – in a complex society, perhaps analogously in accord with something like Quine's opposition to the analytic/synthetic distinction – then the admission of a viable relativism *between* interacting life-worlds will oblige us to admit a viable relativism *within* each life-world as well. Mohanty does not address that difficulty.

Furthermore, once that much is admitted, there is no obvious need to insist that inter- or intrasocietal relativism can or must be overcome. There would be no threatening "chaos" to fear. Nor does Mohanty explain why we should expect success in such an effort. He himself takes the concept of "one world" to be nothing more than a "regulative concept." But that, as we have already had occasion to observe, is entirely compatible with relativism.

In his concluding remarks, Mohanty observes that "Unity [one world, one schema of truth] *is being worked out* rather than being a preexistent metaphysical entity. The process is gentle and tolerant rather than violent and imperious."[18] Just so. But then, of course, relativism can no longer be viewed as a conceptual "chaos." The truth is – or the best interpretation of his worry, given Mohanty's scenario, is – that he construes relativism primarily in terms of the intersection of two non-relativized domains that are incommensurable or strongly divergent. So seen, he concedes that the agents of each life-world may be assigned a noematic structure that, viewed in terms of *their* effort *at* communication, commits them (from *our* point of view) to relativized (specifically, relationalized) notions of truth and meaning ("true in L_1" and "true in L_2" at least). Since (as he claims) "if I am to be able to speak of alternative conceptual schemes, I must be able to translate the others into mine, or mine into the others'," Mohanty really concludes that relativism is always only partial and overcome when the noematic structure of the emerging "one" world (and its corresponding use of "true" *sans phrase*) satisfactorily evolves.[19] The upshot is that Mohanty offers an argument against relationalism which he wrongly construes as ultimately defeating incommensurabilism.

What he does not consider, however, what is essential to Kuhn's and Hacking's thesis, is that *translation and intelligibility do not preclude or eliminate relativism at all*; also, beyond that, *that relativism need not be or entail a form of incommensurabilism*. Mohanty, then, argues from Husserl's and Davidson's point of view, but he offers a kindlier and more gradual strategy for overtaking relativism. In doing that, however, he concedes more (as he must) than he ought if he means to construe relativism as a "chaos" or only somehow on the way to "communication and understanding." Still, he nowhere considers the prospects of a robust relativism that does not depend on incommensurabilism.

VI

Finally, we should add a specimen view or two that would warn us appropriately of the dangers of speaking of plural worlds. There is no better-known example than that presented by Nelson Goodman, and there is none that is more puzzling. We can in fact construct a telling array of alternative models of plural worlds by opposing as extreme options, first, Goodman's explicit view, and then what may (for our carpentered purpose) be drawn from Leopold von Ranke's conception of objective history (and Mohanty's thesis), and, finally, between those two, Kuhn's placement of the plural worlds of Lavoisier and Priestley within the one world in which science progresses through paradigm shifts that often involve conceptual incommensurabilities.

Mohanty's view is actually a little like Ranke's. The noematic structures of different life-worlds, the constitutive conditions of meaning in terms of which the denizens of one society understand their experienced "world" – and we, ours – is *relativized*, on Mohanty's view, to particular life-worlds. But, Mohanty supposes, *truth* is not relativized, not relationalized, to those worlds, *in* those worlds. *What* is taken to be true *sans phrase in* each such world is, from *our* point of view, addressed *in* the relationalist way *in* that life-world.[20] On Mohanty's hypothesis, then, each life-world may be taken to be relatively opaque (although the effort at communication between life-worlds presumably makes it possible for the denizens of each to overcome such opacity and to realize that they are adversely affected by it).

On that view, as Mohanty observes, there is *no* relativism to be found *within* each life-world. We observe a relativism of meaning conditions and a bias in determining truth; but "truth" is *not* "truth in L" *for* the blind creatures of a given life-world. Only *we*, standing somehow outside a given world or two, can treat the "true" that is internal to *each* such world as tantamount to "true in L_1" or "true in L_2" when seen within the space of *our own* life-world. But, if so, *how* do we ever know that we escape? And if we cannot answer, why should relativism (not relationalism) be viewed as a defective stance?

Ranke offers something similar. When he advanced his well-known motto, *"Wie es eigentlich gewesen"* in the context of insisting on archival accuracy, Ranke was committed to the notion of individual historical "worlds" and the need to be "objective" with regard to what was internal to the spirit of each such world. He thought of societies in terms of indissoluble plural *geistlich* individualities penetrable to a certain empathic understanding; he thought of societies as idealized spirits objectively "there" in the whole of the plural histories of peoples, in the sense in which "every epoch is immediate in God."[21]

The important thing is that Ranke was anti-relativistic rather than relativistic – *in* very much the same sense in which Mohanty opposes the "chaos" of relativism and marks it as a failure of "communication and understanding" (unless overcome). In that context, "true in L_1" is a distinction that *cannot* be marked out by the denizens of L_1 – unless, in due time, they become Rankean historians or Mohantyan phenomenologists, or, of course, Kuhnian *rapporteurs* of science. But, within each *Geist* (in Ranke's rather frozen Hegelian space) and within each *Lebenswelt* (in Mohanty's equally frozen Husserlian space), truth is absolute, hardly relativized at all; and, at *our* level of understanding (and only there), the whole discourse of truth of this or that world – what, *there*, is "true" *sans phrase* – *is relationalized by us* to some world *W* or some language *L*. The attribution of relativism, then, is never more than pejorative. But we are not told where to stand to avoid the peril; and, even more important, there *are* relativisms (robust relativisms) that risk no such danger even at the start.

Kuhn's account is superior to Ranke's and Mohanty's, precisely because it never fails to see that the would-be escape from relativism, under the conditions of history, cognitive preformation, horizonal bias, the intransparency of the world, and the like, is merely whistling in the dark.

The incommensurabilist's thesis amounts to the inescapability of relativism *and* the impossibility of saying exactly where it stops and starts at any time. Symptomatically, both the plural worlds of Lavoisier and Priestley and the one world of collected scientific progress are artifacts *of* the incommensurabilist's own horizon, which he knows very well will be similarly interpreted by later historians of science. Hence, for the incommensurabilist as for the protagorean, relativism provides the interior logical space for realism itself, since the world is a flux.

Ranke's and Mohanty's views appear coherent but unconvincing. They are much too sanguine, much too near to closure, much too near to the unchanging limits of change. Kuhn's view risks incoherence though it does not quite succumb, because Kuhn cannot find his way to explaining *what* the relationship *is* between the plural worlds of Lavoisier and Priestley and the one world of objective science. Kuhn lacks Ranke's and Mohanty's confidence, but he has a more uncompromising grasp of the perennial provisionality and flux of what we mark out as "the" world. Neither Ranke nor Mohanty, of course, is a protagorean; but Kuhn *is* – or, is one uneasily. Kuhn, however, is not a relationalist; and no incommensurabilist need be one.

VII

Goodman's version of plural actual worlds is an altogether different vision. It is, in fact, the only one of the four we are considering that is out-and-out uncompromisingly relativist in nature. Goodman says of his own view that it may be "described as a radical relativism under rigorous restraints, that eventuates in something akin to irrealism."[22]

The trouble with Goodman's relativism, quite frankly, is that it makes a stubborn virtue of the self-referential paradoxes. It does not fall victim to them in the usual sense. It celebrates them, and so it baffles everyone. Goodman has no difficulty in acknowledging "conflicting truths and multiple actual worlds":[23]

> To anyone but an arrant absolutist, alternative ostensibly con-
> flicting versions [of a supposed world] often present good and
> equal claims to truth. We can hardly take conflicting statements as
> true in the same world without admitting all statements whatso-
> ever (since all follow from any contradiction) as true in the same
> world, and that world itself as impossible. Thus we must either
> reject one of two ostensibly conflicting versions as false, or take
> them as true in different worlds, or find if we can another way of
> reconciling them.[24]

Apparently conflicting truths cannot be supported, Goodman believes, in the same world, for the reasons he gives. But if we wish to support them nonetheless, we must, he says, assign them to different (actual) worlds; but then, so it would seem, they would no longer be "con-flicting" truths since their home worlds would be entirely different. That is, Goodman nowhere discusses the logical relationship between different actual worlds. One begins to sense Goodman's extravagance.

What a plurality of actual worlds actually is, Goodman also does not explain. He never quite says what the difference is between a genuine inconsistency in truth-claim *within one particular world* and (merely) "conflicting" but not actually inconsistent truths assigned *to different worlds*. He never quite says *where*, in what world or worlds – and *how*, in whatever world or worlds we "make" – *we* may decide the difference between these two alternatives. Also, although Kuhn sees some possible support for his own view in Goodman, Goodman never discusses Kuhn's problem or, indeed, the conceptual relation between plural actual worlds and the "one" world of scientific progress and objectivity in which the puzzles just adduced may in principle be resolved.[25]

VIII

This is perhaps why Quine is so frontal in his review of Goodman's book. In any case, Quine's puzzlement is an honest one:

> Goodman means all his worlds to be actual. Proceeding then to try
> to penetrate what one hopes is a figure of speech [as it tries to be

in Kuhn, we may add], one finds that where the purported multiplicity really lies is not so much in worlds as in versions: world
versions. I cannot quite say [Quine observes] versions of the
world, for Goodman holds that there is no one world for them to
be versions of. He would sooner settle for the versions and let the
world or worlds go by.[26]

Quine's puzzlement here cannot fail to be everyone's. Quine is regis-
tering the difference between his own sort of relativism and Goodman's: "I grant," he says, "the possibility of alternative physical
theories, insusceptible to adjudication." But, given his own work, Quine
is prepared to say (in a sort of Goodmanian lingo) that he is committed
"to physical theory as a world version, and to the physical world as the
world."[27] Goodman denies that there is one world (in the sense in
which, if the pairing will not seem too extreme) Quine and Husserl
agree on the use of the term. Furthermore, Goodman will not permit
(as Quine observes with a certain tact) a disjoining of "world" and
"version" – if we may understand, by "version," a certain perspectival
or horizonal conceptual construction in which "world" is the coherent
and comprehensive internal accusative of each such construction.

It is a harsh judgment, therefore, but hopefully not an unjust one, that
says that Goodman's version of the dialectic of one world and plural
worlds is an object lesson of what to avoid in formulating a viable
relativism. Ranke and Mohanty separate plural worlds too completely to
produce an interesting relativism: there is, for them, no need for relativism *within* each such world (a claim well worth disputing); and relativism itself obtains only *at* the bare incipiently communicative juncture
between two such worlds. As soon as communication and understanding obtain, for Ranke and Mohanty, we are back *within* the "one"
world and, *there*, relativism is otiose again. Kuhn holds on to the
incommensurabilist's relativism, because, for him, there is no articulable
"one" world, though, holistically, we cannot resist admitting that we are
always within it. Whatever we claim, therefore, on Kuhn's view, we
realize must be relativized to some one of plural worlds later observers
will classify like Priestley's, from whatever will later prove to be *their*
world (like Lavoisier's), all within *the* "one" world that none of us can
actually specify. But, in doing that, we are never obliged to favor
relationalism. On the argument, therefore, if he failed to recover his
supposed Husserlian vantage – now, not sufficiently clearly linked to
the very conditions of communication and meaning (since relativists
need not fail here either) – Mohanty would surely count as a relativist
himself.

IX

Mention of the one world we share (hardly equivalent to making reference to it) is merely an expression of our cognizing resolve to admit, interpret, compare, assess, confirm or disconfirm (if we can) *all* enunciative discourse, whatever its provenance. Goodman's play with the language of world and worlds is oddly detached from *any* discussion of the epistemological and methodological puzzles of truth-claims subject to the processes of preformative history, the intransparency of what is real, and the divergence of conceptual schemes. It simply makes no sense to introduce the one set of distinctions (worlds) without addressing in a full-blooded way the other (conditions of truth or truth-like values).

The reader will find it difficult to believe that that's all there is to Goodman's thesis. It *is* all there is, but saying so may not be convincing. At its best, it notes the self-referential puzzles, shows in a formal way what a radical relativism would be like, but abstains from resolving those questions about truth and meaning and reference and "styles of reasoning" (in Hacking's sense) without which we cannot be sure that the option offered is capable of coherent development.

Few seem to share Goodman's sanguine judgment, but no one has as yet shown its actual viability. Goodman himself says: "So long as we keep within a version, 'world' or 'totality' is clear enough, but when we consider conflicting true versions and their several worlds, paradox enters."[28] He also says: "A world is a totality; there can be no multiplicity of totalities, no more than the all-inclusive whole. By assigning conflicting versions to different worlds, we preclude composition of these totalities into one."[29] So Goodman means to avoid the paradoxes. He also sees that, in a sense, the "one" inclusive world is always perspectivally projected as such from within the effective "totality" of whichever one of various plural worlds we happen to inhabit for that purpose.

Still, he does claim that "A true version is true in some worlds, a false version in none. Thus [he concludes] the muliple worlds of conflicting true versions are actual worlds, not the merely possible worlds or nonworlds of false versions."[30] So there is a robust claim about truth and falsity and about their "fit" with (what Goodman calls) the "rightness" of a world made in accord with the evolving practices of inquiry and art and the like.[31] But there is no instruction about *how to use* those notions. At its best, Goodman's account suggests a formal schema for the methodological questions raised by Kuhn and Hacking. Perhaps it is meant to be that. But it is much too elliptical for anyone to be able to say, or to be sure. Whatever its particular future may disclose, we see the ineluctability of admitting "one" world, its compatibility with "plural" worlds, and its compatibility with protagoreanism and incommensurabilism. Also, what begins to dawn on us are the extraordinary lengths to which theorists will go – witness Goodman and Quine – to avoid giving up excluded middle. That they may be hospitable to some forms of relativism seems hardly to affect the matter.

Notes

1 Edmund Husserl, *The Crisis of European Science and Transcendental Phenomenology*, trans. David Carr (Evanston: Northwestern University Press, 1970), p. 143.

2 W. V. Quine, *Word and Object* (Cambridge: MIT Press, 1960), pp. 27, 71. See also Hilary Putnam, "Two Philosophical Perspectives," in *Reason, Truth and History* (Cambridge: Cambridge University Press, 1981), for a clue to Quine's appeal, here, to the Skolem-Löwenheim theorem (pp. 73–4).

3 See W. V. Quine, "Two Dogmas of Empiricism," in *From a Logical Point of View* (Cambridge: Harvard University Press, 1953).

4 See, for instance, W. V. Quine, "Goodman's *Ways of Worldmaking*," in *Theories and Things* (Cambridge: Harvard University Press, 1981).

5 B. F. Whorf, "The Punctual and Segmentative Aspects of Verbs in Hopi," in *Language, Thought and Reality: Selected Writings of Benjamin Lee Whorf*, ed. J. B. Carroll (Cambridge: MIT Press, 1956), p. 55; cited by Donald Davidson, "On the Very Idea of a Conceptual Scheme," in *Inquiries into Truth and Interpretation* (Oxford: Clarendon Press, 1984).

6 Davidson, "On the Very Idea of a Conceptual Scheme," p. 190.

7 T. S. Kuhn, "Reflections on My Critics," in Imre Lakatos and Alan Musgrave (eds), *Criticism and the Growth of Knowledge* (Cambridge: Cambridge University Prss, 1970), pp. 266–7; cited by Davidson, "On the Very Idea of a Conceptual Scheme."

8 Davidson, "On the Very Idea of a Conceptual Scheme," p. 195.

9 Ibid., p. 198.

10 Ibid., p. 165.

11 For the time being, it is perhaps enough to take note here of that much-maligned and misunderstood book by Peter Winch, *The Idea of a Social Science* (London: Routledge and Kegan Paul, 1958). Winch is regularly accused of failing to overcome the self-referential paradoxes of cross-cultural comparison. It may be admitted that his defense could be stronger, but his argument is not at all unaware of these puzzles and makes its way against them.

12 Ian Hacking, "Language, Truth and Reason," in Martin Hollis and Steven Lukes (eds), *Rationality and Relativism* (Cambridge: MIT Press, 1982), p. 64.

13   Ibid., p. 55.
14   Ibid., p. 56.
15   Ibid., p. 64.
16   Mohanty, "Phenomenological Rationality and the Overcoming of Relativism," in Michael Krausz (ed.), *Relativism: Interpretation and Confrontation* (Notre Dame: University of Notre Dame Press, 1989), p. 333.
17   Ibid., pp. 332–3.
18   Ibid., p. 338; italics added.
19   Ibid., p. 333.
20   J. N. Mohanty, "Husserlian Transcendental Phenomenology: Some Aspects," in Robert Sokolowski (ed.), *Edmund Husserl and the Phenomenological Tradition: Essays in Phenomenology (Studies in Philosophy and the History of Philosophy*, vol. 8) (Washington, DC: The Catholic University of American Press, 1988), pp. 180–1.
21   Leopold von Ranke, "A Dialogue on Politics," trans. Theodore H. Van Laue, in *The Theory and Practice of History*, ed. Georg G. Iggers and Konrad von Moltke (Indianapolis: Bobbs-Merrill, 1973), pp. 31–2.
22   Nelson Goodman, *Ways of Worldmaking* (Indianapolis: Hackett Publishing Co., 1978), p. x.
23   Ibid., p. 110.
24   Ibid.
25   See further, Hilary Putnam, "Reflections on Goodman's *Ways of Worldmaking*," in *Philosophical Papers*, vol. 3 (Cambridge: Cambridge University Press, 1983).
26   Quine, "Goodman's Ways of Worldmaking," p. 96.
27   Ibid., p. 98.
28   Nelson Goodman, *Of Mind and Other Matters* (Cambridge: Harvard University Press, 1984), p. 32.
29   Ibid.
30   Ibid., p. 31.
31   See, for instance, *Ways of Worldmaking*, chapter 7, particularly p. 138.

7

Extending Relativism's Domain

I

We have been systematically oversimplifying our treatment of an important theme linking protagoreanism and incommensurabilism. It is a theme that does not affect the bare defensibility of relativism. It does affect our sense of the potential range and variety of circumstances in which, once admitted as viable, relativism may be seen to be a particularly natural and attractive option.

In an obvious sense, protagoreanism affords a more generic, less articulated account of the substantive grounds for favoring relativism than does incommensurabilism. Protagoreanism simply considers that, if we reject the archic doctrine, then a bivalent logic is not the most apt logic for any sustained discourse addressed to truth-claims about whatever stable *Erscheinungen* may strike our notice. Incommensurabilism, on the other hand, isolates a relatively determinate subspecies of experienced cultural change and variety. It has, of course, become quite modish in our time, following the reception of Kuhn's *The Structure of Scientific Revolutions*, but it also obscures somewhat the full pertinence of other manifestations of the flux.

We have, in effect, distorted the picture of the genuinely vast range of application of the relativistic thesis. Nothing perhaps has been permanently lost by it. Indeed, the protagorean and incommensurabilist options are surely the most developed relativistic themes in our own time and throughout the entire history of the matter. But times have changed.

Ours may be the most hospitable of ages in endorsing the theme of the flux. That is, it may be the one most inclined to embrace in a spontaneous, quotidian, even expert and specialized way the following doctrines: (i) the world is cognitively intransparent; (ii) attributions of real structures indissolubly implicate the tacit collective bias and conceptual resources of inquiring societies; (iii) the cultural diversity and non-convergence of conceptual schemes, "styles of reasoning," horizonal prejudice and blindness and the like are an ineluctable feature of the natural history of human inquiry; (iv) there is no principled division between intra- and intersocietal conceptual diversity, and communication and understanding of both sorts are, like the world itself, subject to an incompletely penetrable intransparency; (v) discourse and intelligent behavior function effectively within the flux without any assurance of there being, or of our being able to discern, essential, invariant, universal, exceptionless structures grounding, enabling, or confirming knowledge, truth, validity, proof, rationality, the interpretation or application of formal principles of consistency and coherence or the like; (vi) the distinctly cultural nature of linguistically apt human persons is itself radically alterable through historical change, *sui generis*, not obviously expressible in the terms of the supposed regularities of the physical world; (vii) the very existence of persons or selves is an artifactual evolution uniquely embodied in the biological uniformities of *Homo sapiens*; and (viii) attributions of real structures in both the physical and cultural worlds are radically underdetermined by any and all testing conditions, which are themselves tacitly constrained by the transient conceptual horizons within which particular claims are made.

There you have a strenuous tally of the largest philosophical saliencies of our own day – not, to be sure, uncontested or even altogether clear in their implications, but certainly the focus of the most important current debates about relativism. They are all committed, one way or another, to the doctrine of the profound plasticity of the world; and, taken together, they yield a uniquely popular and ubiquitous disposition to favor protagoreanism. But no combination of them is or entails relativism.

There can be no doubt that the spread of this set of themes – there is, of coures, nothing sacrosanct about the tally – is due in large part to the rise of Western technology and science; the developing sense of the technological alterability of the environing world; cosmic and biological and cultural evolution; the increasing artifactuality of the world we inhabit; our grasp of the unique contingency of distinctly human existence; an increasingly radical sense of history; the genuinely global scope of our understanding of human diversity; the impossibility of locating in any physical, biological, or narrowly sensory sense what constitutes the identity of persons or selves or cognizing agents; and the accumulating pressure of the history of philosophical reflection on all these matters. There may never have been such a protagorean age as our own. Its deepest convictions seem to be encouraged by every form of expertise our own world proclaims.

II

Our theme is a heady one. We are, however, more concerned to locate the contest regarding the fortunes of relativism than to establish any of the detailed claims that might be drawn from the formal and informal tallies just given.[1] It is enough for our purpose to know that our age is hospitable to the protagorean theme: better that than to break off interminably to explain in just what sense we must interpret every complex strand of our developing vision. We need a better and more detailed picture of the relativist's terrain, however.

Incommensurabilism remains a most strategically placed landmark, of course. But it is hardly the only or even the most important oasis of dispute, and it does not quite collect all the caravans of argument drawn to the puzzles of modern science. That it has been singled out as it has is due, of course, to the remarkable impact of Thomas Kuhn's book. We have already set some boundaries to the assessment of incommensurabilism by locating Kuhn's contribution between Davidson's and Hacking's opposed accounts. In doing that, we began to map a larger network of relativist claims. This was, in fact, also the burden of Hacking's strategy in resisting Davidson's charge, quite apart from the hopelessly extreme translatability requirements Davidson sought to impose on the proliferating forms of cultural relativism. The same caveat appears, for somewhat different reasons, in Mohanty's resistance to both Davidson's and Husserl's views.

What we need to collect for ourselves is a suppler and ampler sense of the family of contemporary notions of the features of the flux that would place incommensurabilism as a salient but still limited option among a variety of relativisms. We hardly need a completely inclusive array of such alternatives. Indeed, on the developing argument, it would be impossible and altogether unnecessary to provide such a "totalized" account. The pleasant truth is that a number of important options of the sort required have already been implicitly identified in previous discussions. We were unable to isolate them effectively, because we lacked the preliminary scaffolding that the incommensurabilist dispute itself affords. But now that we have it in place, we may turn back to introduce some further distinctions.

III

It would not be unreasonable to suggest that the protagorean themes developed in rather different ways by Kuhn and Quine and Hacking and Mohanty lead in the direction of quite distinctive forms of relativism, forms that cannot all be characterized in the same way as incommensurabilisms of Kuhn's sort, or that cannot all be satisfactorily illuminated by reference merely to Kuhn's option. Quine, for instance, emphasizes the relativism implicit in his well-known thesis of the "indeterminacy of translation" and the "inscrutability of reference." The two doctrines go hand in hand – in fact, they bleed into a further range of questions of a very large sort regarding *determinacy of meaning and extension* that cannot possibly be confined to the terms of reference of Kuhnian incommensurability. For one thing, although Quine is clearly aware of the historical movement of conceptual schemes, he does not directly examine the contextual embedding of his own exemplars or of anything like Kuhnian paradigms; and, for another, the indeterminacies he draws our attention to are logically more fundamental than that of incommensurabilism, in the sense that incommensurabilist questions do not yet arise in the context of "indeterminacy of translation" or "inscrutability of reference." The justly famous passage in which Quine considers a field linguist's difficulty in interpreting a native's pointing (at a rabbit, as we would say) when he utters the expression, "Gavagai" (or, now, "Gavagai!," as it is often fashionably inscribed)[2] runs as follows:

> Synonymy of "Gavagai" and "Rabbit" as sentences turns on considerations of prompted assent; not so synonymy of them as terms.... Two pointings may be pointings to a numerically identical rabbit, to numerically distinct rabbit parts, and to numerically distinct rabbit stages; the inscrutability lies not in resemblance, but in the anatomy of sentences. We could equate a native expression with any of the disparate English terms "rabbit", "rabbit stage," "undetached rabbit part", etc., and still, by compensatorily juggling the translation of numerical identity and associated particles, preserve conformity to stimulus meanings of occasion sentences [that is, sentences "which command assent only if queried after an *appropriate* prompting stimulation"].[3]

Here, Quine's favored point is that *there is no way to decide* among these and similar parsings of the implicated referential terms of the uttered sentence.

We have already seen that Quine insists that (so far at least) "mishap is impossible" in the translational endeavor, despite these indeterminacies, since the field linguist's effort is executively controlled by his own socially preformed conceptual orientation (his "analytical hypotheses"). The indeterminacies that obtain obtain *within* his own language as well as *between* languages in communication with one another. No mention is made here of conceptual incommensurabilities.

IV

There are grave difficulties with Quine's extremely spare and rigid program, but those do not expressly concern us in the present context of discussion. It may, however, be noted that, in *some* sense, Quine cannot admit a radical "inscrutability of reference" affecting the occasion of "appropriate prompting stimulation," since the indeterminacies alleged presuppose and logically implicate a relatively determinate such stimulation. There is, therefore, an unresolved incipient appeal to a neutral sensory ground (just what Kuhn denied and what Davidson suspected must have been implicit in *Kuhn's* own view); and there is a further set of difficulties affecting Quine's line that has to do with the very intelligibility of the different parsings alleged to obtain just where no behavioral prompting would make any difference and just where the holism of his own one world would have to be contrasted with (for instance) Goodman's insistence on plural actual worlds, or might be compared (favorably, Quine would insist) with Pierre Duhem's influential scientific holism.[4]

The point at stake – it is worth pausing a moment to make it clear – is that Quine obviously requires, and also somewhat surreptitiously inserts, a minimal sensory or minimal sensory/behavioral basis for evidence that is relatively neutral to the alternative "analytical hypotheses" that invite his sort of relativism. The relativism remains, but Quine is not quite as radical (a relativist) as he gives us to believe. (For instance, he is not as radical as Protagoras.) Thus, when he introduces "analytical hypotheses" (that is, the incompletely fathomed presuppositions of anyone's thought – the field linguist's, for instance – in terms of which what is "given" may be parsed), Quine actually *postpones their onset* and influence so that at least *some* relatively neutral data may be admitted. (This concession *is* what Duhem would have insisted on; but it is also not quite consistent with Quine's holism, the rejection of the analytic/synthetic disjunction, and the appeal to sensory and behavioral criteria of so-called "stimulus meaning.")

In any case, Quine himself admits a number of important kinds of sentences (and what they appear to report) as obtaining *prior* to the interference of analytic hypotheses. He explicitly says:

(1) Observation sentences can be translated. There is uncertainty, but the situation is the normal inductive one. (2) Truth functions

can be translated. (3) Stimulus-analytic sentences can be recognized [that is, sentences that are *analytic* for a subject if he would assent to it, or nothing, after every stimulation] (within the modulus) [the modulus of stimulation, the admitted specious present of some range of stimulation]. So can the sentences of the opposite type, the "stimulus-contradictory" sentences which commend irreversible dissent. (4) Questions of intrasubjective stimulus synonymy of native occasion sentences even of non-observational kind can be settled if raised [that, is, where "sameness of stimulus meaning" obtains among sentences "which command assent or dissent only if queried after an appropriate prompting stimulation"], but the sentences cannot be translated.

Immediately following this summary, Quine asks rhetorically, "how does the linguist *pass* these bounds," which he answers at once by invoking the notion of "analytical hypotheses": roughly, by introducing (tacitly) a speaker's contingent prejudices *about what* terms designate in the world, as opposed to merely admitting *sentences* of the sorts just mentioned.[5] In short, Quine is *not* a relativist regarding sentences conforming with the characterizations given in (1) to (4), though he nowhere explains his bias and nowhere squares it with the central doctrines of his own account.

Much the same kind of restriction appears (also unexplained) in Kuhn's rather different, strongly historicized, account. For Kuhn does actually attempt to sort out, not algorithmically of course, transhistorical criteria of rational choices among competing theories.[6] In a word, drawing on earlier connections: Goodman is far more radical than Quine, and Feyerabemd far more radical than Kuhn. But the first pair, Quine and Kuhn, run much less risk of explicit incoherence than do the second; and yet, they also disappoint us by the obvious arbitrariness with which they manage to secure the safety of their respective nonrelativistic theories.

Nevertheless, there is good reason to believe that the limited (but still important) indeterminacies Quine draws attention to do obtain. *If* the case can be made out, then, at that level of analysis at which the alternative parsings obtain (according to various jungle-to-English manuals Quine mentions) – parsings that confirm "indeterminacy of translation" partly at least because they cannot overcome "inscrutability of reference" – Quinean relativism does remain empirically intelligible. ("Indeterminacy of translation" is not merely "inscrutability of reference," but the latter is not entirely separable from the former.) One may still be able to show that alternative parsings – intelligible and operative, *ex hypothesi* – could not be satisfactorily sorted through all relevant instances merely on grounds (Quinean grounds) of behavioral prompting, nor (one supposes, relaxing the Quinean program) on grounds of speaker's intentions or the like, under real-time terms. There is, then, on Quine's view, and on the view of many who would not subscribe to Quine's program, a certain indeterminacy of *ontology* (an indeterminacy of *terms*) implicated in natural-language use. This, for instance, would be entirely hospitably received by anyone who subscribed to the themes tallied just above as (i) to (viii). In fact, Quine's entire question quite vividly recalls Peirce's striking remarks about the ubiquitous vagueness and indeterminacy affecting the whole of nature. To recall them now (since they are cast in semiotic terms, since they accommodate the symbiosis Quine and Peirce share through rather different devices: remember Quine's "analytical hypotheses") may perhaps incline us more favorably toward admitting the further, distinctive indeterminacies of *intentional* and cultural phenomena (which, of course, Quine will have no truck with). But the matter does bear directly on the fortunes of what, in the prologue, we very briefly identified as "ontic relativism."

V

Quine presents his thesis as a logical possibility, which he believes cannot fail to obtain in the context of actual human life. The least review of his account shows unmistakably a further source of ineliminable relativism (somewhat repressed in Quine himself). For one must realize that, on the Quinean view, the would-be contradiction of affirming and denying the same things applied to the experienced world must surely generate the self-referential paradoxes Protagoras is supposed to have been unable to resolve. Quine offers us a way of resolving those paradoxes, a way that, along the lines already drawn, is radically different from Goodman's would-be resolution of conflicting truths. Both solutions are extravagant because they are intransigently committed to bipolar truth-values: Quine allows truth-value *gaps* to intrude where incompatible (ontic) parsings threaten; and Goodman allows actual *worlds* to proliferate to accommodate in the tamest possible way truths that would otherwise threaten self-contradiction. Neither opts for the more obvious conceptual economy: that of abandoning excluded middle. We have already seen how Goodman maneuvers in this regard. Quine is content to admit "the unverifiable consequences" of would-be "translations" of sentences "not covered by (1) – (4)." "They can be defended," he says, "only through the analytical hypotheses now and forever."

"Where cultural contrasts begin to be threatened with meaninglessness," he adds, "is . . . where they depend on analytical hypotheses."[7] So Quine abandons any comprehensive program for adjudicating between incompatible parsings; but he also provides (no more than) dubious grounds for supposing that we could distinguish (in principle) between such unresolvable disputes and straightforward empirical disputes where no such difference of parsings obtains. That we cannot explain the distinction in a principled way is a disastrous consequence of his own thesis.

Quine's lesson is strategically centered on the analysis of reference and referring expressions. We are advised to avoid the use of proper names like "Pegasus" that (on Quine's view) name nothing real, because, in speaking of Pegasus, we merely pretend to speak of something that is imaginary. It is also centered on the need to regularize, syntactically, our treatment of proper names whether or not we do name something real or actual in sentences (particularly when names occupy referential position, as in sentences like "Pegasus flies"). As a result, Quine recommends that we reinterpret proper names predicatively. Shifting to the use of "Socrates," which (after all) does name Socrates, Quine remarks:

> The "is" [of apparent identity, as in "Socrates is the teacher of Plato"] is now treated as a copula which, as in "is mortal" and "is a man", serves merely to give a general term the form of a verb and so suits it to predicative position [say: "The teacher of Plato socratizes"]. "Socrates" becomes a general term that *is true of just one object*, but general in being treated henceforward as grammatically admissible in predicative position and not in position suitable for variables.[8]

What we now see, attending to the italicized expression in the citation, is that the determinacy of reference, whether in the original form captured by proper names or in the now Leibnizianized predicative replacement intended *works in a cognitive way only if man can* (as he obviously cannot) *claim to fathom the all-comprehending mind of God*. This, of course, is precisely what Quine had already obscured by employing his schema of types of sentences (1) to (4) that are not to involve analytical hypotheses. For anyone – in effect, for a consistent protagorean – who refuses any neutral stance (the provisional neutrality of "stimulus synonymy" and "stimulus analyticity" Quine does not and cannot defend), a much more radical indeterminacy threatens, an indeterminacy *affecting all reference and predication*. This is, in fact, the current philosophical situation.

Quine never addresses *that* question directly: it would of course entrench certain profound puzzles of intentionality at the very heart of his own extensional program. That is the point of worrying Quine's account of "analytical hypotheses"; for, if we grant the force of the worry, then there is no possibility that Quine could escape subscribing to a very extreme form of relativism. That he resists nevertheless is worth conjuring with.

Beginning with Quine's own alternative to incommensurabilism, therefore, we can see how easily one may provide a basis for developing a great many varieties of relativism of a sort congenial to a general protagoreanism but more specifically concerned with puzzles affecting the use of conceptual categories, while not being characterizable as mere incommensurabilisms.[9] On the protagorean argument – in effect, on Quine's use of that argument – relativism is bound to affect all employments of reference and predication just as it is bound to affect the parsing of classificatory terms, ontic determinacy, or any fixity of meaning. We could not come to a more radical finding. But that's just the way things are, and yet we *do* actually succeed linguistically, and specifically in science. The protagorean, as we may say, is hardly a skeptic or a nihilist.

VI

We may secure another bit of philosophical turf by nagging at, and extending, Quine's own admissions. Consider what Quine says about vagueness, for instance: "Vagueness does not perturb the truth values of the usual sentences in which vague words occur.... A sentence affirming the approximate height of Mount Ranier is independent of the vagueness of that singular term. Not so a sentence affirming the approximate area or population of Mount Ranier; but these are unusual aspects of a mountain to talk about."[10] When "pressure arises" for a new convention or a greater precision of meaning, we may reasonably take steps to restrict particular instances of vagueness, Quine pleasantly recommends. So there would seem to be no principled difficulties about vagueness.

But all that presupposes that the required reform be straightforwardly available; and, indeed, it would be, *if* Quine's simple sort of behaviorism (regarding *sentences*) could be trusted – could be trusted to ensure a measure of cognitive neutrality. But it cannot be trusted, at least *if sentence and term are indissolubly linked, conceptually*. If inscrutability of reference and indeterminacy of translation affect terms, then they cannot fail to affect sentences as well. The illusion of adequate technical resources depends not only on the bifurcation of sentence and term and the blessing of a kind of cognitive neutrality among discriminated behavioral changes and sensory stimulations, but also on a refusal to countenance the ubiquity of historicized and preformed conceptual orientations.

Quine admits the preformational only in the coyest way; for to admit it generously and holistically would be to risk infecting all his own well-laid schemes. It would be to install the protagorean thesis without the prospect of external constraint. So Quine tends to equate the drift toward conceptual incommensurability with the threat of "meaninglessness," because he sees that possibility as depending on the scope of analytical hypotheses. (Nevertheless, Quine himself often signals from a distance that his own thesis – that sentences of the kinds he privileges by his categories (1) to (4), said to be unaffected by analytical hypotheses, said to be relatively neutral in a cognitive sense, are *posited* as such – is a guess that may or may not work. We may well have to change our mind about these from time to time.)[11]

But *if* we concede, with Quine, the relativism of reference and translation, then, *if* we also insist (*contra* Quine) on the inclusive role of "analytical hypotheses," we must challenge Quine's own terribly bland assurance that "Vagueness does not perturb the truth values of the usual sentences in which vague words occur." Vagueness does threaten to become ubiquitous, in the way of indeterminacy, just insofar as it generates the same sort of truth-value gaps (or irrelevance of assigning truth-values) that Quine has already defended. What holds for reference and predication and ontic commitment holds for vagueness and ambiguity and conceptual incommensurability, and, indeed, for the extension of universal terms beyond any paradigm or (nominalist) exemplar.

Quine would eliminate all "abstract objects" ("classes, attributes, propositions, numbers, relations, and functions"), wherever he can.[12] But that again is a sanguine possibility *only if* the relativism Quine himself espouses *can* be constrained *within* the rough cognitive neutrality *he* needs and affirms. But of course it can't be constrained: it is impossible, under the cognitive conditions Quine himself admits. Hence, his entire endeavor may be pressed hard enough to show that a progression of relativist scenarios can lead us from a spare and simple protagoreanism to incommensurabilism and to indefinitely many proliferating forms beyond. There are no assured boundaries that can confine the play of relativism.

If we add to this array such considerations as: the radical underdetermination of theory by data at the level of scientific explanation, the need to appeal to a principle of charity in reidentifying theoretical entities, the theory-laden nature of perception itself (already broached), the ineliminability of interpretive consensus in applying conceptual distinctions, cognitive uncertainty and unperceived error and the absence of canonical examples in every sector of inquiry, even the provisionality of logical laws, we see that it is quite impossible to hold the line against the invasion of comparatively vigorous forms of the relativist thesis going well beyond Kuhn's incommensurabilism.

VII

A strategic illustration or two may help us to appreciate the sense in which protagoreanism cannot fail to extend its domain to a large number of relatively well-defined questions that have generally not been treated relativistically.

Thus, in an earlier moment in his own inquiries, Hilary Putnam subscribed to a quite sanguine reading of the regulative principle, "Terms in a mature science typically *refer*."[13] Even in the form in which it was originally intended, the principle required the admission of a relativism somewhat congruent with Quine's, even though Putnam had pressed the thesis in a strong realist sense (which he shared with Richard Boyd),[14] in a sense intended to counteract the "idealist" (and threateningly deep-relativist) views of Kuhn and Feyerabend. What Putnam claimed at that time was that we are bound to admit: (i) that the executive terms of a "mature science" functioning at the explanatory level "typically refer" in the usual realist sense of successful reference; and (ii) that alternative theories that appear to compete with one another in the actual process of scientific work nevertheless, "typically refer" to the *same* theoretical entities for which they offer diverging or incompatible characterizations. The trouble is that, contrary to doctrines (i) and (ii), the existence and nature of the entities in question may be no more than artifacts of the theories themselves.

That reading – (i) and (ii) – Putnam came to see could not be readily squared (probably could not be squared at all) with his own continuing sympathy for Quine's view on translation and reference, together with his sympathy for Goodman's speculation about plural worlds and

Davidson's very decided attempt to subordinate reference to truth (more or less in Quine's spirit).[15] More than that, Putnam came to realize that, to the extent he shared with Michael Dummett that part of the "anti-realist" thesis that rejects a correspondence (or "realist") relation between statements and a "mind-independent" world – consistently with his other commitments – he had to give up (even on his own "internalist" or deprivileged view of cognitive access to reality) any pretense that the regulative principle, given above, *could* yield, distributively, anything like a determinately confirmed (or converging) reference to given theoretical entities.

Putnam's reflection here is rather touching in its candor:

> There is a sense of "correct" in which to understand a sentence *is* to know when that sentence is correctly asserted, Dummett claims. If this sense is equated with correspondence to mind-independent states of affairs, as it is by the correspondence theory of truth, then we are driven to either an infinite regress or else to the myth of comparing signs directly with unconceptualized reality, ... Dummett contends [Putnam nearly agrees with that much] that truth (or "correctness") in this sense is simply the epistemic notion of justification. "A statement is true if its assertion would be justified." Dummett calls this the *external* notion of truth. It is a non-realist sense (sentences are not "made true", in this sense of "true", by mind-independent states of affairs, but by states of affairs as *perceived and conceptualized*); and it is in *this* sense of "true" that to know the meaning of a sentence is to know under what conditions it is true.

What Putnam then proceeded to do was to distance himself from Dummett's strong intuitionism, reject the view that simply "identifies truth with justification," avoid as much relativism as possible, and treat "truth as an *idealization* of justification."[16] But now, explicitly following Davidson, Putnam conceded "that *truth is prior to reference*" – which effectively repeated Quine's untenable division between sentence and term, thereby yielding no more than another version of Quine's indefensible sort of relativism.[17] As a result, the strong realist reading of reference to theoretical entities could no longer be squared with the regulative principle Putnam had adopted in (i) and (ii). In fact, that principle could not fail to invite a strongly relativist reading of realism, *wherever the principle was intended to have a realist force*; in particular, it could no longer provide grounds for distinguishing Putnam's own view from the frankly relativistic view favored by Kuhn and

Feyerabend, or for repudiating the latter as a false or incoherent doctrine. We can no longer say (on the adjusted view) precisely *what* we are referring to in a "mature theory," and we cannot hope to confirm that, in shifting from one theory to another (say, in theories about the nature of genetic determinants developed somewhat before and around the turn of the century), we are, we must be, refering to the very same entities.

When he first introduced the issue, Putnam found himself already obliged to appeal to "the principle of charity on this matter."[18] Now, with the additional concessions we have been collecting, it becomes quite clear that Putnam's resistance to Dummett's view of truth (which is by no means the only option available) itself dissolves. For there is now no clear regulative sense in which the intended "idealization of justification" can be expected to lead to a unique or strongly convergent specification of the entities that competing explanatory theories share in a realist spirit. Relativism senses here an incipient victory – and an enlarged domain.

One can only suppose that a similar fate awaits the review of all the other issues we have assigned to a burgeoning protagoreanism distinguished from incommensurabilism. So, for example, once the reason for Putnam's reversal is rightly construed, we begin to see that we cannot even ensure a realist reading of explanatory theories or a straightforward realist reading in terms of empirical truth. Relativism threatens once again, even with respect to the proper way of construing the relationship between explanatory theories and observational findings in science.

Thus, on Wilfrid Sellars' view, the phenomenal world does *not* really exist: the regularities we pretend to find "there" form distorting and fragmentary approximations to the real microtheoretical processes of explanatory theories strictly governed by universal and invariant laws.[19] Alternatively, Bas van Fraassen is persuaded that "scientific realism" is better served by construing explanatory theories as "empirically adequate" (to observational phenomena, more or less in Duhem's sense) rather than as simply true (in Sellars' sense): if it "correctly describes what is *observable*," van Fraassen says, then the *truth* of proliferating theories is quite beside the point. The trouble, here, is that van Fraassen cannot (and admits that he cannot) provide a demarcation line between the "observable" and the "theoretical"; but trouble also arises because we are unable to decide the matter disjunctively as between Sellars' and van Fraassen's general strategies.[20]

The point is not to side with one or the other of these theorists, or others like them, but to come to appreciate the sense in which: (a) different parts of the history of science are likely to favor incompatible forms of realism; (b) no single theory is likely to win out against all opposing views (even within this very broad-gauged sort of disagreement); and (c) each promising theory is bound to improve its own competitive standing on grounds that build on a favorable use of the principle of charity. These subtleties are not likely to attract our attention until we actually attempt to adjudicate between well-formed and detailed alternative proposals. There is good reason for believing that the problem is endemic.

What we now see is that the symbiosis, the intransparency, the stubborn indeterminacies encountered in all our dealings with the physical or natural world conspire to make the avoidance of relativism a distinctly arbitrary pose. But if that is so, then merely to admit that there *are*, also, intentionally complex objects and phenomena that are as *real* as any physical objects and phenomena would be to oblige us to attend to certain extreme alternative forms of relativism that could not be easily assimilated to the usual specimens of protagoreanism or incommensurabilism. Properly developed, they form a distinct variety of (robust) relativisms that we had earlier labeled, somewhat mysteriously, as "ontic relativism." (We shall mention the thesis again, somewhat later, in a slightly fuller way.)

VIII

We may close this bit of our discussion by lingering a little longer on Bas van Fraassen's remarks on theory and observation in the sciences. We noted, just a moment ago, that disputes about the demarcation between the "observable" and the "theoretical" probably cannot be resolved in principle along bivalent lines, and that therefore the profoundly incompatible ontologies favored by Sellars and van Fraassen might both be entitled to a strong inning when "fitted" to the accumulating history of the physical sciences and the philosophy of science. Van Fraassen's position, however, is much more subtle than this confrontation suggests.

In fact, although there are "elements" of skepticism, relativism, and realism in his rather carefully crafted view, van Fraassen specifically declares that his "new epistemology is driven into neither skeptical despair, nor feeble relativism, nor metaphysical realism."[21] He treats skepticism and metaphysical realism fairly conventionally – there need be no quarrel with him there. For instance, he says: "Skepticism . . . comes two-fold: even if there is such a thing as objective rightness or truth, there is (3) [the point of the numbering will be clear in a moment] no possibility of attaining it, and (/or) (4) no possibility even of rational opinion."[22] Regarding realism, of course, van Fraassen opposes "foundationalism" and a strong "scientific realism" like Sellars'.[23] But when he addresses relativism ("irenic relativism," as he calls it), he says that it maintains: "there is (1) no objective criterion or rightness for opinion, and(/or) (2) no non-trivial criterion of rationality – anything goes, there is no truth except truth-for-you."[24] So it is clear that van Fraassen construes relativism in the relationalist way at least (his item 2).

On (1), he goes on to say:

> To begin then with the question of objective truth and right opinion. Certainly our opinion is right or wrong, and this depends on what the world (the facts we make judgments about) is like. Of course, this must be properly construed. The vaguer my judgments are, the less decisive the criterion can be. If I judge that it will rain today, then I am exactly right if it does rain, and wrong otherwise. If I judge that it is three times as likely to rain today as not, then what? Do not confuse this with the judgment that the chance of rain is ¾ – an entirely different question, which falls under the first heading of "true/false" judgment. No, if my judgments are of the "seems ... likely ..." form, the criterion is very insensitive if applied to single judgments, and becomes sensitive only if applied to a substantial body of judgments.... It may be that this criterion does not go very far. Very well; this is exactly how far opinion sticks its neck out with respect to the facts. To this extent only can it be objectively in or out of tune with the facts. We have other criteria as well for evaluating opinion, but the point at issue was whether there is one, non-trivially applicable, objective criterion of rightness – and there is. Along the way, we have rejected not only claim (1) but also claim (3) of skepticism for we can certainly attain this rightness, if only by accident.[25]

Here, it is clear, first, that van Fraassen pretty well accepts the ancient characterization of Protagoras' brand of relativism and, second, that he does not countenance any relativism that would accept just *this* very thin sense of "objective truth," "right opinion," realism, and bivalence. But what we have already said discounts that line of attack: no respectable relativist need go that way – nor, as we have also noted, the relationalist's way.

Still we have mentioned van Fraassen's account for another reason altogether. The point is simply this: what van Fraassen recommends *may* be quite easily construed in the robust relativist's way, though he himself is not so inclined. Van Fraassen is concerned to avoid the "scientific realist's" thesis (also, the "instrumentalist's") and to steer a middle course that he calls "constructive empiricism." His main moves are these. First, he agrees with the scientific realist "that a theory is the sort of thing that can be true or false, that can describe reality correctly or incorrectly, and that we may believe or disbelieve. All that is part [he adds] of the semantic view of theories. It is needed to maintain the semantic account of implication, inference, and logical structure." Nevertheless, says van Fraassen, even on the "traditional" view of theories, though they "*may*" be true or false, "it is nevertheless literally meaningful information, in the neutral sense in which the truth value is 'bracketed'," that theories primarily convey.[26] Hence, in proposing an "alternative" to scientific realism, van Fraassen retreats from truth to belief (which not only invokes the "desire for truth" but harbors other "ulterior motives") and then straightforwardly affirms:

> *Since therefore there are reasons for acceptance* [reasons for accepting a theory] *which are not reasons for belief* [reasons for believing the theory true] *I conclude that acceptance is not belief.* It is to me an elementary logical point that a more informative theory cannot be more likely to be true – and attempts to describe inductive or evidential support through features that require information (such as "Inference to the Best Explanation") must either contradict themselves or equivocate.

This intermediary step leads on to van Fraassen's "anti-realism" or "constructive empiricism": "the aim of science [he holds] is not truth as such but only *empirical adequacy*, that is, truth with respect to the observable phenomena."[27]

Now, there are all sorts of difficulty with van Fraassen's theory, not the least of which is the one regarding the demarcation of the "observable" and "not observable" or between the "theoretical" and "non-theoretical." Here, van Fraassen pits his view against that of the logical positivists, who make the division "a philosophical one, that is, [one] imposed from outside." On the constructive empiricist view, the distinction is drawn only "from within science," that is, without any epistemic privilege.

Van Fraassen nevertheless insists that his position "denies what is called conceptual relativism." He adds at once: "To be more precise, it denies it *on this level*, that is, on the level on which we interpret science and describe its role in our intellectual and practical life." And then he adds further, significantly again: "Philosophy of science is not metaphysics – there may or may not be a deeper level of analysis on which

[the] concept of the real world is subjected to scrutiny and found itself to be ... what? I leave to others the question whether we can consistently and coherently go further with such a line of thought."[28]

One might well claim, first, that there may be, on van Fraassen's own view, alternative, nonconverging ways in which the demarcation of the observable and nonobservable could be drawn, since foundationalism is out, also inferences to the best explanation (also "laws of nature");[29] secondly, that there can be, for that very reason, no strong disjunction between the philosophy of science and metaphysics, that is, that drawing the line regarding the first distinction just is implicating one or another metaphysics in one's philosophy of science; hence, thirdly, that van Fraassen's own insistence on the "criteria" (his term) of objective truth cannot fail to be affected (however marginally in our quotidian life) in a way that need not disfavor relativism at all.

In fact, it is just here that van Fraassen characterizes his own view as "Voluntarist." He means by this, first, that "the deliverances of experience [are not] propositions, though still intimately connected with them"; second, that we make "a primary response" to experience, "*the acceptance of some constraint* [because of those 'deliverances'] on what your opinion (henceforth) should be" – so, he adds, "the deliverances of experience are not propositions (but commands to oneself)"; and, third, that this very response has a voluntarist and variable aspect "because of the crucial role of the term 'accept', 'constraint', 'command'."[30] But, then, there is literally nothing that van Fraassen says here that could not be straightforwardly construed *as* a robust relativist's conception of science. One has merely to acknowledge explicitly that, for these very reasons, incongruent judgments are bound to obtain.

We have made this somewhat extended detour for the sake of a strong example of how relativism might arise in the physical sciences, not merely in the interpretation of artworks and the like, in a context in which neither incommensurabilism nor ontic relativism is invoked, and in which relationalism may be safely set aside. But, of course, van Fraassen's is not the only option of this sort that recent work in the philosophy of science offers. (We shall, by the way, return, in our closing chapter, to the "temperamental" feature of what van Fraassen may have had in mind in favoring a strong bivalence regarding "objective truth," all the while he weakens every prospect at arriving at it uniquely, and all the while he marks off, as with metaphysics, that about which there seems to be "no fact of the matter." We are suggesting, in short, that here, there is a distinct similarity between van Fraassen's way of avoiding relativism and Quine's. We shall examine the matter primarily in Quine's company.)

Notes

1 A systematic attempt to ground these themes in the prevailing controversies of current Western philosophy is provided in Joseph Margolis, *The Persistence of Reality*, 3 vols (Oxford: Basil Blackwell, 1987–9).

2 See David Premack, *Gavagai! or the Future History of the Animal Language Controversy* (Cambridge: MIT Press, 1986).

3 W. V. Quine, *Word and Object* (Cambridge: MIT Press, 1960), pp. 53–4, 35ff; italics added.

4 See Pierre Duhem, *The Aims and Structure of Physical Theory*, trans. Philip Wiener (Princeton: Princeton University Press, 1954).

5 Quine, *Word and Object*, p. 68; italics added. (The material in square brackets appears at pp. 25, 35–6, 46, 55.)

6 See, for instance, Thomas S. Kuhn, "Objectivity, Value Judgment and Theory Choice," in *The Essential Tension: Selected Studies in Scientific Tradition and Change* (Chicago: University of Chicago Press, 1977).

7 Quine, *Word and Object*, pp. 73, 77.

8 Ibid., p. 179; italics added.

9 In a recent paper, "Truth and Object," delivered at Temple University, March 1989, Quine returns once again to his master thesis: "By beginning with observation sentences rather than terms [which the latter, as he says, the empiricist tradition never tires of preferring, to his chagrin] we find a reasonable *criterion* of observationality, we accommodate the question of theory-lading, and we dispense with bridge principles" (italics added). But Quine fails to explain here (as, unfortunately, he always has) *how* to disjoin sentence and term, or how to identify criteria of assent to sentences that do not implicate (neutral) terms. There appears to be no satisfactory answer.

10 Ibid., p. 128.

11 Cf. ibid., p. 4.

12 Ibid., chapter 7; cf. p. 233.

13 Hilary Putnam, "Meaning and Knowledge" Lecture II, in *Meaning and the Moral Sciences* (London: Routledge and Kegan Paul, (1978), pp. 20–1.

14 See Richard N. Boyd, "Realism, Underdetermination, and a Causal Theory of Evidence," *Nous* VII (1973), pp. 1–7.

15 See Donald Davidson, "Reality without Reference" and "The Inscrutability of Reference," in *Inquiries into Truth and Interpretation* (Oxford: Clarendon Press, 1984).

16 Hilary Putnam, "Reference and Truth," in *Philosophical Papers*, vol. 3 (Cambridge: Cambridge University Press, 1983), pp. 83–4.

17 Putnam, "Beyond Historicism," in *Philosophical Papers*, vol. 3, pp. 291–2.

18 See Hilary Putnam, "Language and Reality," in *Philosophical Papers*, vol. 2 (Cambridge: Cambridge University Press, 1975), pp. 274–7; cf. N. L. Wilson, "Substances without Substrata," *Review of Metaphysics* XII (1959), pp. 521–9.

19 Wilfrid Sellars "The Language of Theories," in *Science, Perception and Reality* (London: Routledge and Kegan Paul, 1963).

20   Bas van Fraassen, *The Scientific Image* (Oxford: Clarendon Press, 1980), pp. 38, 12; italics added.
21   Bas C. van Fraassen, *Laws and Symmetry* (Oxford: Clarendon Press, 1989), p. 151.
22   Ibid., p. 176.
23   Cf. van Fraassen, *The Scientific Image*, chapter 2.
24   *Laws and Symmetry*, p. 176.
25   Ibid., pp. 176–7.
26   Ibid., p. 192.
27   Ibid., pp. 192–3; italics added. Cf. *The Scientific Image*, chapter 2.
28   *The Scientific Image*, pp. 81–2.
29   *Laws and Symmetry*, p. 183 and the rest of chapter 8.
30   Ibid., p. 320.

8

Extending Relativism
a Little Further

I

We may continue the line of discussion of the preceding chapter by shifting rather abruptly to an altogether different family of protagorean options – different, that is, in what they explicitly emphasize rather than in their ultimate significance. These options afford the additional benefit of showing in a very natural way the convergence of recent Anglo-American and Continental European philosophical currents along relativistic lines.

Here we must risk reviewing an extremely obscure, but remarkably influential, passage in Heidegger. We shall need a little patience.

Consider the following remark from Heidegger's much-discussed essay "The Question concerning Technology":

> Occasioning has to do with the presencing [*Anwesen*] of that which at any given time comes to appearance in bringing-forth. Bringing-forth brings hither out of concealment forth into unconcealment. Bringing-forth comes to pass only insofar as something concealed comes into unconcealment. This coming rests and moves freely within what we call revealing [*das Entbergen*]. The Greeks have the word *alētheia* for revealing. The Romans translate this with *veritas*. We say "truth" and usually understand it as the correctness of an idea.[1]

Heidegger's point is approximately captured by the following three distinctions. First, "truth," the local logical property of distributed statements or propositions, said to "correspond" with reality or the "facts," is ascribed only in radically contingent, holist, shifting, incompletely fathomable contexts of human life and linguistic usage. Here Heidegger speaks of what can only be called the ultimate surd of undifferentiated Being [*Sein*], which has no discernible structure of its own. Being "reveals" itself to man as plural beings [Seiende], because of man's special aptitude [Dasein] for ontic, discursible structure: roughly, very roughly, that is what Quine had in mind in speaking of the parsing of sentences. This mythic process – as mythic as analytical hypotheses – proceeds by way of "unconcealment" or alētheia [Truth]. Second, the sequence of worlds thus revealed is the result of a historicized habituation or sedimentation of cognitive and active commitments on the part of human societies. In an important sense, man survives through precognitive resources, through an incipient technology that does not as yet posit the conceptually frozen hypostatized entities of any particular phase of alētheia. Third and most important, the capacity of a human society to become aware of such an array of entities ("unconcealment") is itself symbiotically linked to a form of blindness or "concealment" that makes other similar revelations inaccessible. (This, again, is rather like Quine's insistence that there is no "truth of the matter" in choosing among alternative viable ontologies, except that Heidegger invents a specific myth to suggest why "truth" is merely local to what is perceived to be a phase of alētheia.)

That's a mouthful, of course, and possibly too purple to be worth taking seriously. But the passage does actually repay attention.

On Heidegger's view, the kind of "revealing" that technology makes possible is peculiarly intransigent and limited, not at all as open to new possibilities as is poiēsis (creative or free activity or invention).[2] Heidegger uses the notion to criticize the peculiar narrowness of vision of modern man. There may be some justice in it, but it is not our particular concern here.[3]

What is genuinely interesting in Heidegger's account, what has been developed by others in ways that bear explicitly on the fortunes of relativism, rests with the third of the distinctions given above. This is the meaning of Heidegger's otherwise quite mysterious summary: "Enframing [Ge-stell: roughly, an inflexible ordering of objective things for technologically effective purposes] conceals that revealing which, in the sense of poiēsis, lets what presences come forth into appearance."[4] The idea is that every conceptual scheme that a society employs blinds that society to the possibilities of alternative such schemes that it or other societies might employ, synchronically or diachronically, intra- or inter-societally. Every conceptual scheme, itself the contingent artifact of a contingent societal history, embodies an implicit horizon – an endogenous limitation of vision that cannot as such be penetrated merely by the cognitive and practical aptitude of all those who are preformed by its particular habits of mind and life. (This theme will reappear later, in connection with Gadamer's views.)

One important immediate consequence that we may draw from this way of putting things is that it disallows, at a stroke, any and every appeal to conceptual scenarios that invoke "all possible worlds"; hence, it disallows all universalisms that pretend to reach or even approximate logical or phenomenological or conceptual necessities by totalizing somehow over the extensions (and the interrelations among them) of any and every conceptual scheme. Horizonal limitation, whether historically induced (on Gadamer's and Foucault's views) or praxically (on Marx's view) or by the inherent exclusionary power of conceptualization itself (on Heidegger's and Lyotard's views) preclude any and every presumption of capturing strict conceptual invariances that bear on defining the conditions of human knowledge. For example, it completely subverts the various sorts of progressivism associated with Husserl, Peirce, Popper, and Habermas; and, in doing that, obviously strengthens the relativist's hand.

If we may risk another purple passage, this time from *Being and Time*, Heidegger holds that:

> *The world is already presupposed* in one's Being alongside the ready-to-hand [*Zuhandenheit*: man's precognitive, instrumental aptitude for surviving in the world] concernfully and factically, in one's thematizing of the present-at-hand [*Vorhandenheit*: the reflexive technological tendency to regularize the objects of science and successful practice in the very space of *Zuhandenheit*], and in one's discovering of this latter entity [the objects of science and technology] by Objectification; that is to say, all these are possible only as ways of Being-in-the-world [*in-der-Welt-sein*].[5]

Heidegger goes on to say – in what one cannot deny is an unusual analogue of Quine's thesis, now cast in terms of the contingency and historicity and preformed orientation of man – that

> the significance-relationships [roughly, the conceptual categories, phenomenologically discerned] which determine the structure of the world [the world of appearances, the world as we encounter it, the world of our science and technology] are not a network of forms which a worldless subject has laid over some kind of material. What is rather the case is that factical Dasein [in effect, man as historically subject to *alētheia*], understanding itself and its world ecstatically in the unity of the "there," comes back from these horizons to the entities encountered within them. Coming back to these entities understandingly is the existential meaning of letting

them be encountered by making them present; that is why we call them entities "within-the-world" [*innerweltlich*].[6]

(We may see in this a fundamental objection to Husserl's views examined in a previous chapter.)

In a word (much delayed), what we perceive, discern, understand is a function of our own historicized conceptual horizon; that horizon, developed in accord with the interests of science and technology, blinds us to other possibilities just where we pursue those that it makes accessible.

This is a deeper theme than that of Kuhn's conceptual incommensurabilities, but it supplies something of a rationale for those as well, for the mythic intercourse between *Sein* and *Dasein* resists our yielding to any simple realism or idealism or any simple disjunctive assignment of invariant realist and idealist elements (Kantianism). In the Kuhnian context, we may *understand* incommensurable schemes; in the Heideggerean, we do not really perceive at all the accessibility of other distinct ways of construing the world. (If we did, they would not be "other," which rather neatly subverts the point of Davidson's sort of stonewalling.)

The point is this: *if* what we call the intelligible world is, in some sense, an artifact of the indissoluble symbiosis of a (mythically assigned because impenetrable) cofunctioning of cognized world and cognizing agent (*Dasein*), then the threat of a radical relativism can never be allayed. The entire *objective* order is no more than a contingent posit of a certain phase of conceptual history.

We have traced certain currents in analytic philosophy – in Quine, in Goodman, in Putnam, in Kuhn – that fasten on the bare logic of attempting to recover realism, objectivity, truth, reference, progress within the constraints of holism and conceptual preformation. Here, reviewing Heidegger, we turn instead to a more speculative account of human existence within the terms of which the puzzles of the more analytic theorists, for instance, Putnam's problematic use of the principle of charity, are rather easily located in such a way that no merely nonrelativistic solution could possibly win out.

II

Once we have mastered his thesis, we may drop Heidegger's heavy-handed prose. The relevant claim is simply this: that man's cognitive and discursive powers are radically historicized, preformed, contingent, largely tacit, horizonal, and capable of supporting objective truth-claims only within the logical space of its own horizon. Heidegger supplies a variety (perhaps a mere jumble) of ontological, existential, phenomenological, and hermeneutic reasons for endorsing all sorts of relativisms, whereas so-called analytic thinkers (of the Anglo-American sort) offer more formal reasons for supporting (or opposing) particular doctrines.

The two strategies converge, nevertheless, simply because on either argument: Quine's rejection of the analytic/synthetic disjunction or Heidegger's advocacy of *alētheia*, all rules of reason, all logics, all mathematics, all methodologies have the scope they do only as applied or interpreted in or for an assigned domain of inquiry. There is no assurance that *any* merely abstractly formulated principle – noncontradiction, *modus ponens*, double negation, excluded middle, *tertium non datur*, Leibniz's law, Euclid's parallel lines axiom, Church's thesis, the analytic/synthetic distinction, Mill's canons, and similar rules – holds everywhere in some uniquely specifiable way, or simply holds everywhere, or holds transparently and without any need for piecemeal interpretation. But *that* concession itself, the recognition that the would-be invariances of our most strenuous conceptual resources are artifacts inseparable from the tacit encompassing conditions of ongoing life and inquiry, confirms the inseparability of the ultimate strategies of Anglo-American and Continental European philosophy, of which Quine's and Heidegger's idioms are merely particularly instructive and polarized samples.[7] Wherever we embrace the doctrine of the flux, or wherever we embrace doctrines of deep contingency and intransparency short of the flux (as with Quine and Heidegger), we present a picture of the world regarding which it becomes impossible to exclude any number of relativistic options.

III

Heidegger's "concealment/unconcealment" distinction, for instance, has now begun to figure quite prominently in formulating arguments affecting the competence of computers to simulate or equal human intelligence. Terry Winograd, for example, a specialist in computer science and long committed to the feasibility of a comprehensive computer analysis of human knowledge and human language, the inventor in fact of SHRDLU (thought to be, in its time, one of the more promising programs for getting on with artificial intelligence projects), has now completely reversed his view of the matter.[8] Our concern here is not with the fortunes of artificial intelligence as such, but rather with the bearing of quarrels about its fortunes on the issue of relativism.

Winograd is now persuaded that the very question of computer design in simulation contexts cannot be separated from the question of "designing ways of being" – in particular, the ways of "being" peculiar to humans (with special attention to problems of absorbing a living tradition, preformative factors, open-ended contexts, so-called "frame" problems, problems of relevance in pattern recognition, improvisational and consensual factors, and the like) – and that these instantiate Heidegger's "concealment" distinction in an ineliminable way, without regard to the difference between inter- and intralinguistic communication.[9]

Here, for instance, is an example of Winograd's deliberately Heideggerean reading of the phenomenon of natural (human), culturally formed facility and its implicated problem of artificial simulation:

> The essence of our Being is the pre-reflective experience of being *thrown* [cf. Heidegger's *Geworfenheit*] in a situation of acting, without the opportunity or need to disengage and function as a detached observer.... Whenever we treat a situation as present-at-hand [cf. Heidegger's *Vorhandenheit*], analyzing it in terms of objects and their properties, we thereby create a blindness. Our view is limited to what can be expressed in the terms we have adopted. This is not a flaw to be avoided in thinking – on the contrary, it is necessary and inescapable. Reflective thought is impossible without the kind of abstraction that produces blindness.[10]

Winograd's interesting point is this: (i) that the use of any conceptual scheme occludes the perceivability of others; (ii) that the effective use of any conceptual scheme entails a strong tendency toward its functioning in a spontaneously horizonal and naturally exclusive way; and (iii) that the very facility with which humans use their conceptual schemes, naturally acquired in living in a society, is grounded in a precognitive and existential condition (of being): (i) to (iii), of course, signify forms of "blindness."[11]

One may easily grasp, therefore, that not only the differences in conceptual orientation *between* societies, synchronic or diachronic, but also the differences in conceptual orientation *within* a given society (as a result, say, of the division of social and conceptual labor and of the contingency and informality with which the members of any new cohort of human infants are first introduced to the practices and habits of their own society) are bound to generate indefinitely many small instances of mutual and reflexive blindness.

Those differences, however, can be and normally are tolerated by any encompassing viable society to the extent that it functions smoothly enough at critical moments, or functions in a sufficiently cross-grained way, that such discrepancies are hardly perceived or are automatically neutralized by other stabilizing or compensating consensual forces that are of an equally generous gauge. *Incipient* conditions, therefore, for construing human judgment relativistically lie everywhere. It is not so much that the Heideggerean thesis *is* itself relativistic as that it provides a global picture within which it becomes impossible to preclude relativistic options alongside *any* analyses of language and thought that would eschew relativism altogether. For example, it poses an insuperable objection to the sort of progressivism that Mohanty has constructed along phenomenological lines.

IV

A similar conclusion may be drawn from Hans-Georg Gadamer's use of the Heideggerean model, applied in the hermeneutic manner:

> The overcoming of all prejudices [that is, the historical preformation of judgment and perception], this global demand of the enlightenment, will prove to be itself a prejudice, the removal of which opens the way to an appropriate understanding of our finitude, which dominates not only our humanity, but also our historical consciousness ... the idea of an absolute reason is impossible for historical humanity. Reason exists for us only in concrete, historical terms, i.e., it is not its own master, but remains constantly dependent on the given circumstances in which it operates.[12]

Gadamer's critical thesis (which, as we shall see later, he himself cheats on) is simply that: (a) reason has a history (or, better, is a historicized talent); (b) reason functions only and always in an existential and interpretive way; and (c) reason is itself preformed, a manifestation of horizonal "prejudice."

Once again, this is not so much an explicit relativism as it is a view of the globalized human condition within which relativism cannot be avoided. In the hands of someone like Protagoras, it would have been an explicit relativism. Gadamer, however, is an opponent of an out-and-out relativism; although, like Quine and Putnam, he is clearly hospitable to certain rather mild relativistic tendencies. The question stands, whether Gadamer or any other Heideggerean who wishes to remain consistent with the terms of reference of *alētheia* can convincingly resist extreme relativistic pressures. The bet, here, is that they can not. In any case, Gadamer *does* relativize reason in a historicized way which, in effect, provides a holist hermeneutic analogue of the "analytic" thesis we were developing earlier on, namely, that logical, mathematical, and methodological principles (taken distributively) cannot fail to be relativized to their contexts and domains of application.

What the most recent Continental European philosophical currents provide, then, is a compendious overview of the human condition (an overview said to be, in various ways, ontological, existential, phenomenological, or hermeneutic) that distinctly favors – though it normally does not argue the case for – increasingly radicalized versions of relativism. The important thing is to see the relevance of that overview: *we* can supply (and to some extent have already supplied) the explicit argument for relativism.

Continental currents tend to emphasize the following themes, all of which, singly or collectively, favor one or another form of relativism: cognitive intransparency; the symbiosis of world and word; preformation; the historicized nature of man; the deep contingency of conceptual schemes; horizonal blindness; and, most particularly, the indefensibility of all conceptual assurances regarding the *apodictic*, the *originary*, and the *totalized*.

The point of the last trio of distinctions is plain enough. There can be no conceptual scheme that is sufficiently systematic and closed ("totalized") that, for any given sector of inquiry, it would be true that no further supplementation of categories would ever be spontaneously elicited. Any such enlargement would inevitably affect the *relational* or *differential* import of all conceptual distinctions already in place. Similarly, no viable scheme of concepts can be shown to rest on some *first* point of entering into the match of world and category ("originary"), so that every further distinction could be systematically and invariantly related to *that* beginning. Finally, at no point in our application of concepts to the phenomena of the world can we claim to have found a particular self-disclosing truth so powerful that it is unquestionably true, and that whatever we take to be true (and important) in our inquiries flows from *that* first indubitable truth, or can be shown to have a heightened reliability regarding its own truth as a result of that relation ("apodictic").

V

We have, in fact, traced a version of these problems, just a moment before, in reviewing Quine's and Putnam's theories of reference. There, we saw the relativistic implications of the failure to reach a closed and comprehensive conceptual system (with respect to predicates, in Quine's case; with respect to the meaning and intent of theories, in Putnam's). Here the most inclusive strategies of avoiding relativisms are collected as variations on one and the same theme. In practice, they have all been dubbed "logocentric" or "privileged," and have been notoriously (though effectively) attacked, by way of a peculiar sort of conceptual subversion, by Jacques Derrida, in pursuing what Derrida calls "deconstruction."

One could say that deconstruction generalizes over all forms of conceptual "blindness," of which the forms pursued by Winograd and Gadamer are simply specialized versions. Deconstruction is also indebted to Heidegger's notion of *alētheia*, though in a leaner way and in a way that subverts the related universalizing or totalizing or privileging tendencies in Heidegger himself. It is also perhaps more profoundly indebted to Nietzsche, which is to say, to an orientation as close to advocating the doctrine of the flux as any conceptual orientation the modern world has yet produced. In any case, Derrida practices deconstruction chiefly (or did so originally) against the pretensions of Husserlian phenomenology and Saussurean structuralism, which two programs he effectively shows converge in requiring some extremely sanguine commitment to the apodictic, the originary, and the totalized.

Derrida thus proposes to pursue what he ironically (but nevertheless productively) calls "the science of writing – *grammatology*." Of this he says – we must allow his extreme indirection – that "such a science of writing runs the risk of never being established as such and with that name. Of never being able to define the unity of its project or its object. Of not being able either to write its discourse on method or describe the limits of its field." For essential reasons

> the unity of all that allows itself to be attempted today through the most diverse concepts of science and of writing, is, in principle, more or less covertly yet always, determined by an historico-metaphysical epoch of which we merely glimpse the *closure*. I do not say the *end*. The idea of science and the idea of writing – therefore also of the science of writing – is meaningful for us only in terms of an *origin* and within a world to which a certain concept of the sign (later I shall call it *the* concept of science) and a certain concept of the relationships between speech and writing, have

already been assigned. A most determined relationship, in spite of its privilege, its necessity, and the field of vision that it has controlled for a few millennia, especially in the West, to the point of being now able to produce its own dislocation and itself proclaim its limits.[13]

In effect, Derrida's strategy is to *use* the various forms of logocentric thought and language so as to uncover, by internal subversion, evidence of a breach of the necessary, the originary, the closed, the privileged, the certain, the totalized, the invariant, which is to say, to enable our most comprehensive science to "proclaim its limits."[14] The point is that pretensions of these sorts *cannot* be defended on conceptual or evidential grounds but are nevertheless almost ineluctably favored within the horizonal blindness of any such usage. Derrida's project is, however, a conservative one: *not* to disturb the effectiveness of any particular discourse, but to nag interminably at its heels so as to remind us of the faulty pretensions that it cannot help assuming. There is in this sense a remote similarity between what Derrida has undertaken and the much thinner (but also doctrinally more quarrelsome) "deconstruction" that Richard Rorty has pursued largely within the Anglo-American philosophical literature.[15] That shared tendency, hospitable to relativism, is often misleadingly dubbed a relativism in its own right.

What is more important to notice is that the Heideggerean-like strategies of Winograd, Gadamer, and Derrida are not so much explicit relativisms as confirmations of certain conceptual limits and blindness *that others, we for instance, could exploit relativistically.* They prepare the ground for extending alternative forms of a relativism (robust relativism), but they are not themselves primarily concerned to endorse them. And where they seem to, for instance, in Gadamer's view of the nature of reason, it is usually the case that the explicit formulation of a relativistic position is never really taken up. Nothing is lost by this. But we must, for the time being, content ourselves with noticing that many discussants who seem remarkably sanguine about claims that would support a relativistic position are themselves quite often vigorous opponents of relativism. Certainly, as we have already seen, this is true of such thinkers as Quine and Putnam and Rorty. There is no reason why it should not also be true of Heidegger and Gadamer and Derrida.

Notes

1   Martin Heidegger, *The Question Concerning Technology and Other Essays,* trans. William Lovitt (New York: Harper and Row, 1977), pp. 11–12.
2   Ibid., p. 14.

3   Cf. ibid., pp. 19–23.

4   Ibid., p. 27.

5   Martin Heidegger, *Being and Time*, trans. from 7th ed. by John Macquarrie and Edward Robinson (New York: Harper and Row, 1962), p. 416 (p. 365 in the German pagination).

6   Ibid., p. 417 (p. 366 in the German pagination). We are not, it should be noted, equating Heidegger's sense of technology in the essay "The Question concerning Technology" with the sense in which he raises what may be regarded as the "technological" aspect of *Zuhandenheit*, in *Being and Time*.

7   See W. V. Quine, "Two Dogmas of Empiricism," in *From a Logical Point of View* (Cambridge: Harvard University Press, 1953) pp. 20–46; Hilary Putnam, "Introduction: Science as Approximation to Truth," "The Logic of Quantum Mechanics," in *Philosophical Papers*, vol. 1 (Cambridge: Cambridge University Press, 1975), pp. vii–xiv, 174–97; Judson C. Webb, "Gödel's Theorems and Church's Thesis: A Prologue to Mechanism," in Robert S. Cohen and Marx W. Wartofsky (eds), *Language, Logic, and Method* (Dordrecht: D. Reidel, 1983), pp. 309–53; and John Stachel, "Comments on 'Some Logical Problems Suggested by Emergent Theories' by Professor Dalla Chiara," in the same volume, pp. 91–102.

8   See Terry Winograd, *Understanding Natural Language* (New York: Academic Press, 1972); also, Joseph Weisenbaum, "ELIZA – A Computer Program for the Study of Natural Language Communication between Man and Machine," *Communications of the AMC*, IX (1968), pp. 36–45; and Marvin Minsky (ed.), *Semantic Information Processing* (Cambridge: MIT Press, 1968).

9   Terry Winograd and Fernando Flores, *Understanding Computers and Cognition* (Norwood, NJ: Ablex Corporation, 1987), p. xi, cf. also p. 8, chapters 2, 9. See, also, Hubert L. Dreyfus, *What Computers Can't Do: The Limits of Artificial Intelligence*, rev. ed. (New York: Harper and Row, 1979); and Hubert L. and Stuart E. Dreyfus, *Mind over Machine* (New York: Free Press, 1985).

10 Winograd and Flores, *Understanding Computers*, p. 97.

11 Cf. ibid., chapter 8.

12 Hans-Georg Gadamer, *Truth and Method*, trans. Garrett Barden and John Cumming from 2nd German ed. (New York: Seabury Press, 1975), pp. 244–5.

13 Jacques Derrida, *Of Grammatology*, trans. Gayatri Spivak Chakravorty (Baltimore: Johns Hopkins University Press, 1976), p. 4; I have italicized "origin."

14 See *ibid.*, part two; and Jacques Derrida, "Différance," in *Margins of Philosophy*, trans. Alan Bass (Chicago: University of Chicago Press, 1982).

15 See Richard Rorty, *Philosophy and the Mirror of Nature* (Princeton: Princeton University Press, 1979).

9

Resisting Relativism

I

We have just been attempting to extend the domain of relativism. In a way we have done so, but in another way we have not. The reason is that we have not quite taken care to force a confrontation at every decisive point. There is, in fact, a veritable army of theorists who would concede *many* of the themes we have just been collecting, particularly those associated with historicizing human existence and human inquiry, who would *then* go on to deny that their admission *entails* relativism or at least any troubling or sinister form of relativism. They are absolutely right in this: not that their conclusion holds, but rather that the clinching argument is not yet at hand.

Here there is some danger of oversimplifying our catalogue of the population of would-be opponents. They pretty well fall into three groups. One maintains that relativism is incoherent, self-defeating, self-contradictory, incapable of escaping self-referential paradox. (This group obviously supposes that relativism can never escape the admittedly fatal weakness of relationalism.) It is an extraordinarily confident and widely distributed brotherhood. We have seen that it includes Plato and Aristotle – what more need be said? – and is rather glibly, also rather unceremoniously, championed in our own time by formulaic pronouncements that can hardly be taken to be the result of strenuous new inquiries. We have seen, for instance, the almost insouciant ease with which theorists like Newton-Smith, Putnam, and Rorty have tossed off the comfortable finding that, "of course," relativism (pressed in a serious way) inevitably runs into self-referential paradoxes.

Newton-Smith is a strenuous opponent of all forms of relativism, at least in his *The Rationality of Science*.[1] But Putnam and Rorty are themselves distinctly attracted to *some* form of relativism, which they are inclined to discount as *not* leading to the virulent form, *or* as not being potent enough to constitute a conceptual crisis for those (themselves, to some extent) who favor a form of "objectivism" that catches up the mainstream tradition of science and philosophy.

Also, it should be remarked, classicists who devote themselves to the nearly pious transmission of the supposedly fixed discoveries of Plato and Aristotle (as in defeating Protagoras) tend to raise only the narrowest textual doubts about their vulnerability or the consequences of their vulnerability. M. L. Burnyeat, for instance, in a much-admired analysis of Plato's *Theaetetus*, says flat out: "No amount of maneuvering with his relativizing qualifiers will extricate Protagoras from the commitment to truth absolute which is bound up with the very act of assertion."[2] Burnyeat takes a strong "absolutist" line (that is, one that is at least committed to bivalence and opposed to relationalizing truth) and shows no sympathy at all for the difficulties besetting truth-*claims* and the epistemic use of realism under conditions of intransparency. But let that ride.

For all his care in explicating the *Theaetetus*, Burnyeat does not quite manage to feature the troublesome possibilities that Protagoras' argument offers – partly in terms of what the text may be made to support, partly in terms of what the general connection might be between relativism and Protagoras' argument. Burnyeat certainly slips easily from what he believes the text will support to what he thinks Socrates' reconstruction of the argument comes to, to what might be said of Protagoras' text apart from that, to what might be said of relativism itself. But all the purely scholarly skills he has will avail him nothing in Protagoras' case, unless he has an independent insight about what new maneuver might be possible. Since he subscribes to the canonical defeat of relativism (since he means only to give it greater precision), he *has* nothing new to say about the matter or about the novelty of Protagoras' maneuver.

II

Burnyeat's most important contribution in analyzing the *Theaetetus* and the discussion, ancient and modern, about the issues raised rests with this: he is very clear, first, that the expression "true for x" ("true for Socrates," say) is a "novel locution" introduced by Protagoras and (usually) is so featured by Plato, in offering what Burnyeat terms "an adequately formulated relativism":

(*M*) Every judgment is true *for* the person whose judgment it is;[3]

second, that it is not true that that locution in (*M*) "simply means the same as the more familiar 'seems true to [*x*]' or 'is believed by [*x*]'";[4] and third, that the meaning of that phrase is the linchpin of Protagoras' argument. Burnyeat gives us a reading of (*M*) but *not* an analysis of the "original locution"; and, of course, he draws the conclusion already cited. He also ventures "a philosophical claim which [he is] anxious should stand in its own right – namely, the claim that the argument under (*M*) is not the harmless thing that defenders of Protagoras have always taken it to be." And then he adds his own clincher:

> a proposition of the form "*x* is *F*" is true (relatively) for person *a*, if and only if "*x* is *F* for *a*" is true (absolutely) [that is, *sans phrase*, without any relativizing qualifications whatsoever].[5]

But that is simply Burnyeat's extraordinary prejudice: he is merely saying he cannot see how it could be otherwise.

Now, the trouble with all of this is that Burnyeat *cannot* say what Protagoras means by his "novel locution"; hence, he cannot say how it bears on the fortunes of all the canonical moves. Yet he persists in believing that *those same moves* may continue to be taken in their standard way, in the face of what remains an utter mystery for him. He himself is not in the least clear about what possible maneuvers regarding "true" may be made by the clever relativist, possibly including Protagoras. For example, he never directly discusses the following three essential issues (that we, of course, have had in mind all along): first, whether Protagoras may, in the modern sense, have been talking about truth-*claims* (in speaking of "man the measure") rather than about the *meaning* of "true," so that the "absolute" meaning of "true" may not be at issue at all; secondly, whether, in talking about the alethic and epistemic aspects of using the predicate "true," Protagoras was defining "true" in the relationalist way (which would explain the phrase "for *x*") or was not, or whether, in not talking about the meaning of "true," he was concerned only with *what a relativist might claim*, *if* indeed "man is the measure," *if* indeed we are confined to how things "seem to *a*" in deciding whether "*x* is *F*"; and third, whether Protagoras may have deliberately "violated" excluded middle (as Aristotle believes) and, if he did, how that bears on the fate of his argument.

It's hardly a question of Plato's being dishonest in presenting Protagoras; it's more a question of whether Plato adequately understood Protagoras (since *we* don't, reading the *Theaetetus*, wondering about the "novel locution"). After all, there is no handbook on relativism to be consulted.

Take just one or two illustrations from Burnyeat's own analysis, to judge how reasonable these caveats are. Burnyeat begins with a passage from the *Theaetetus* (170c): "What seems to each person is so for the person to whom it seems." This lays it down, Burnyeat says, that (for all persons *x* and all propositions *p*)

P1. If it seems to *x* that *p* [or, if *x* believes/judges that *p*], then it is true for *x* that *p*.[6]

Perhaps. But notice that the analysis says nothing about the meaning of "true for *x*" except that the consequent is entailed by the antecedent (whatever it means): it says nothing about *how* the antecedent bears evidentially on determining the truth-value of the consequent, or how it does so in virtue of what the consequent means. Furthermore, it is clearly made to lead, in the relevant passage in the *Theaetetus*, to the absurdity that no one supposes that another is ever ignorant or mistaken at all; in that sense, it implicitly reduces what Protagoras is claiming to what would be nonsense on the canonical view of truth. So the whole affair is a charade.

Burnyeat goes on to suggest that, on Plato's account, Protagoras is also committed to

P3. If it does not seem to *x* that *p*, then it is not true for *x* that *p*.[7]

Well, again, perhaps. But notice that the "normal" reading of the antecedent invokes "seems to *x* that *p*" in just the sense in which *x* *would not* (pertinently) *claim that p*, in the "absolutist," *not* in the (still mysterious) "relativist" sense of "true" (whatever the latter sense may be: the sense in which the phrase "for *x*" cannot be omitted). So, once again, we cannot say just *what* Burnyeat is arguing for, unless it is the complete irrelevance of the "novel locution" for the analysis of "true." And if it is that, then, of course, we may as well admit we have no new interesting or strong account of Protagoras that might validate him after all, nothing more than further evidence that modern commentators are disposed to repeat the ancient arguments again and again.

The truth is that Burnyeat's account is subject to an elementary *reductio*, just the one the ancient critics never faced up to. It is this: if you concede Protagoras' thesis, "man is the measure," then it becomes impossible to reconstruct a plausible version of his argument – assuming that he is the clever man he is said to be – by adducing logical or conceptual constraints that are invariant or necessary *a priori*, that are, *in the sense being contested*, antecedently binding on *whatever* Protagoras may have meant. For you will then surely have contradicted Protagoras' thesis.

You may well say that it is impossible to defend Protagoras' claim. Fine. But why say that you are presenting Protagoras accurately when you characterize his position in a way that is flat-out incompatible with his most famous pronouncement? All Burnyeat's talk about the "absolutist" account of truth cannot mean anything but (as he himself explicitly says) that the relativist thesis (*whatever* it is) must remain constrained by conceptual restrictions regarding the relation between truth and the world *that take precedence over "man the measure."* "No amount of maneuvering with his relativizing qualifiers [Burnyeat says, you remember] will extricate Protagoras from the commitment to truth absolute which is bound up with the very act of assertion." "Protagoras' theory [he says elsewhere] is, after all, a theory of truth and a theory of truth must link judgments to something else – the world, as philosophers often put it, though for a relativist [he adds, unhelpfully, even superstitiously] the world has to be relativized to each individual."[8] There *is* no way to interpret Burnyeat's assessment and his gloss on the *Theaetetus* except in the sense that the ancient "archic" doctrine is correct: *man is not the measure.*

The gloss, by the way, confirms the plain fact that Burnyeat attributes to Protagoras a view that could not fail to generate paradox and self-contradiction; though it does, indeed, afford *a* reading (an utterly hopeless reading) of the mysterious phrase "true for x": "When it seems to x that p, it is true for x that p, *because* the *world* is, then, whatever it seems to be for x." (Needless to say, this last is a caricature of what Burnyeat actually says, but it *is* what his analysis entails.) We may never know what Protagoras really claimed. Or perhaps he wasn't clever after all. But the defense of relativism we have been slowly building signifies that, if he can be redeemed at all, Protagoras must have been leaning in that direction in which some part of the following prevails: (a) the archic doctrine is false; (b) we may abandon, or restrict the scope of, excluded middle, without contradiction; (c) there is an indissoluble symbiosis between word and world; (d) we oppose the relationalist definition of truth; (e) incongruent claims may be defended. If he did not favor any significant part of (a) to (e), then, we may say, Protagoras was not an interesting relativist – or else he was not clever enough.

III

Of the more equivocal discussants, Rorty *appears* to be radical, because he means to subvert the pretensions of canonical philosophy. But the truth is that that subversion is *not* offered in a relativistic but in a skeptical spirit – an entirely different kettle of fish. The evidence is that

Rorty has become even more optimistically insistent (without "philo-sophical" backing, now) about the *first-order* objectivity of our sciences. This has inevitably taken the form of a *laissez-faire* doctrine: in fact, the use of the expression "first-order objectivity" would not be admitted by Rorty, since it necessarily invokes second-order or philosophically legi-timative discourse, which Rorty will have none of. The resultant opti-mistic and lax attitude about science and morality may well be a sort of "relativism" (for others), *but not in the legitimative sense the relativist shares with the objectivist* (whom Rorty also necessarily discounts).[9] That attitude may also, understandably, be viewed as rather dangerous and silly, because it simply refuses to answer for what it quite arbitrarily excludes from responsible review.

Putnam's effort, by contrast, is meant to accommodate the *kind* of relativism theorists like Quine and Goodman and Davidson concede (to the extent those views do actually remain coherent: where, it must be said, Putnam has grave misgivings about the views of Goodman and Dummett in particular); but *he* acts at once to recover a nonrelativist conception of both science and philosophy, in offsetting the troubling possibilities of the others.[10] Broadly speaking, Putnam's strategy is to separate the question of the nature of reality, of what there is, from the question of the nature of truth.

Where he worries the views of Goodman and Dummett, for instance, Putnam stresses the danger of confusing the two issues or of linking them so closely that concessions on the first adversely affect answers to the second. This is the point of his attempt to recover what is salvage-able in the correspondence theory of truth without subscribing to "metaphysical realism" (in congenial accord, therefore, with Quine *and* Goodman *and* Davidson *and* Dummett).[11]

For instance, this is the reason Putnam sides with Dummett in remarking that "reductionistic philosophers" (and other "metaphysical realists") disagree "with other philosophers ... over *what there really is*, and not over the conception of truth";[12] and why he ultimately distances himself from Dummett (as well as from Goodman), because *truth* (he believes) cannot be restricted to verification or confirmation or the selection of "right versions" or the like. It is true, he would say, that "the world is not descritable independently of our description" (which might encourage a certain incipient relativism as well as a convergence with Kuhn and Feyerabend, whom he vigorously opposes); but the *revisability* of any statement makes sense only in a logical space in which we hold (he would add) to the conception of objective truth (correspondence, in effect), which verificationism (positivism) and de-cidability (Dummett) and right versions (Goodman) do not and cannot make provision for.[13] Effectively, then, Putnam supports a bivalent logic and regards himself as a sort of Peircean optimist.

IV

This won't do, however, and it is important to know why. With Quine, Putnam opposes "*absolute* unrevisability": "Any statement can be 'revised'." Nevertheless, speaking more cautiously than would Quine, Putnam says that "the revisability of the laws of Euclid's geometry, or the laws of classical logic, does not make them mere 'empirical' statements. This is why I have called them *contextually a priori*."[14]

The point is that Putnam favors a kind of "Kantianism" – his interpretation, in effect, of the Quinean program he pretty well accepts. Also, although *that* yields *some* (as it does in Quine) in the direction of relativism, the *plural* (perhaps more than the relativist) theories of reality our *social* inquiry cannot fail to support do still capture *what is real*. That, Putnam somehow supposes, precludes a serious relativism. Of course, it does no such thing, or at least it does not on the strength of Putnam's argument. There is a lacuna there.

The "metaphysical realist" fails to see why realism must be "internalist" (internalism being "Kantian"); but the anti-realist (Dummett in particular) fails to see that verificationism or decidabilism (as we may call Dummett's view) cannot fail to be hostage to relativism, because it cannot in principle make room for the continuous *realist* revisability *of* verifiability and decidability claims.

That won't do either, however, simply because: first, the verificationist and decidabilist *can* make such provision *if* Putnam can; and second, Putnam's own adjustment is never more than holist (as it must be to remain consistent with his own internalism), and it is ultimately obliged to side, in practice, with verification and decidability.[15] The symbiosis of realist and idealist elements that *Putnam* adopts ("Kantianism") is entirely available to his would-be opponents (except, of course, the "metaphysical realist"). Furthermore, there just is a logical gap in Putnam's argument, one that fails to grasp the possibility that *realism* (internal realism) *and relativism are compatible*. This is obscured by Putnam's objectivism and optimism (his Peircean pragmatism), for which he offers no supporting grounds.

The truth is that the rather casual attack on relativism that views it, when fully formulated, as self-defeating or prone to self-referential paradoxes depends *entirely on the supposed irreplaceability of a bipolar logic* (a logic committed to bivalence or at least *tertium non datur*). This is almost never explicitly mentioned. But, for one thing, it strongly suggests just how closely even the most attenuated Quinean program (or any of its analogues: positivist, Popperian, unity of science) hews to the deepest conservative ontological themes Plato and Aristotle had already appealed to in opposing Protagoras; and, for another, it explains just why the relativism that seems fairly patent in the work of Quine, Goodman, Davidson, Popper, Kuhn, Putnam, Rorty and others is treated by all of them as entirely benign.

The clue lies at hand in what we have already drawn attention to in the opposed visions of Quine and Goodman. For, you will remember, *wherever* a relativistic option surfaces for Quine – for instance, in matters touching on the inscrutability of reference and the indeterminacy of translation – Quine *always* insists that there is "no fact of the matter," *there is no truth to decide*; and *wherever* Goodman is faced with the apparent need to support incompatible "truths," he *always* does so by assigning them disjunctively (in principle: only in principle, for he has no idea how to do so in actual practice) to "different actual worlds."

If, now, we ask *why* these two sterling philosophers do what they do, the answer stares us in the face. They simply do not wish to have any truck with weakening our adherence to a bipolar logic. For, according to what may well be the best insight about why that stubborn resistance prevails: *to* give up excluded middle looks very much like accommodating a whole family of arguments that are bound to install the puzzles of intentionality and relativism in an utterly ineliminable way.

So the countermove against the first sort of opponent of relativism simply holds that he is stonewalling, arguing dialectically from a premiss (the fixity of excluded middle, or the fixity of admitting invariant structures that entails admitting the fixity of excluded middle). The wonderful truth is that an enormous philosophical edifice rests precariously on that single conceptual feather. One might reasonably say that, here, unnecessary philosophical fears are leading us by the nose.

What we need to emphasize is that the abandonment or restriction of excluded middle (and *tertium non datur*, of course) would permit us to apply a many-valued logic *to* particular domains of inquiry in science, in morality, in the interpretation of the arts, in philosophy itself. That alone would not be *to* install relativism, to be sure, but it would lay the necessary ground for any number of protagorean-like (or "robust") theories that would permit us to honor *incongruent* claims. In that sense, by exposing the arbitrariness with which theorists like Quine and Goodman and Putnam and Popper and Dummett resist yielding on excluded middle, we see how easy it would be to introduce what we have earlier termed *robust relativism*, that is, a relativism that, for cause and with regard to carefully selected contexts of substantive inquiry, replaces bivalent truth-values with many-valued values and is prepared to entertain incongruent claims where, otherwise, on the bipolar model, only contradiction and inconsistency would pertinently arise. Furthermore, in grasping this possibility, we grasp as well the peculiarly one-sided nature of the attack on relativism that hardly ever pays attention to the option now beginning to surface. For the standard attack on relativism has always obscured the vulnerability of excluded middle and, as a result, has spent its cartridges entirely on exposing the self-referential paradoxes of *relationalism* (or, on the flat stupidity of brazening it out that one and the same proposition can be determinately true and false at once). Of course, the attack on relationalism trades on the regulative constraint of excluded middle.

V

But what we have been presenting is the view of only the first cohort of the opponents to relativism. Well, it is a little more, of course, because, *in* Putnam, Rorty, Quine, and Goodman, a second strategy may be more than glimpsed. Each of these discussants finds a way of admitting (what looks like) a bona fide form of relativism (where it is indeed unavoidable) and then finds a further way of construing that admission: (i) as not entailing contradiction or the self-referential paradoxes; and (ii) as being benignly eligible, when suitably thus tamed, for a larger nonrelativist theory of our knowledge of reality. In short, these theorists very nearly construct a form *of* (robust) relativism themselves, which they quickly block by an utterly arbitrary maneuver. *They*, therefore, are *not* (robust) relativists at all, and they are certainly not relationalists either. But their maneuver demonstrates (by its "formal" success: fiddling with excluded middle) that (robust) relativism cannot be precluded from being viably applied to their own puzzles, and cannot be defeated by attacks suited only to defeating relationalism. QED.

Here, the characteristic strategy is simply one of providing evidence of the coherence of an adjusted realism (say, Putnam's or Kuhn's or Popper's or Lakatos's or Davidson's), a realism that then quite ingeniously absorbs the potentially threatening relativist admissions. This is why one finds (and why one may be puzzled by) the strong progressivism of thinkers like Kuhn and Popper and Lakatos – and Charles Sanders Peirce, for that matter, who long ago fatally betrayed the inherent weakness of the entire (second) strategy. The fact is that "progressivism," notably in science, just *is* an expression of a strong realism (internalist, in Putnam's sense, or at least symbiotized in a Kantian-like sense) that clings, in spite of its concessions to relativism, to a bipolar logic and a distinct objectivism.

The point is that to insist on bipolar truth-values *in* the context of admitting complications like the inscrutability of reference has the ineluctable effect of making that admission a logically or ontologically *shallow* one. That is, the admitted complication construed as not requiring a fundamental change of logic, is, then, not a fundamental complication. The question remains, of course, whether such a maneuver is a reasonable one, whether it is the only reasonable maneuver, whether it genuinely accords with the spirit of Ockham's razor (a distinction it usually claims), and whether it precludes a more thoroughgoing relativism.

VI

Let us step back a bit to see the field a little better.

Quine had already exposed the weakness in Peirce's fallibilism, in *Word and Object*. One cannot really improve on the argument, and there is no need to attempt to. At a certain moment in his own account Quine had finished saying that, "whatever [the] details [of scientific method, and however] customary [it may be] to doubt that ... a more detailed body of canon can be brought together ... can be [produced] finally and definitely, [nevertheless, there is a good] sense in which [science] *is* the last arbiter of truth."[16] What could Quine possibly have meant by the phrase "the last arbiter of truth"? Whatever else may be supposed, the remark would have made no sense if Quine *had* meant to abandon excluded middle. For then, no uniform order ranging over *all* aggregated judgments could have been imposed on such judgments in a way that progressivism or verisimilitude or approximative or inductivist forms of realism could still be pursued or trusted. The irony remains that *Quine*, who, as we shall see, exposes the futility of the second strategy (in Peirce), is himself a vestigial victim of that same strategy and must remain one.

Having thus protected "objective science" in the noticeably vague way he does (a way that Putnam takes to be sufficient for his own purpose), Quine turns to Peirce:

Peirce was tempted to define truth outright in terms of scientific
method, as the ideal theory which is approached as a limit when

the (supposed) canons of scientific method are used unceasingly on continuing experience. But there is a lot wrong with Peirce's notion, besides its assumption of a final organon of scientific method and its appeal to an infinite process. There is a faulty use of numerical analogy in speaking of a limit of theories, since the notion of limit depends on that of "nearer than," which is defined for numbers and not for theories. And even if we by-pass such troubles by identifying truth somewhat fancifully with the ideal result of applying scientific method outright to the whole future totality of surface irritations, still there is trouble in the imputation of uniqueness ("*the* ideal result").[17]

This devastatingly accurate and straightforward criticism of Peirce's fallibilism may not unfairly be said to undermine Putnam's pragmatist effort as well (just the one we looked at a moment ago, that conveys a sense of progressivism not terribly different from Peirce's own, or from Kuhn's or Popper's for that matter). Also, of course, it is just here that Quine very slyly leads us into his alternative to a full-blooded relativism.

We can now appreciate the dialectical connection between the first two strategies. The first simply holds that relativism is incoherent or self-defeating *because* it fails to abide by the formal constraints of excluded middle and similar rules "properly" construed (that is, interpreted in such a way that it would make the charge of incoherence unavoidable: for example, by insisting on the unchanging structures of the real world, as in Plato and Aristotle; or by insisting on the inadmissibility of intentional complexities, as in Quine[18]). (The self-referential paradoxes of relationalism simply fall out as a historically instructive specimen.) The second strategy holds that excluded middle and similar formal constraints (or, similar formal constraints "materially" interpreted in the ways just indicated) just *cannot* or *ought not* be rationally abandoned, *and* that their being in place is, methodologically, sufficient to ensure a measure of objectivity or realism or progress or confirmation sufficient for first-order science.

Peirce had, if we now flag the implication of Quine's argument, utterly failed to notice that, in the "long run," the very choice of rational method *for* testing the fallibility of particular rational or scientific beliefs would itself have to undergo fallibilistic revision. The result is that our question cannot be merely a question of what first-order *beliefs would remain believable in the long run*; it becomes a question also of *second-order beliefs of how to test the truth of distributed first-order beliefs*. That means, however, that radical conceptual discontinuities cannot fail to obtain in the *continuous* testing of particular beliefs. *That's* what Peirce failed to grasp, what Popper[19] and Kuhn fail to grasp and, ironically, what Quine and Putnam[20] and (in the most egregious sense) Rorty fail to grasp. *The inherent discontinuities of history and method and rational policy cannot be overcome or rendered neutral by such formal strategies as clinging to excluded middle.* Only consider that the notion of the long run encourages the belief (the Enlightenment prejudice, as it is often said) that: (a) humanity forms one inclusive inquiring community over the whole of time; (b) human reason, by which that inquiry is guided, remains essentially invariant over the length of its history; (c) cultural relativity, therefore, functions entirely benignly with respect to the long-run goals of objectivism (even within internalist constraints); and hence (d) a bivalent logic need never be abandoned during the diachronic run of approximations to objective truth. There you have a rather plausible version of the secret argument shared by Husserl, Peirce, Quine, Putnam, Davidson, Mohanty, Popper, and Habermas. It is all too stunning – but, of course, it is also utterly unconvincing.

What is required is a fresh interpretation of what may be meant by objectivity or methodological rigor under the conditions indicated (discontinuity, incommensurability, horizonal blindness). Those conditions are too substantive, too material, for mere formal devices. That is really what Quine demonstrates and then ignores. Hence, the bipolar model offers much too little (for the purpose of ensuring the "objective science" Quine and the others mean to defend) and offers it much too late (once the profound discontinuities and intransparencies of inquiry those same champions have admitted are allowed to impress us).

Peirce, as we have already seen, *was* initially hospitable to weakening (or abandoning) excluded middle in certain sectors of inquiry. But he, too, overtakes the concession (*in the long run*) by linking abduction, the mysterious human power to produce fruitful scientific hypotheses here and now under conditions that, treated in a mere, mathematically formal sense, would be hopelessly and endlessly swamped by a constant infinity of alternative hypotheses. Peirce's solution is to turn to the interesting (realist) myth that there must be a certain affinity between Nature and the inquiring mind of man, such that the results of finite inquiry can be counted on to offset the impossibility of progress under the terms of blind infinity. So Peirce says: "every simple truth of science is due to the affinity of the human soul to the soul of the universe, imperfect as that affinity no doubt is"; the laws of nature are, "by logical necessity, incorporated in [man's] own being."[21]

Hence, man's "natural beliefs" (that is, his distributed beliefs) are abductively fruitful for reasons that have nothing to do with the methodological rigors of exhausting an infinity of possible beliefs. There's the *reductio* of Popper's and Lakatos's sanguine methodologies. But then, Peirce absorbs his own provisional accommodation of a relativistic strategy by recovering the adequacy of excluded middle within the terms of his (holist) evolutionary myth construed in cognitive and realist terms. That's what Quine exposes as unconvincing and inapt. But, by the same token, Quine's excellent exposé cannot fail to apply reflexively to his own reading of indeterminacy and inscrutability. Why should we subscribe to the myth that a science committed to a bipolar logic, to a reductive materialism, to an uncompromising extensionalism, to a mode of inquiry essentially unaffected by the discontinuities and preformative forces of history *could possibly function well or best (among all options) as "the last arbiter of truth"*? There's no reason at all, and there's none that is actually given.

If there were no further opposing strategy to consider, we should now have to conclude that relativism had won hands down. "Fortunately," there is at least one other strategy, one in fact that may reasonably be said to be the dominant doctrine of our own day.

VII

Look at the possibilities again. The anti-relativists of the first strategy insist on the timeless, the discernibly timeless, structures of reality (in our own time, at least in terms of the fixed relevance of excluded middle). Man is said to be cognitively competent enough for that. If so, of course, there's no point in abandoning a bipolar logic. Protagoras, then, was mistaken in trotting man out as the measure of all things; he could not possibly have escaped the self-entangling paradoxes of reference and truth-claims. The anti-relativists of the second strategy yield some in Protagoras' direction by conceding that all apparent invariances, the work of any actual inquiry, *are* encumbered by the executive intransparencies and preformative influences of inquiry itself. Hence, there are always bound to be, on the terms of a bipolar logic, incompatible perceptual or ontological parsings of the world we inhabit. On that reading, *some* accommodation of relativism seems unavoidable. But, say the champions of the second strategy, *all* such *intervening*, all such proliferating divergences are no more than superficial evidence of the self-corrective cognitive hygiene of every realist inquiry; in the limit, truth wins out, science *is* the last arbiter, claims do correspond to reality, the fixed order of things *is* recovered, though, of course, *we* never actually reach the limit, and we never need to.

As a result, it is the progressive, the approximative, the verisimilitudi-
nous, the self-corrective, the more or less "finally" rigorously confirmed
beliefs (with whatever small eddies of relativistic variety may continue
to nag at the more solid posits of our continuing science) that take
precedence over just those nuisances, just those relativistic ephemera.

Goodman once put his finger on the required assurance – quite a
while ago, when he had not yet committed himself to the radical notion
of "worldmaking." Speaking of his justly famous paradoxes involving
emeralds and "emerubies" and related demarcations of color, Goodman
made it quite clear that competing "projectibles" (projected scientific
hypotheses) may be tested once and for all, "progressively" if not
exhaustively, *if* they are to exhibit "inherited extrenchment" and to be
eligible (as they must be) for "elimination" in the normal process of
inquiry. So he says, for instance, offering a "rule" of induction: "The
underlying principle is that where a consequent [of some candidate
hypothesis ranging over a would-be projective class] could have been
projected over the extension of a given antecedent by a hypothesis, any
other hypothesis is illegitimate if it has nothing additional in its evidence
class and yet uses a much less well entrenched antecedent to project the
same consequent over other things."[22] So the early Goodman also
belongs to the "evolutionary" optimists.

This is at least one very suggestive clue as to *why* the partisans of
the second anti-relativistic strategy sense no strain in superseding the
limited relativism they themselves allow. Goodman's assurance, of
course, is quite irreconcilable with his own later "radical relativism,"
in spite of the fact that he himself believes his theories form a single
seamless cloth.[23] For to admit history, preformation, the artifactual
nature of inquiring and active humans, the discontinuities of reflexive
critique – for example, along the lines of Kuhn and Gadamer and
Foucault, and, more blandly, of Peirce and Quine and Putnam – is to
subvert the very confidence with which the redemption of a bipolar
logic (and whatever else may be "materially" added to it) may be
assured. There is no way to redeem such programs as Quine's and
Goodman's, once the discontinuities, the intransparencies, the incommensurabilities already admitted are allowed to deepen. Peirce's optimism pervades, but cannot justify, the entire analytic tradition wedded,
in a variety of ways, to a bipolar model of truth, to a materialism and
extensionalism and realism congruent with presuming the adequacy of
such a logic.

We have yet to examine the third strategy of the anti-relativists. But
for convenience and a certain neatness of argument, we shall separate
that account and make a fresh start.

Notes

1 In the last few years, Newton-Smith has significantly departed from the thesis of that book. We shall have to see whether he has also become more hospitable to relativism. The two matters are related, but they do not necessarily function in tandem.

2 M. F. Burnyeat, "Protagoras and Self-Refutation in Plato's Theaetetus," *Philosophical Review* LXXXV (1976), p. 195.

3 Ibid., pp. 174, 180.

4 Ibid., p. 180.

5 Ibid., pp. 189, 193.

6 Ibid., pp. 177–8. The wording of the passage from *Theaetetus* (170c) is Burnyeat's. Cf., also, M. F. Burnyeat, "Protagoras and Self-refutation in Later Greek Philosophy," *Philosophical Review* LXXXV (1975), pp. 44–69.

7 Ibid., p. 178.

8 Ibid., p. 187.

9 See Richard Rorty, *Philosophy and the Mirror of Nature* (Princeton: Princeton University Press, 1979); "Pragmatism and Philosophy," *Consequences of Pragmatism (Essays: 1972–1980)* (Minneapolis: University of Minnesota Press, 1982); and "Postmodern Bourgeois Liberalism," *Journal of Philosophy* LXXX (1983), pp. 583–9.

10 See, for instance, Hilary Putnam, "Reflections on Goodman's, *Ways of Worldmaking*," in *Philosophical Papers*, vol. 3 (Cambridge: Cambridge University Press, 1983); and "Realism and Reason," in *Meaning and the Moral Sciences* (London: Routledge and Kegan Paul, 1978).

11 See Hilary Putnam, *Reason, Truth and History* (London: Routledge and Kegan Paul, 1981), pp. 56–69.

12 Ibid., p. 57.

13 Putnam, "Realism and Reason," pp. 135–8; cf. also, "Reference and Understanding," in *Meaning and the Moral Sciences*.

14 "Realism and Reason," pp. 137–8.

15 Cf. ibid., pp. 123–30.

16 W. V. Quine, *Word and Object* (Cambridge: MIT Press, 1960), p. 23; italics added.

17 Ibid. Cf. also, *Collected Papers of Charles Sanders Peirce*, ed. Charles Hartshorne and Paul Weiss (Cambridge: Harvard University Press, 1934), vol. 5 par. 407; cited by Quine.

18 Cf. Quine, *Word and Object*, pp. 219–21.

19 Cf. Karl R. Popper, *Realism and the Aim of Science* (from *Postcript to the Logic of Scientific Discovery*), ed. W. W. Bartley, III (Totowa, NJ: Rowman and Littlefield, 1983), pp. xxxvii, 56–62, for Popper's second thoughts on verisimilitude (that is, Popper's analogue of Peirce's long run).

20 For a good sense of Putnam's Peircean confidence – philosophically quite unguarded – see Hilary Putnam, "Why Reason can't be Naturalized," in *Philosophical Papers*, vol. 3.

21 Peirce, *Collected Papers* vol. 5 pars. 47, 603.
22 Nelson Goodman, *Fact, Fiction and Forecast*, 2nd ed. (Indianapolis: Bobbs-Merrill, 1985), pp. 103–5.
23 See, for instance, Nelson Goodman, *Of Mind and Other Matters* (Cambridge: Harvard University Press, 1984), pp. 36–9.

10

Avoiding Relativism

I

The partisans of the third strategy know all about the implausibility of the first two strategies: their own claims presuppose it. They therefore abandon any pretense of fiddling with the adequacies of a ramified formal logic. Not that they actually attack it or defend it. They simply ignore it, and turn to other presumed assurances of the avoidability of relativism.

Their essential maneuver involves two steps: by the first, they freely admit the effect on cognition of all the intransparencies and preformative factors that may be reasonably adduced; and by the second, they insist that there is still a third way between the stubborn denial of such intransparency and preformation and the disastrous relativism that that denial itself must spawn. Nothing could be simpler.

They reject the first and second strategies, because (as they see matters) the first is false to our present understanding and because the second (to the extent they address it at all) is a cheat that ultimately retreats to the privileges of the first. There is a fair claim in this, in fact the one we have pursued up to this point. On that line of argument, the extreme blindness of those strategies appears to leave no option but the option said to be favored by the relativist, that is, by that parasitic skeptic anarchist nihilist irrationalist who is prepared to destroy everything if the champions of the first and second strategies will not relent. This explains, for example, the reception of Feyerabend's scientific anarchism and Rorty's repudiation of philosophical legitimation wherever it is not felt that the radical views of those two (or similar) theorists are not merely a pose for the third strategy itself (which, of course, they are not).[1]

The theme of the third strategy is this: relativism, construed only in terms of the "worst scenario" we offered at the very beginning of this account, is no more than the sinister side of the *first* strategy (or of the first with whatever additions from the second we may allow). Call that position *objectivism*. So used, the expression is a term of art more or less popularly installed through Richard Bernstein's summary analysis. "Objectivism" was, of course, originally introduced as a term of philosophical opprobrium by Husserl in his effective criticism of all forms of naturalistic cognitive privilege, critique, apodicticity, and adequacy that fell short of phenomenological correctives – in particular, it was applied to the work of all forms of reasoning modelled on the practice of Galileo, Descartes, and Kant.[2]

In Bernstein's hands, the term loses that particular distinction – in fact, it would not be amiss to apply it (in Bernstein's usage) to Husserl's own familiar presumptions of having achieved results that *were* apodictic and free of historicist and naturalistic taint. In any case, Bernstein characterizes the notion as follows:

> By "objectivism," I mean the basic conviction that there is or must be some permanent, ahistorical matrix or framework to which we can ultimately appeal in determining the nature of rationality, knowledge, truth, reality, goodness, or rightness.... The objectivist maintains that unless we can ground philosophy, knowledge, or language in a suitably rigorous manner we cannot avoid radical skepticism.[3]

II

Protagoras does not figure in Bernstein's analysis; but it is pretty obvious that what Bernstein calls the objectivist position is simply the canonical tradition of philosophy beginning with Parmenides and Heraclitus and Plato and Aristotle (that Protagoras clearly opposed) and continuing until our own day (in the various forms we have been tracing). In fact, his own characterization of the relativist oscillates between the condemned position anciently ascribed to Protagoras himself (by Plato and Aristotle) and the suggestive (but still equivocal) position he (Bernstein) associates at least with what he means to redeem in Kuhn and Feyerabend and in Gadamer as well. For the relativist, on Bernstein's say-so, denies that "there is [a] substantive arching framework or single metalanguage by which we can rationally adjudicate or univocally evaluate competing claims of alternative paradigms." The relativist therefore relativizes "all such concepts" (as of rationality, truth, reality, right) "*to a specific conceptual scheme*, theoretical framework, paradigm, form of life, society, or culture."[4] (Bernstein is none too clear, here, as to whether he intends his finding in a strictly alethic or in a more relaxed evidentiary sense. When he attacks the relativist, he apparently means to appeal to the first; but when he embraces Kuhn, Feyerabend, Rorty, and Gadamer, he clearly means the second.)

Bernstein shares the relativist's objection against the objectivist; but he does not accept the relativist's own conclusion. That is, he does not accept the conclusion of the "relativist" as he defines relativism. Of course, there is absolutely no reason why he should to do so: *his* "relativist" is a hothouse product of his own imagination. There is no serious "relativist" of the sort he has in mind *among the theorists he reviews* (that is, a flat-out relationist or a caricature of Protagoras). He is perfectly justified in suggesting, therefore, that there must be a "third" strategy that affords a way between the other two. The philosophical crunch comes in saying what that strategy must be like.

Clearly, Bernstein's objection to relativism – to relativism in the modern or contemporary sense, to what we have been calling the incommensurabilist and other "robust" options (to distinguish them from the ancient protagorean theme) – is directed against *the disjunctive and distributed use of such relationalized notions as "true in L_1," "true in L_2" and the like*. Bernstein's view is that either this leads to conceptual chaos, in that no *comparative* assessments are possible across the extensions of relevantly disjoined predicates (contrary to what we obviously want to preserve), since they do not function within "one world"; or else that they produce paradox and self-contradiction just where we do allow a comparative use, since we thereby clearly exceed the scope of the relationalized truth-predicates supposed.

This is the point, for instance, of Bernstein's effort to domesticate Kuhn's and Feyerabend's views sufficiently to accord with his own version of the would-be *third* strategy. On the incommensurability issue, Bernstein warns us:

If we are to sort out what is and what is not involved in the incommensurability of paradigm theories, we must carefully distinguish among *incompatibility, incommensurability*, and *incomparability*. Frequently these three notions have been treated as synonymous by Kuhn's critics, and even by his defenders. For example, Kuhn's (and Feyerabend's) remarks about incommensurability have been taken to mean that we cannot *compare* rival paradigms or theories. But such a claim, I will argue, is not only mistaken but perverse. The very rationale for introducing the notion of incommensurability is to clarify what is involved when we do compare alternative and rival paradigms.[5]

168   AVOIDING RELATIVISM

This correctly catches up the intuition of what is wrong with Davidson's strenuous objection against incommensurabilism, though it does not actually show us why that objection won't work or just how Kuhn's thesis will work. But never mind.

The important thing is that Bernstein conflates the *recovery* of a conceptual basis for *comparative* judgments with the *vindication* of his supposed third strategy. And that is simply a conceptual mistake. For one thing, it fails to make room for the possibility that, as we have already seen, the mere rejection of *relationalized* truth-predicates ("true in L_1," "true in L_2") *does not as such directly bear* on the fortunes of a relativized use of nonrelationalized truth-predicates or truth-like predicates – what we have been calling robust relativism; and, for another, such a formal maneuver *cannot possibly decide the substantive question* of the viability and reasonableness of the third (or any "third") strategy. There you have the deep lacuna in Bernstein's account. Metonymically, it may be made to stand in for the similar arguments of Gadamer, Habermas, Hans-Otto Apel, MacIntyre, Taylor, Popper, Lakatos – and Kuhn as well.

The essential thrust of the third strategy, then, entails: (1) that "logical incompatibility" presupposes "a common *logical* framework within which we can show that two theories are logically incompatible"[6] – right; (2) that, according to Kuhn, "there is [no] 'third,' completely neutral language or framework within which rival paradigmatic theories 'could be *fully* expressed and which could therefore be used in a point-by-point comparison between them'"[7] – right again. So (1) and (2) are meant to undermine "one of the pillars of a common variety of objectivism – the idea that there is (or must be) a single, universal framework of commensuration."[8] But, somehow, the defeat of objectivism is taken by Bernstein (and all of his allies) to be tantamount to a defeat of all pertinent forms of relativism. And *that's* not possible unless, contrary to what we have been suggesting, relativism is never more than the ancient form of Protagorean self-defeat favored by Plato and Aristotle or a relationalized interpretation of contemporary incommensurabilism. Put in another way, given (1) and (2), *there is still a great deal of room for a relativistic and a nonrelativistic reading of the third strategy*. Bernstein does not see this – in particular, regarding incommensurability.

Step back a pace, once again. As far as (1) and (2) are concerned, Bernstein and the relativist agree – in fact, so far, Bernstein agrees with Protagoras. Nevertheless, (1) and (2) are *not* equivalent to the third strategy, for the point of the third strategy (on Bernstein's argument) is to disallow relativism *tout court*. The story is a little complicated since Bernstein construes relativism *only* in the form in which it is straightforwardly self-contradictory *or* in the form in which it generates self-referential paradox by supporting radically relationalized truth-predicates.[9] But if we concede that Bernstein *may* have conflated (1) and (2) *with* the conclusion disallowing *only that* sort of relativism that his own (and any similar) *anti*-relativist "third" strategy intends to scuttle, then we must insist as well that he has simply failed to consider a *further* form of relativism also implicated in the original dispute (robust relativism or, more particularly, a "robust" interpretation of incommensurabilism or of what we have alluded to as ontic relativism). Robust relativism does not favor the *relationalized* option *and* it does freely accept doctrines (1) and (2). So there is a definite lacuna in Bernstein's argument.

Now, the extraordinary thing is that *no one* prominently committed to the third strategy *has actually shown us how to proceed from (1) and (2) to the exclusive conclusion of Bernstein's "third" strategy*. That's all. Of course, no one can.

III

We have proceeded in a deliberately measured way with Bernstein's account although, in all candor, it is not very compelling in itself. It is not, because it does not actually provide anything like a well-formed argument. It *is* important, nevertheless, just because it does *not* yield an argument, because it really cannot do so, and because there is a very large army of influential theorists who are committed to precisely the same maneuver. They are all partisans of what may be called *traditionalism*.[10]

By traditionalism, we may understand any theory that holds: (a) that objectivism (more or less in Bernstein's sense) or cognitive privilege or transparency or essentialism or any similar doctrine is false or indefensible; and (b) that, nevertheless, the historical movement of human traditions contingently yields norms and principles and criteria of truth and value that are effectively invariant or that progressively and favorably converge toward the kind of invariance the objectivist supports, without yet being committed to any doctrine rejected in (a). The gymnastic possibilities stare one in the face. In fact, by the argument of the previous chapter, the partisans of the second strategy (Peirce and the rest) clearly join hands here with the partisans of the third. (That marriage is surely very close to the heart of Bernstein's philosophical trade.)

The contest that remains, of course, is just the one in which we see that it is formally quite impossible – once (a) is conceded – to disallow a *relativist* alternative to (*b*) from yielding a bona fide version *of the "third" strategy*. *Why*, if (a) is conceded, and if relativists do accept (a), should we ever suppose that traditionalism is the only possible (or the best) option available to us?

Now, it will not be believed but it is nevertheless true that traditionalists disallow *any* attack on (b). They particularly object to views that do not accept the traditionalist's unflattering characterization of relativists, as incoherent, self-defeating, anarchical, irrationalist, or nihilist. Put more manageably, traditionalists either subscribe to the strong bipolar logic of the objectivists *they oppose* (which is already strange) or else they ignore or fail to see the logical possibility (and import) of giving up excluded middle and *tertium non datur* (which is equally strange). They simply confuse the point of these options with the avoidance of the disorders just mentioned.

Once we allow the (robust) relativist's option, there is no hiding-place left for the traditionalist. He cannot be more than an objectivist or essentialist *manqué*. He reclaims the fixities, invariances, objectivities of the *objectivist* (or something very close to that), but he gains his advantage by pretending to discern *in* the very fluidities of history, experience, practice, interest and the like certain *normatively significant objective stabilities* that converge as closely as you please to whatever the objectivist had supposed he could salvage by way of direct cognitive privilege.

There's the charge. Now for a bit of supporting evidence.

We have already taken note of the progressivism and naive fallibilism of such thinkers as Peirce, Popper, Lakatos, Putnam, and Kuhn. Their views are, in a sense, versions of a general scientific inductivism – even Popper's falsificationism falls within its terms, as Lakatos was honest and perceptive enough to admit – with whatever tact he could command.[11] So, in a curious way, it's entirely possible that the defenders of the second and third strategies may combine forces, just as it is possible for the defenders of the first and second to do. What we need, however, are clearer specimens of the third strategy separated from such complications. Consider Charles Taylor.

In his careful criticism of Peter Winch's apparent (but only apparent) radical incommensurabilism, Taylor makes the following observations regarding cross-cultural comparison:

> There is a definite respect in which modern science is superior to its Renaissance predecessor; and this is evident not in spite of but because of their incommensurability.... This is not to say that

there is some common criterion by which one is proved inferior to the other, if that implies some criterion, already accepted by both sides.... What we have [rather] is not an antecedently accepted common criterion but a facet of our activity ... which remains implicit or unrecognized in earlier views, but which cannot be ignored once realized in practice.... And out of this can arise valid transcultural judgments of superiority. Of course, I must repeat, there is no such thing as a single argument proving *global* superiority.[12]

Taylor's curious argument has it that first, we do (and must be able to) make *comparative cross-cultural judgments*; second, that such judgments do not presuppose or entail *universally binding or uniquely valid cross-cultural criteria*; and third, that, nevertheless, within the historicized practices of such comparative judgment, *globally valid distributed judgments of superiority with respect to truth and value* may always or regularly be counted on, or may be counted on in at least decisive contexts.

There is a serious multiple mistake here (that includes but goes beyond a sin of omission). What Taylor does not grasp is first, that relativists (just as objectivists and traditionalists) *can* consistently admit comparative judgments; second, that comparative judgments, like any judgments claiming a measure of objectivity, *can be* treated relativistically; and third, that it is a sheer *non sequitur* to suppose that if, in particular contexts, evidence tends to support exclusive or strongly convergent judgments, then relativism must be untenable. (In fact, there is no logical reason why relativists should deny that, in *some* contexts – however many and however important, so long as they are not exhaustive or nearly exhaustive, or so long as they do not preclude *other* contexts from behaving in a different way – comparative judgments *do* favor or do appear to favor exclusively correct findings. That is, relativists need not suppose that if their thesis holds in this or that domain, then it must hold in all domains as well.)

In a word, Taylor somehow conflates the question of the epistemic viability of comparative judgments with an analysis of their alethic structure. Alternatively put, he does not see that *the admission of comparative judgments is logically compatible with the rejection of excluded middle and tertium non datur*. He falls back to a bipolar logic which was, we may recall, the particular favorite of the objectivist, of just those committed to the first and second strategies. So it is ironic, to say the least, that an opponent of those strategies should himself accept so easily a constraint that puts him more or less in their own camp. There's no reason for it at all.[13] Also, of course, there is lurking here a distinctly "archic" presumption regarding the continued reliability of reason or rational judgment – across history, across conceptual discontinuity, incommensurability, divergence, diachronic change, vagueness and indeterminacy, ideological bias, horizonal blindness and the like – that is simply never independently supported. It is, we may say, just the thread that binds the partisans of the second and third strategies to one another.

Taylor also betrays the weakness of the traditionalist's position in a more pointed way, simply because he tries to address the question of truth-values and then criteria. Other traditionalists, Bernstein for instance, certainly Gadamer, tend to ignore the alethic and epistemic question and content themselves with the sheer optimism that it will all work out in a way that precludes any relativistic challenge. This is why, although Taylor is also remarkably sanguine, theorists like Peirce, Popper, Lakatos, Kuhn, Bernstein, Gadamer, and Habermas are more notable for that more primitive form of traditionalism that we have dubbed progressivism.

As a matter of fact, Kuhn himself, who, after all, is an ardent defender of the notion of scientific progress, has, in recent years, become much more careful (and much more candid about his own puzzlement) regarding the conceptual analysis of progress. So he says, for instance:

> The pragmatic success of a scientific theory seems to guarantee the ultimate success of its associated explanatory mode. Explanatory force may, however, be a long time coming. . . . Is there some sense in which the explanatory canons of modern physics are more advanced than those of, say, the eighteenth century and in which those of the eighteenth century transcend those of antiquity and the Middle Ages? In one sense the answer is clearly yes. The physical theory of each of these periods was vastly more powerful and precise than that of its predecessors. Explanatory canons, being integrally associated with physical theory itself, must necessarily have participated in the advance: the development of science permits the explanation of ever more refined phenomena. It is, however, only the phenomena, not the explanation, that are more refined in any obvious sense. . . . Studied by themselves, ideas of explanation and cause provide no obvious evidence of that progress of the intellect that is so clearly displayed by the science from which they derive.[14]

What this helps us to see is that there is no simple or straightforward connection between the *holist* impression of progress and the *distributed* proof of progress. For similar reasons, there is no simple connection between holist impressions of objectivity or reasonableness and distributed and determinate criteria of *rationality, objective truth, objective value*, or the like. Still, Taylor is noticeably slippery in his own attempt to assess the sort of evidence Kuhn considers, or the bearing of such evidence on, say, Winch's sort of incommensurabilism. So he argues as follows – it will pay us to have his precise wording:

> From our point of view within this culture, we may want to argue that our science is clearly superior [to Renaissance science]. We point to the tremendous technological spin-off it has generated in order to silence many doubters. But a defender of relativism *might* retort that this begs the question.... In these circumstance [in circumstances involved in comparing scientific and pre-scientific views of what is edible], it is difficult to understand how an increase in scientific knowledge beyond pre-scientific common sense could fail to offer potential *recipes* for more effective practice.... The basic point is that given the kind of beings we are, embodied and active in the world, and given the way that scientific knowledge extends and supersedes our ordinary understanding of things, it is impossible to see how it could fail to yield further and *more far-reaching recipes* for action ... one culture can *surely* lay claim to a higher, or fuller, or more effective rationality, if it is in a position to achieve a more perspicuous order than another. It seems to me that a claim of this kind can be made by theoretical cultures over against atheoretical ones.[15]

Now, none of this is incompatible with relativism, although Taylor insinuates that the opposite is true. None of this is incompatible with what Winch says, for instance, or with what Kuhn says (in the passage cited). The reason is that Taylor somehow lets it be supposed that because the holist impression (and judgment) of progress or superiority is conceded, *we must, as a result, be able to derive distributed criteria of objectivity, rationality, progress and the rest from the encompassing practices in which the holist judgment appears to be quite reasonable.* Taylor simply does not see that relativistic disputes about *such* success are as yet quite ineliminable, entirely pertinent, and certainly not weaker, logically, than is his own conviction; *and* that the relativist's position is actually strengthened by the traditionalist's (his own) admission that "no single argument proving *global* superiority even obtains." In this regard, Kuhn is finally more careful and more candid than Taylor.

IV

As a matter of fact, Taylor has recently been emboldened by the plausibility of the sort of argument we have just rehearsed, and has gone on to
suggest a much stronger objectivism *manqué* born of traditionalist convictions. He has taken to diagnosing the "objective" bewilderment and
disorientation of the entire modern Western world. The tendency is
quite characteristic of current traditionalism – it is explicit, for instance,
in the work of Alasdair MacIntyre[16] and is certainly at least implicit
in Hans-Georg Gadamer's speculations about the objective grounds of
morality.[17]

In any case, Taylor now considers that a society may have taken "a
wrong turn" in the development of its own form of judgment and
commitment in the face of responding to its own historical situation. We
must, he thinks, try to *retrace* our history back to the "earlier" moment
of understanding so that we can *correct* the mistake. We have trusted to
certain interpretations of past practice to function paradigmatically or
foundationally or regulatively in the present, and that may turn out
(and, in our time, has turned out) to be a mistake. "It suffices," he says,
"that, for whatever reason, some earlier formulations [judgments, prac-
tices] *have* been taken up, and have been given some kind of founda-
tional or paradigm status in the development of a practice." Some
"original theory" about an earlier stage of our economy, say, worked
quite well in the past and has now begun to generate conceptual and
practical problems which we could perhaps resolve, if only we could
recover a more balanced sense of how that theory and those earlier
economic practices actually once worked. So, Taylor goes on, amiably
enough:

> This reformulation requires that one can get clear *on the original
> form*. It is not that this original formulation is somehow the true
> articulation of what underlies today's reality. On the contrary,
> a great change has patently taken place, with the rise of giant,
> bureaucratic, multinational corporations, and contemporary state
> structures. But because today's reality is what has arisen through
> the drift, and hyper-development, of a society *informed by the
> original model, recovering this is essential to our being able to
> understand what now exists. The society is out of true with the
> original.* We are dealing with a society which is characterized by
> the fact that it is out of true with *this* original. That makes it all the
> more important to understand the original, if we are to understand
> the society.[18]

Taylor, therefore, is obviously committed to the thesis that, in spite of the "drift" of history – which should, in principle, affect human nature, human knowledge, human rationality as well – the events of the historical past are somehow sufficiently frozen in time that *they can be objectively, more or less uniquely recovered*. It is perfectly fair for Taylor to make the claim. But the fact remains that *he* never supplies the supporting argument, and *we* are hardly obliged to follow him in this. In any case, he betrays in this way the peculiar prejudice of the traditionalist: that the claims of the objectivist can be defended without subscribing to objectivism itself, that the mere drift of historical tradition, rightly recovered, will save the day.[19]

There is a bit more to be said. For, *if* we follow Taylor *now* in worrying about our society's having taken *a wrong turn* ("being out of true"), then, obviously, *all* of Taylor's intuitions about the comparative validity of one's society's claims over those of another will be put at risk – in particular, just those that undermine the traditionalist's confidence (without necessarily advocating preposterous possibilities). Furthermore, if we do that, then why should it not also be the case that Taylor's own intuition about where the society is "out of true" be as unreliable as, or as incapable of being managed in a legitimate way as, our own society's "errors"? In short, Taylor is conceding here the full force of the deep theory of horizonal blindness and the rest (which gives relativism a good inning); but he is also, at the same time, redeeming in the most desperate way the stubborn confidence of the cornered traditionalist (which would deny once again the benefits conceded). The minuet is clear enough.

V

We may perhaps allow ourselves the luxury of one final example of the bolder forms of traditionalism. Without a doubt, Gadamer is the *doyen* of traditionalists, if for no other reason than that he is the most uncompromising advocate of *the radically historicized nature of man*. In this regard he effectively subverts the sort of confidence we have just seen Taylor display:

> The naiveté of so-called historicism consists in the fact that it does not undertake this reflection [that is, the reflection on the inherent nature of historical consciousness], and in trusting to its own methodological approach forgets its own historicality. We must here appeal from a badly understood historical thinking to one

that can better perform the task of understanding. True historical thinking must take account of its own historicality. Only then will it not chase the phantom of an historical object which is the object of progressive research, but learn to see in the object the counterpart of itself and hence understand both. The historical object is not an object at all, but the unity of the one and the other, a relationship in which exist both the reality of history and the reality of historical understanding. A proper hermeneutics would have to demonstrate the effectivity of history within understanding itself.[20]

There *is* no historical past to recover as an epistemic "object" of any sort. That is precisely what, following Heidegger's lead, Gadamer repudiates in so-called Romantic hermeneutics, to which, of course, Taylor (not unlike Ranke) subscribes. But, by the same token, there is, for Gadamer, no fixed subject or historical self that *can*, in history, function epistemically to collect historical "objects" from any distributed points in historical time. Gadamer is as explicit about this as one can be:

We say, for instance, that understanding and misunderstanding take place between I and thou. But the formulation "I and thou" already betrays an enormous alienation. There is nothing like an "I and thou" at all – there is neither the I nor the thou as isolated, substantial realities. I may say "thou" and I may refer to myself over against a thou, but a common understanding [*Verständigung*] always precedes these situations.[21]

Gadamer's thesis is that historical understanding is always the effect and work of "effective history" (*Wirkungsgeschichte*). This is not a procedure for which one could formulate a rational methodology; it is rather the inherent nature of any form of human understanding. It actually defies universalized or invariant methods, cannot be regularized, belongs to the "ontology" of existence itself. (There is, in this respect, not a negligible similarity between Gadamer's thesis and Feyerabend's, though, temperamentally and doctrinally, the two could not be further apart.)[22] "The historical movement of human life," Gadamer affirms, "consists in the fact that it is never utterly bound to any one standpoint and hence can never have a truly closed horizon. The horizon is, rather, something into which we move and that moves with us. Horizons change for a person who is moving." In fact, *we* change in the process of historical understanding, as a result of that unending process: "In the process of understanding there takes place a real fusing of horizons [of interpreted past and posited present], which means that as the historical horizon is projected, it is simultaneously removed."[23] "In fact," says Gadamer, "history does not belong to us, but we belong to it."[24]

There can be no question that a casual reading of such remarks from Gadamer's account would justify the strong impression that Gadamer was a protagorean, certainly a friend of relativism. But that would be an utter mistake. It is plain enough that Gadamer concedes a very rich version of the notion of historical process; but he is adamantly opposed to construing it as a flux, in spite of the fact that he denies that there are fixed structures in the historical process. He is a genuine traditionalist. His account obviates the possibility of a methodology of historical understanding; although, in spite of his strong emphasis on the in- herently "prejudicial" (that is, prejudged or preformed) nature of his- torical understanding, he very clearly is committed to some constraints of historical accuracy. We are prejudiced, he holds, simply because we perceive and understand everything we do within the preformed hori- zon of our perspectived vision, we understand what we understand "by [means of] the prejudices that we bring with us."[25]

On the other hand, one understands oneself "as the placing of oneself within a process of tradition, in which past and present are constantly fused."[26] *That* placement is constrained in a way that leads toward what (in another, perhaps an alien idiom) could be treated as a sort of "objectivity."

Gadamer indicates at least two essential constraints on *tradition*. First of all, he very clearly insists that "that which has been sanctioned by tradition and custom has an authority that is nameless, and our finite historical being is marked by the fact that always the authority of what has been transmitted ... has power over our attitude and behavior.... Tradition has a justification that is outside the arguments of reason and in large measure determines our institutions and our attitudes."[27] Secondly, we actually understand and overcome our "finitude," we understand matters hermeneutically, only when we are able to fuse our limited horizon with *the horizon of the whole of human history*. To be sure, that project can never be completed but it can be achieved again and again. Here is the knockdown proof that Gadamer means to retrieve *from* the very fluidities of history something very much like what the objectivist would lay claim to by way of cognitive privilege:

When our historical consciousness places itself within historical horizons, this does not entail passing into alien worlds unconnected in any way with our own, but together they constitute *the one great horizon* that moves from within and, beyond the frontiers of the present, embraces the historical depths of our self-consciousness. It is, in fact, *a single horizon* that embraces everything contained in historical consciousness.[28]

In fact, the effect of these joint constraints is the recovery of what Gadamer calls the "classical": "a historical reality to which historical consciousness belongs and is subordinate, . . . something retrieved from the vicissitudes of changing time and its changing taste," something "of significance that cannot be lost and is independent of all the circumstances of time . . . a kind of timeless present that is contemporaneous with every other age."[29] This is, of course, nothing more than an analogue of what Taylor had in mind in thinking that we could reorient our society (which is "out of true"). It is also, though it is surely not progressivist (for instance, in Habermas's sense), very close in spirit to what Peirce and similar-minded progressivists have in mind regarding the "objective truth" at the end of the "long run's" rainbow.

Gadamer offers absolutely no defense of this conviction. It's a charming one, of course, but it's utterly preposterous to suppose that, given his own views of historicity, it is either consistent or defensible or, indeed, exclusively or strongly plausible as opposed to a relativistic reading. The important point is that it represents the ultimate prejudice that traditionalists cling to, the belief *that there is in the very movement of history* (even if human existence is historicized) *a power of understanding that can retrieve a normative, changeless, universally valid core of judgments, tastes, criteria or the like.* It remains an objectivism or archism *manqué*, simply because it pretends that it makes its claim without subscribing to any of the objectivist's own prejudices.

We have taken a good deal of space in order to present Gadamer's view fairly. But there can be little doubt that it captures the essential theme that, in a thousand alternatively attenuated ways, either is shared by, or parallels, the traditionalist spirit that we have ascribed to Peirce, Popper, Kuhn, Lakatos, Putnam, Taylor, Bernstein, MacIntyre, Habermas, and others. There is no point to multiplying cases further. But one can begin to see what the counterstrategy would be, for instance, against the pretended recovery of the universal norms of communication and meaning and truth that is the hallmark of Jürgen Habermas's influential and familiar thesis. It is obviously impossible to ensure the approximative or asymptotic progress that Habermas enthusiastically promotes within the space of historical existence formed by his own general adherence to Marxist, Frankfurt Critical, and hermeneutic currents.[30]

There are no other traditionalist strategies that offer any stronger prospects.

VI

We may take advantage here of Gadamer's remarks, cited just above, to press an issue somewhat tangential to those we have been pursuing. The discussion has become rather tangled as it is; it would certainly not be a good idea to launch an entirely new line of reflection at this point. But there is an economy to be gained.

Gadamer, you will remember, denies that persons – any "I" and "thou" – have *natures*, that is, "natures" taken in the canonical sense in which particulars are individuated relative to the kinds of things they are (the "natures" they have): where, on the familiar assumption, such natures cannot change *qua* natures so long as the particulars in question remain the particulars they are. Gadamer favors what is really a profoundly radical conception, one that also certainly appears in the work of Michel Foucault: that human persons have "histories" rather than "natures" (or have historical or historicized natures), in the sense that *they may remain the same individuals they are, even though their "natures" change as a result of the hermeneutic features of their history.*

There are, of course, interesting conceptual puzzles about how to manage reidentification of pertinent particulars under the circumstance proposed (persons, artworks, words and sentences, theories, institutions, traditions, actions, histories, and the like: in short, all culturally distinctive entities and phenomena). By and large, though we cannot pursue the matter here, the trick is turned by treating reference and reidentification in accord with *narrative* strategies, which is to say, in strongly intentionalist ways.[31] The coherence of disjoining singularity and (essential) nature – which is not to say that particular things are not of this or that "kind" – is assured by the coherence of narratized and historied individuation. Our interest, here, is not in such complications, however, but in the bearing of the thesis that Gadamer advances on the fortunes of relativism. Of course, Gadamer ultimately reneges on his radical proposal because, as we have seen, he manages to pull the Hellenic tradition out of his hat as the invariant normative tradition of all human history. But that is also not our concern.

No. The important point is that *if* we concede that there *are* such phenomena: cultural things and processes that have histories, that is, that have intentionally interpreted, narratized forms of temporal persistence assignable to them *as* individuated, histories that (furthermore) can be profoundly altered by interpretation, by self-interpretation, by historical intervention, and the like, then it is certainly plain that an entirely new field of application may be claimed for the practice of robust relativism. This is precisely what we had in mind, earlier on, in introducing the notion of *ontic relativism*. It would be too strenuous to try to vindicate that possibility here. It would require a full discussion of its own; also, it is obviously controversial and bound to be resisted in many quarters.[32] But *if* we allowed such a picture of the world of human culture – for example, regarding real artworks and real histories – then, on a view pretty much in accord with what Gadamer here concedes (*not* with his fallback traditionalism) regarding the "fusion of horizons" and "effective history" in particular, it would then surely be impossible to disallow a whole raft of robust relativisms of the sort suggested. For, if one interpretation of the intentionalized "nature" of a poem or painting or history were thought defensible (plausible or reasonable rather than true, say), it would be impossible in principle to disallow other "incongruent" claims about the same profoundly intentionalized individual.[33] Let us here take note of this option as an intriguing possibility. To venture much further might well encourage opponents of the larger argument to seize an undue advantage that we should take care to deny. The argument for ontic relativism can be made out, but we do not need to do so here; and what has been claimed up to this point has not depended on its validity.

Still, the decisive clue to this entire domain is worth illustrating. We may do so in terms of the theory of history. What may be said of history may be said with equal aptness of the interpretation of art and action and language.

By and large, all accounts of descriptive history are of two principal sorts, what we may call *monadic* and *relational*. Relational conceptions of history[34] maintain: (a) that whatever persists temporally may be assigned a history; (b) that the time of physical nature and human history is one and the same and is adequately characterized in terms of the role time plays in the physical sciences; (c) that histories are constructed narratives assigned to persisting things in accord with variable interests humans happen to favor – hence they are relationally applied and are assessed in terms of how they serve other truth-oriented objectives, scientific explanation for instance; (d) that there is no sense of match, however loose, between a constructed historical narrative and the narratizable structures of the actual referents of history, that bears as such on historical truth. Relational theories, therefore, are particularly hospitable to reductive accounts of the real world along the lines of the unity of science conception, though such theories need not actually be reductive.

Monadic conceptions maintain, on the contrary: (a') that only things of certain kinds are intrinsically historical, have historied "natures" intrinsically, persist in distinctively historical ways (which need not preclude, of course, invoking relational histories, where wanted, with regard to mere physical phenomena that lack such natures – Olduvai Gorge, for instance); (b') that historical and physical time are different in nature, although historical time is inseparably (that is, complexly) incarnate (or emergent) in physical time;[35] (c') that narratized histories take truth-values or truth-like values in precisely the same sense in which all other enunciative or assertoric discourse does, since their proper referents intrinsically possess historical properties (persons, actions, speech acts, artworks, institutions); (d') that things that intrinsically possess historical "natures" do so in virtue of possessing *intentional* properties open to interpretation and open to change as a result of interpretation – so that such things may be said to have (narratizable) histories and to lack (fixed) natures.

For our present purpose, there are two decisive differences at least between these two conceptions of history. For one, on the relational conception, the past is fixed and changeless;[36] but on the monadic conception, even if the physical past is fixed, the historical past (incarnate in the other) may change under ongoing interpretation. (In that case, of course, only a sense of narrative continuity – a sense of history – could secure sameness of reference.) For a second, on the relational conception, there is a principled distinction between the referent of a history and the narrative or interpretation assigned it; on the monadic conception, *since* the "nature" of the referent of a history (which is alterable under interpretation) is a function of the interpretive or historical narratives assigned it, there *is* no principled demarcation between genuinely historied particulars and the histories assigned them. Artworks, for instance, change in "nature" within a tradition of interpretation; and human persons may change their own "nature" by their behavior (without, however, changing the nature of the species, *Homo sapiens*, in which they are indissolubly incarnate or embodied).[37] (The monadic theory is in a way a kind of intentional analogue of Quine's view of the connection between "analytical hypotheses" and the ontic "nature" of whatever we may refer to.)

There's no question that these last two distinctions are strenuous ones. But the monadic conception is certainly not incoherent and may even be distinctly favored in discourse about cultural phenomena. In any case, we have elaborated just enough of what is essential to the cultural disciplines to have a sense of the pertinence and promise of "ontic relativism." The relational conception tends to favor pluralism over relativism (in terms of variable interests) or else it may deny truth-values to history and interpretation altogether. The monadic conception resists both moves, clearly favors a strong relativism. The question remains: which of the two is the suppler and more convincing? But that is a matter for another time.

Still, having supplied this much, we may risk a few words more. The relational theory of history restricts historical narrative – *not* the relatively atomic *elements*, atomic facts, regarding changing pasts and changing presents caught up in the hermeneutic *relata* of the historical narrative itself – to an imaginative, unified *representation* of those temporally ordered elements. Or, perhaps more exactly, "narrative" order may be mere *chronicle*, the merely temporally united sequence of dated atomic events with or without causal connection (where time is simply physical time and causality implicates universal causal laws); or, much more ambitiously, it may be a *hermeneutically significant, "geistlich" story* or the like incarnate in chronicle, the intentionally unified career of an appropriately selected referent (cultural entity, process, or event). On the (relational) argument, the story thereby told, the history, is true or false only in the sense of preserving what is true or false about the individuated elements or atomic facts collected in the chronicle, never the full hermeneutically unified story itself. There is, after all, nothing for that to be true about.

This comes as a surprise, since one might have supposed that if a history is a "representation," then there is (must be) a structured something that it "corresponds" to. But, on the relational theory, a history is a representation only in the sense that *we* take a certain historied interest in the discrete elements or causal connections of any temporal sequence which we may weave into a narrative unity. Consequently, the relational historian favors pluralism merely in favoring the shifting interests of history-minded humans. Narrative history remains relational only, whether as chronicle or story: a "historical sentence" is merely "a sentence which states some fact about the past" (for instance, the dating of the Thirty Years' War or its causal connections).[38]

The odd result is that full historical narratives are neither true nor false *qua* narratives. They answer to nothing in the world: narratized phenomena are not real or actual. It is only that we *believe* that the histories of things are thus and so or, more sparely, that we *take an interest in construing* them thus and so. It is therefore entirely possible (as Arthur Danto concedes, speaking as one of the principal relational theorists of history) that the Romans construed Virgil's *Aeneid* as a true narrative of their own origins. Hence,

> The historical Dido [he says] may have been a Carthaginian slut who rented rooms to the shrewd mercenary from Dalmatia. The point is that whether their beliefs were false or inflated or accurate and true, we identify what the past was for the Romans by identifying their beliefs about the past. The past *for them* was what it was, whatever history-as-science may ultimately say about their representations.[39]

"History-as-science," of course, is occupied ("objectively") only with atomic facts regarding the past or the causal connections that they involve.

Here, truth enters at two points only: first, we may determine whether it was or was not the case that the Romans believed what they are said to have believed about their own narrative history; and second, we may determine whether the discrete temporal elements collected only as the intentional accusatives of their own story were or were not correctly reported (as by chronicle). The upshot is that "the past *for them*" (in Danto's telling phrase) is part of the real world all right, *not* (on the best reading) a propositional claim *about* the world.

Danto is admirably clear about this:

> It was the theory of [historical] relativists [he says] that history is just a set of pasts-for-*x*, as though the *en soi* of the past were its *pour autrui*. Questions of truth-or-falsity do not really arise for pasts-for-*x*. Pasts-for-*x* are, after all, just parts of historical reality. The past-for-the-Romans was an objective feature of Roman life, as much so as Roman architecture and Roman sewage, and in just the way in which the past-for-us is part of contemporary American reality.... To hold an historical belief is to hold that there is (was) some bit of history-as-reality it describes, external to the belief in question.... Historical beliefs are thus internal and external to historical reality, and it was the curious muddle of relativism to have denied the latter by having discovered the former. "Right you are if you think you are," which is the title of a play of Pirandello, condenses unfairly the relativist attitude.[40]

This certainly supplies the sense in which the relational theorist of history favors pluralism: pluralism, you see, escapes relativism, leaves no room for relativism, and permits one to construe relativism as merely muddled. Very neat. But the price one pays is rather steep: now, there are in principle no "objective" (heremeneutic) biographies or histories to be recorded. The monadic theorist, on the other hand, risks recovering the genuine question of whether *narratized representations* correspond to actual *narratively structured events and lives*. But the monadic theorist is well aware that, in doing that, he cannot possibly disallow a fair inning for the (robust) relativist with respect to historical truth.

The "historical relativist" (Danto is thinking of theorists like Ranke, probably) is guilty of two confusions: first, he is tempted to think that "internal" beliefs to the effect that the world has a significant narrative structure (the Romans' belief about the *Aeneid*, for instance) *could* correspond to an "external," genuinely narratized order of reality (some *geistlich* or cultural sector of the world, in Ranke's sense); and, second, by way of the first confusion, he believes, in the sense the relationalist favors, that what is narratively true about the world is only "true-for-x" ("true-for-the-Romans," say). Danto, therefore, gives up full-blooded truth-claims about historically narratized structures: beliefs that there are such structures are *real* beliefs, but they cannot be *true*. There is no narrative truth. There is perhaps only the thin "adequacy" of chronicle relative to atomic and causal truths;[41] furthermore, if narrative beliefs are treated as eligible for truth-values, then, given the plurality of such beliefs, only a relationalist theory of truth could be favored – and then only at the usual price of self-referential paradox. But these are extravagant fears no one need honor.

Notes

1 Without a doubt, the most energetic advocate of taming the extreme and quite uncompromising views advanced by Rorty and Feyerabend is Richard Bernstein. Bernstein has been actively attempting to reconcile the advocates of what we are here calling the second strategy (notably, Kuhn) with their own most extreme critics (notably, Rorty and Feyerabend) *and* with the champions of what we are here calling the third strategy (notably, Bernstein himself, together with Gadamer, Habermas, Charles Taylor, Alasdair MacIntyre, and others). See, for instance, Richard J. Bernstein, *Beyond Objectivism and Relativism: Science, Hermeneutics, and Praxis* (Philadelphia: University of Pennsylvania Press, 1983) and *Philosophical Profiles: Essays in a Pragmatic Mode* (Philadelphia: University of Pennsylvania Press, 1986). For a clear sense that this homogenizing undertaking would

not be at all acceptable to either Feyerabend or Rorty, see, for example, Paul Feyerabend, *Farewell to Reason* (London: Verso, 1987) and Richard Rorty, "Postmodern Bourgeois Liberalism," *Journal of Philosophy* LXXX (1983), pp. 583–9, and "Solidarity or Objectivity" in John Rajchman and Cornell West (eds), *Post-Analytic Philosophy* (New York: Columbia University Press, 1988).

2 See, for instance, Edmund Husserl, *The Crisis of European Sciences and Transcendental Phenomenology: An Introduction to Phenomenological Philosophy*, trans. David Carr (Evanston: Northwestern University Press, 1970) and *Phenomenology and the Crisis of Philosophy*, trans. Quentin Lauer (New York: Harper and Row, 1965).

3 Bernstein, *Beyond Objectivism and Relativism*, p. 8.
4 Ibid.; italics added.
5 Ibid., p. 82.
6 Ibid., p. 84.
7 Ibid., p. 85; italics added by Bernstein.
8 Ibid.
9 Perhaps it is unnecessary to remind ourselves again that theorists like Gilbert Harman do believe that a noncognitivist analogue of the relationalized reading of truth-predicates *is* viable. We may also note that some theorists even subscribe to a fully cognitivist *and* relationalized reading of truth-predicates opposed to Harman's views. See, for instance, David B. Wong, *Moral Relativity* (Berkeley: University of California, 1984). Wong's essential formula is given as follows: "A moral principle can have universal scope; that is, it can apply to all moral agents in the sense of directing them to perform certain actions; and it may be *true of all* agents given a certain set of truth conditions that a group or society assigns to the principle; but since there may be more than one set of truth conditions for the principle, it may not be *universally justifiable* to all agents" (p. 189). In effect, Wong relativizes the criteria of "true," but he does not explain the meaning of "true" and he does not explain the legitimation of his criteria. If, however, the disjunction between the theoretical and the practical is denied or opposed, one begins to see the weakness or even incoherence of Wong's (otherwise) interesting alternative. Cf. also, Bernard Williams, "The Truth in Relativism," in *Moral Luck: Philosophical Papers 1973–1980* (Cambridge: Cambridge University Press, 1981) and Joseph Margolis, "Moral Realism and the Meaning of Life," *Philosophical Forum* XXII (1990), pp. 19–48.

10 I introduce and explore the notion in Joseph Margolis, *Pragmatism without Foundations: Reconciling Realism and Relativism* (Oxford: Basil Blackwell, 1986), part I.

11 See Imre Lakatos, "Popper on Demarcation and Induction," in *Philosophical Papers*, vol. 1, ed. John Worrall and Gregory Currie (Cambridge: Cambridge University Press, 1978). Cf. also, Larry Laudan, *Progress and its Problems: Toward a Theory of Scientific Growth* (Berkeley: University of California Press, 1977). For a strong statement of scientific realism and

objectivism, see C. A. Hooker, *A Realistic Theory of Science* (Albany: State University of New York Press, 1987), chapter 8.

12 Charles Taylor, "Rationality," in Martin Hollis and Steven Lukes (eds), *Rationality and Relativism* (Cambridge: MIT Press, 1982), pp. 102–3. Cf. Peter Winch, "Understanding a Primitive Society," *American Philosophical Quarterly* I (1964), pp. 307–24.

13 I may perhaps be permitted to say that, at a small party at Bernstein's house, after a conference some years ago, Taylor and Bernstein both pressed on me the incompatibility of relativism and the admission of comparative judgments. Bernstein, who offered then, and who offers now, no distinctive supporting argument of his own, pretty well accepts Taylor's lead.

To some extent, Taylor and Bernstein have been misled by excessive or ambiguous claims made by "relativists" (who, as it happens, often deny that they *are* relativists just when they make the claims they do). Usually, the point is made by such theorists against "relativists": the practice is a little baffling. The company includes Quine and Putnam, who deny that they are relativists; Kuhn, who is sometimes ambivalent; Feyerabend, who is the most explicit "relativist" of the stripe in question; Imre Lakatos, who could hardly be classified as a relativist; Barry Barnes and David Bloor, who, as sociologists of knowledge, come in as close seconds to Feyerabend; Rorty, who is tagged by his opponents as a relativist but who opposes both relativism and the thesis here being attributed to relativists; and, rather more distantly, Wittgenstein and Peter Winch, who draw attention to understanding "forms of life" other than our own.

An excellent summary of the general line of argument (in effect, attacked by Taylor and Bernstein) is handily sketched (but not supported) in one of the most recent little books on relativism – a dialogue on issues in the philosophy of science: Larry Laudan, *Science and Relativism: Some Key Controversies in the Philosophy of Science* (Chicago: University of Chicago Press, 1990), particularly pp. 54–7 (including the footnotes) and chapter 3 (on holism). The position sketched, drawn primarily from Kuhn and Feyerabend – in effect, "epistemic equivalence" (cf. p. 65) – is actually cast (by the "relativist") in terms of quite specific difficulties regarding demonstrating the evidentiary superiority of any hypothesis over any other, as opposed to merely avowing our "reasonable" intuitions about their comparative validity. These challenges are *not* skeptical, in at least the strong sense that they admit truth-claims and the viability of inquiring into their epistemic credentials. Laudan himself identifies a "radical relativism about knowledge" or "strong forms of epistemic relativism" which he defines "to a first order of approximation" as: "the thesis that the natural world and such evidence as we have about that world do little or nothing to constrain our beliefs. In a phrase, the relativists' slogan is 'The way we take things to be is quite independent of the way things are'" (p. viii). Laudan himself thinks "the contemporary state of the art in philosophy of science" will not support the claim (ibid.) The dialogue he constructs is certainly inconclusive

– against the "relativist"; although the relativist's position ("epistemic equivalence") hardly seems convincing (cf. pp. 169–70).

In any case, relativism in this sense is not equivalent to, or entailed by, our own robust relativism; nor does it require or endorse it. Its defeat would not entail the defeat of relativism, and its vindication (apart from an obvious self-referential paradox) would be much too strong for (our) relativism; it would, in fact, be a form of intellectual anarchism. See, also, Barry Barnes, *T. S. Kuhn and Social Science* (New York: Columbia University Press, 1982), p. 76; and David Bloor, "Reply to Buchdahl," *Studies in History and Philosophy of Science* XIII (1982), p. 306. (Both are cited by Laudan.)

14 Thomas S. Kuhn, "Concepts of Cause in the Development of Physics," in *The Essential Tension: Selected Studies in Scientific Tradition and Change* (Chicago: University of Chicago Press, 1977), pp. 29–30.

15 Taylor, "Rationality," pp. 100–1, 104; italics added.

16 See Alasdair MacIntyre, *After Virtue*, 2nd ed. (Notre Dame: University of Notre Dame, 1984).

17 See Hans-Georg Gadamer, *The Idea of the Good in Platonic-Aristotelian Philosophy*, trans. P. Christopher Smith (New Haven: Yale University Press, 1986).

18 Charles Taylor, "Philosophy and Its History," in Richard Rorty *et al.* (eds), *Philosophy in History; Essays on the Historiography of Philosophy* (Cambridge: Cambridge University Press, 1984), p. 25; italics added (except for the final term "this," which was italicized in the original).

19 See further, Charles Taylor, *Philosophical Papers*, 2 vols (Cambridge: Cambridge University Press, 1985). The materials in the introduction, "Interpretation and the Sciences of Man," and "Theories of Meaning" pretty well demonstrate that Taylor does commit himself to something very much like an objectivist view of the natural sciences and does attempt to bring his hermeneutic view of the human sciences as much into line with that as is possible.

20 Hans-Georg Gadamer, *Truth and Method*, trans. Garrett Barden and John Cumming, from 2nd German ed. (New York: Seabury Press, 1975), pp. 266–7.

21 Hans-Georg Gadamer, "The Universality of the Hermeneutical Problem," in *Philosophical Hermeneutics*, trans. David E. Linge (Berkeley: University of California Press, 1976), p. 7.

22 See Paul Feyerabend, *Against Method* (London: Verso, 1975).

23 Gadamer, *Truth and Method*, pp. 271, 273; cf. the whole of the passage, pp. 267–74.

24 Ibid., p. 245.

25 Ibid., pp. 244, 269, 272.

26 Ibid., p. 258.

27 Ibid., p. 249.

28 Ibid., p. 271; italics added.

29 Ibid., p. 26.

30 See, for instance, Gadamer's excellent exposé of Habermas: Hans-Georg Gadamer, "On the Scope and Function of Hermeneutical Reflection," trans. G. B. Hess and R. E. Palmer, *Philosophical Hermeneutics*. Cf. also, Jürgen Habermas, *The Theory of Communicative Action*, vol. 1, trans. Thomas McCarthy (Boston: Beacon Press, 1981). For a brief summary of the essential objections, see Margolis, *Pragmatism without Foundations*, chapter 2.

31 For a favorable overview of the issue, see Joseph Margolis, *Texts without Referents; Reconciling Science and Narrative* (Oxford: Basil Blackwell, 1989), chapters 6, 8.

32 For a sustained defense with regard to the interpretation of art, see Joseph Margolis, "Reinterpreting Interpretation," *Journal of Aesthetics and Art Criticism* XLVII (1989), pp. 237–51.

33 For specimens of recent tendencies to think along these lines, see Roland Barthes, "From Work to Text," in *Image-Music-Text*, trans. and edit. Stephen Heath (New York: Hill and Wang, 1977); and Harold Bloom, *A Map of Misreading* (New York: Oxford University Press, 1975).

34 See Arthur C. Danto, *Narration and Knowledge* (New York: Columbia University Press, 1985). Cf. also, Adolf Grünbaum, *The Foundations of Psychoanalysis: A Philosophical Critique* (Berkeley: University of California Press, 1984), introduction, for a sense of a similar view not fully worked out.

35 See Margolis, *Texts without Referents*, chapter 8.

36 Danto, *Narration and Knowledge*, chapter 8.

37 This clearly applies to Harold Bloom's and Roland Barthes's conceptions of reading. A suggestive reading of Michel Foucault's conception of the human subject along these same lines is offered by Reiner Schürmann, "On Constituting Oneself an Anarchistic Subject," *Praxis International* VI (1986), pp. 294–310.

38 Danto, *Narration and Knowledge*, p. 258.

39 Ibid., pp. 328–9.

40 Ibid., pp. 329–30.

41 The term "adequacy" (as opposed to truth) is offered by way of analogy with the account of scientific realism developed in Bas C. van Fraassen, *The Scientific Image* (Oxford: Clarendon Press, 1980), chapter 2.

11

Order Restored

We have now vindicated relativism, that is, the generic form of robust relativism as opposed to relationalism. The principal lines of objection have proved decidedly weak. That is, *if* we understand the defense of relativism to depend on rescuing it from the kinds of objection we have been considering – those favored by traditionalism, objectivism, progressivism, inflexibility regarding bivalence and *tertium non datur* – then we are home free. There is, however, or there seems to be, a deeper sort of objection to consider. It is not an objection merely to relativism as such, an objection that means to leave the other sorts of doctrine standing, whatever their distinctive merits may be. It attacks relativism, if it may be said to attack it at all, from a point of view addressed in exactly the same way to relativism's opponents. Some might indeed insist that *that* sort of attack *is* an expression of relativism proper, the real thing. There certainly is some evidence that discussants like Bernstein and Putnam make room for a would-be radical critique that is not merely anarchical or skeptical or incoherent on the usual grounds (on grounds drawn from Plato and Aristotle or reinvented by discussants like Newton-Smith and Putnam and Rorty) but one that also intends, in its own terms, to scuttle every pretense at the rational legitimation or second-order defense of any discourse that supports truth-claims, or supports truth-claims as *objective* claims.

The nature of such a critique is hardly pursued by the philosophers in question, with the possible exception of Rorty advocating the thesis in one particular way (at least) and by Putnam (in his rejection of Rorty's own maneuver).[1] In any case, although Rorty's view raises a kind of objection that may be tagged as relativist in the sense intended, the "deeper sense" is deeper still, hardly captured by maneuvers of Rorty's sort.

The charm of what we have been calling relativism up to this point rests with the fact that, whatever its varieties, it is as much committed to accommodating first-order truth-claims as the more conventional theories it opposes. Its opposition is based on two sorts of consideration: first, that on purely formal grounds, there is and can be no compelling argument against the sheer viability of a logic that either gives up or restricts the range of use of excluded middle (or bivalence) and *tertium non datur*; and, second, that, on substantive grounds, there are many compelling reasons for holding that, in particular sectors of inquiry, a relativistic logic (that is, one relevantly conformable with giving up or restricting bivalence and *tertium non datur* and with accommodating "incongruent" claims) is at least as reasonable and as well suited as – or more reasonable and better suited than – the formal management of truth-claims offered by the standard view in just such sectors.

These two considerations are clearly too general to yield a fully formed position by themselves, but they are the essential minimal conditions of any relativism of the sort we have been examining up to now: *LF*, in the notation of the prologue. Any coherent and ramified position that pertinently satisfies these two conditions is a *robust or moderate relativism*.

Of course, the tag is self-serving. But why not? We have been able to show that protagoreanism and incommensurabilism are in themselves, or can be made to incorporate, robust relativisms; and, further, that there are many other substantive versions of relativism that cannot easily be characterized as versions of incommensurabilism, or are too detailed and too distinctive to be helpfully characterized as mere versions of protagoreanism. That is just what we have been trying to demonstrate most recently, in extending the boundaries of genuinely relativistic options.

We are now at a point where the "robust" alternative is taken to be *too concessive regarding the objectivity of truth-claims*. If it is entitled to be called a relativism, the argument goes, it is still much too tame a position to be thought to have oriented us to the main issue the philosophical tradition has been debating for millennia. It is hardly better than the objectivist doctrine that (admittedly) it opposes. Anyone really interested in the genuine article will want to defend a deeper claim that undercuts *both* that sort of relativism and the objectivism it opposes. But that, of course, was just where we had entered the lists earlier on in order to examine the force of Bernstein's claim and the claims of allied traditionalists. We found them all uncompelling *and* incapable of disqualifying the credentials of any robust relativism. Now the counterargument has been revved up a notch or two. We have, it is said, been satisfied with much too little. Not that what we have shown is not a tenable position in its own right. Only that *that is not* the relativism one wants to see defended – *if* relativism is to be defended at all. That, of course, is what Bernstein says.

He cheats a little, it must be admitted, because he asks us to defend a position (flat self-contradiction or relationalism) that, *ex hypothesi, is* incoherent and self-defeating. That is, Bernstein is pretty nearly explicit in claiming that any thesis that is not incoherent – "robust relativism," of course – just is not sufficiently responsive. Well, there's no point in playing that game for long. It's the same game, mind you, that we found Putnam and Rorty and Newton-Smith and Popper playing. Nearly everyone plays it. And so nearly everyone is amazed to find that it *is* actually possible to formulate a self-consistent position that captures a good deal of what belongs to the central tradition of debate: questions regarding bivalence, real invariant structures, and degrees of conceptual incommensurability at least.

But we need to go the extra mile. What can be said in favor of the "deeper" sort of relativism that attacks the presumption of objectivity itself? The issue is not nearly as simple as one might suppose. In order to do it justice – and in order to do it justice consistently with what we have already attempted to defend – we must insist on two very general concessions needed to give the dispute a genuine sense of reality, a sense of trying to come to terms with more than paper doubts. There is a risk, of course, that the concessions may not be generous enough, may actually still disallow the challenge we mean to entertain. But that's a risk one cannot avoid. In any case, the two concessions are these: first, that every viable human society supports a well-entrenched practice of making truth-claims, every society is committed to *enunciative* or *assertoric* or *constative discourse*, every society is committed to making reference to this or that and to predicating of it what we wish to say is true of it;[2] second, that, among all human societies, there is little reason to doubt that, in general, modern physical science has made significant, relatively systematic factual discoveries about the nature of the actual world. That's all.

It is certainly true that these two constraints place a considerable burden on all those who would worry (in the name of relativism or not) the sheer objectivity of scientific truth-claims. But that's not to say that they could not possibly reinterpret both constraints in such a way that they could then go on to make their own case. It would be unreasonable not to impose *any* dialectical limits on what they might say: the constraints we are advancing are no more than constraints of pertinence and responsiveness, certainly not indisputable truths that would disallow the intended challenge any footing at all. Anyone who said, for instance, that these considerations just *were* question-begging would not be responsive. At least that's the prejudice of the present argument. We also want to ask our objectors *for* an *argument*. That's all. In fact, quite a number of those who attack the thesis of objectivity – or do what they call attacking the thesis – *are* entirely willing to mount an argument. This is true, for instance, of Rorty and Jean-François Lyotard and Feyerabend and Barbara Hernnstein Smith and Jacques Derrida and Michel Foucault and Gilles Deleuze and, some would say, Protagoras.

There are some loose ends here. But perhaps we may postpone their discussion, or even waive them altogether for our present purpose, if we can mount a satisfactory defense against this last line of attack. Because it is the "last" line of attack. Of course, we must assume that, *if* any nonrelativist conformity with the two concessions mentioned is, or can be made, coherent, then the same holds true of any relativist conformity. So we may retire Bernstein's sort of objection as *hors de combat*, but we shall need to distinguish between relativist and nonrelativist ways of satisfying our two constraints.

II

All this scaffolding encourages suspicion. We need to move as smartly as possible to specimen disputes. As it happens, once we do that, we cannot fail to be struck by the enormous power of our two constraints: the obvious fact that enunciative or constative discourse is ubiquitous, and the equally obvious fact that the physical sciences do have a very strong claim to having formed a reasonably objective picture of a good part of the actual world.

Hold back a bit, however, so that the point of these constraints is clear enough at the start. They are, first of all, proposed only *dialectically*, that is, as reasonable considerations that mark the pertinence of opposing views. They may be overtaken, modified, even rejected by some ingenious maneuver that *first* addresses the seeming pressure of each claim. Secondly, the constraints collect certain *saliencies* of experience, that, whatever we would make of them, remain arresting and relevant enough that no argument ignoring their force altogether could (as we now understand matters) even be taken to be serious. Thirdly, as saliencies, they register *apparent invariances* (what, in the Hegelian idiom, have come to be called *Erscheinungen*), not truly or strictly exceptionless universals, but strong "empirical" open-ended uniformities that we now see no way of resisting and that do not yet entail conclusions that are question-begging with respect to the dispute at hand.

We may call such "invariances" *indicative universals* – like mortality – that: (a) need not, as normally interpreted, prove to be strictly exceptionless, certainly not necessarily exceptionless, or incapable of contrary interpretation (think of bionic engineering even with respect to mortality); (b) do not entail any distributed cognitive or legitimative norms ensuring or authorizing the confirmation of strictly invariant objective first-order claims; but (c) may well include holistic presumptions – pragmatic constraints, for instance – regarding debates of the sort we are trying to air here (just the three constraints we are featuring, in fact).

The effect of (a) to (c) is to permit us to be entirely open about our prephilosophical prejudices in entertaining particular philosophical disputes. Here, "prephilosophical" clearly does not signify distinctions that are utterly *without* philosophical import: no, they signify, rather, admitted prejudices of debate, preformed dispositions that favor weighing subsequent philosophical arguments one way rather than another; but they also signify a willingness to acknowledge the fact and to try to appreciate the force of dialectically engaged antagonists who, though similarly but perhaps differently prejudiced, intend (through philosophical argument) to alter certain of the prephilosophical biases of their opponents and to risk their own.

The point is that both sides are clearly at risk in such a proceeding and that there is, on the conditions granted, *no* indisputably neutral (or absolutely "objective") conditions outside of, prior to, unaffected by the terms of the debate itself. The conditions of debate are substantively encumbered *by* the intended debate. But saying *that* does not, by itself, preclude the reasonable formulation of some *second-order* legitimative (or philosophical) account of *objectivity*, in virtue of which, say, relativists (and nonrelativists) could consistently defend their own view of what they take objectivity to require. To draw the opposite conclusion from the foregoing concessions alone, namely, *that a relativistic conception of objectivity regarding truth-claims is self-contradictory or incoherent as such*, would be to go for a merely question-begging argument (or, very possibly, to go for one of those self-referential paradoxes regularly assigned Protagoras).

The subtlety of these matters is not well understood. But the essential issue on which we need to fix a very steady grip is simply this: that we cannot, honoring the coherence of the challenge posed, presume that we antecedently possess *objective* rules and constraints *of* argument that are not substantively affected by, or at risk in, pursuing the argument itself; *and* that we cannot, engaging that challenge, disallow the possibility that we *may* reasonably posit a compelling and resilient picture of what, under the circumstances, objective argument requires. The results will continue to be prephilosophically prejudiced; but they will now be "critically" disciplined as well, within the terms of such prejudice; and they will be able to be reported to be thus disciplined and to be open to further critique. And that's the best we can hope for under the conditions granted. To mention the point is to begin to understand how "objectivity" may be construed (relativistically), so that one need not fall back to objectivisms or privilege of any sort, and one need not embrace mere skepticism or incoherence.

One further caveat will be needed, but it will arise in a natural enough way as a result of entering particular debates.

III

Consider, now, one quite extraordinary reinterpretation of science, that is, of what, regarding its truth-claims, science is up to. In a notorious essay, *The Postmodern Condition*, Jean-François Lyotard offers the following observation:

> Science has always been in conflict with narratives. Judged by the yardstick of science, the majority of them prove to be fables. But to the extent that science does not restrict itself to stating useful regularities and seeks the truth, it is obliged to legitimate the rules of its own game. It then produces a discourse of legitimation with respect to its own status, a discourse called philosophy. I will use the term *modern* to designate any science that legitimates itself with reference to a metadiscourse of this kind making an explicit appeal to some grand narrative, such as the dialectics of Spirit, the hermeneutics of meaning, the emancipation of the rational or working subject, or the creation of wealth. For example, the rule of consensus between the sender and addressee of a statement with truth-value is deemed acceptable if it is cast in terms of a possible unanimity between rational minds: this is the Enlightenment narrative, in which the hero of knowledge works toward a good ethico-political end – universal peace.... Simplifying to the extreme, I define *postmodern* as incredulity toward metanarratives.[3]

This is a marvelously cockeyed summary of what, one cannot deny, holds the key to the most fashionable attacks on philosophy that are being made in our own day – hence, according to its own buzz-word, it is itself a deep-relativist (a *postmodern*) attack.

The sense in which this *is* a "relativist" attack – in fact, a Protagorean attack – rests with the double consideration: first, that it disallows the legitimation of any universal exceptionless truths as such (the reverse side of what Plato and Aristotle inveigh against); and second, that it redeems human claims to knowledge without the restoration of such truths and without the cognate presumption of inviolate, universal, apodictic rules of argument and reason.[4]

Nevertheless, Lyotard's argument is not entirely obvious. The following distinctions need to be borne in mind in assessing the force of what he claims. First of all, he *opposes* the notions of knowledge (*savoir*) and science. Science, he says, is "a subset of learning [*connaissance*]."[5] Evidently "knowledge" is not. Secondly, science (but not knowledge) "cannot avoid raising [the problem of its legitimacy] with all of its implications, which are no less sociopolitical than epistemological."[6] Thirdly, science aims at "the truth," but knowledge does not. It is because it aims at the truth that science is in need of legitimation. Fourthly, legitimation is a "philosophical" or second-order procedure for establishing the first-order effectiveness of science *in* gaining the truth (with which "knowledge" may apparently dispense). Fifthly, legitimation is a laughable, paradoxical, self-serving, question-begging, sociopolitically sly, altogether indefensible and unnecessary undertaking. But, sixthly, the distributed *affirmations of "knowledge"* are themselves enunciative or constative, in the sense sketched a short while ago.

We must say at once that Lyotard's package is utterly incoherent as it stands. But if it is, it is so on grounds internal to its own apparent claims. To explain its indefensibility, then, should go a long way toward redeeming the kind of relativism we were trying to put in place before this last line of attack had surfaced.

Lyotard is right, however, about one extremely important matter: *if* science aims at what is true – at what, more pointedly, is "objectively true" – then it is quite impossible to acknowledge *that* normatively specified aspiration or achievement without conceding the need for *some* legitimation of its practice. Put in the simplest terms: distributed *first-order* scientific claims (truth-claims about the way the actual world is) make no sense *as* truth-claims, except in the context of *second-order* efforts to legitimate the aptitude on which they rest; second-order claims of the legitimative sort have no function except to provide a critical and reflexive sense *of* such first-order aptitudes; and the distinction between first-order and second-order claims is itself a second-order distinction subject to all the vagaries of such speculations. There is, therefore, a conceptual symbiosis that cannot be avoided between first-order truth-claims and their second-order legitimation. *But that has nothing as such to do with presumptions of cognitive privilege, of transparency, of strict universality, contextlessness, apriority, or anything of the sort.* On the contrary, it is entirely possible (the relativist, our relativist, would say) that legitimative discourse is *not*, and cannot be shown to be, any of those lovely things.[7]

Remember: this means that second-order legitimation may trade on mere saliencies of experience (rather than strict exceptionless universals), may be subject to all the vagaries to which first-order claims are prone (horizonal blindness and the rest), need not claim any cognitive privilege at all or any superior standing to the first-order claims it reviews (being subject to the same intransparency), need not be put forward as necessarily or apodictically true (which, in any case, would be inconsistent with the concessions just allowed), and may be open to incongruent alternative options and profound historical revision (which would catch up all the philosophical saliencies of our own age). In short, a legitimative claim is merely a reflexive critical claim about why we should suppose that this or that way of making and testing claims about what is true about the world (first-order discourse) is a more reasonable bet than any competing such rationale (a second-order judgment). None of this, of course, accords with Kantian transcendental arguments, but that hardly matters. What *is* important is that arguments of this sort *are* needed (since, otherwise, science would be merely a matter of brute luck, utterly blind – which is preposterous), *are* viable and coherent (since they may be corrected, though only under the same sort of constraints joined to a change of experience), *and are* themselves fully reconcilable with a robust relativism.

IV

We are indebted to Lyotard for focusing on the thesis – difficult to resist – that the reflexively identified pursuit of truth *cannot be disjoined from second-order legitimative discourse.* As we shall see shortly, this fixes the deep incoherence of Richard Rorty's try at the so-called deep-relativist maneuver. Lyotard's incoherence rests rather with his presumption that *we can dispense with the pursuit of truth.* This appears in several guises. First of all, Lyotard evidently supposes that what he says, by way of his own theory, *is true* regarding science, knowledge, and philosophy (or has at least some truth-like status – possibly relativistically construed); he actually calls his essay *A Report on Knowledge* ("*Rapport sur le savoir*"). He fails to tell us whether the report is a manifestation of *savoir* or of *science* or of something else. Secondly, he himself ascribes to *knowledge* (*savoir*) properties that ineluctably implicate the very search for truth that calls for legitimation. Thus he says:

> What is meant by the term *knowledge* is not only a set of denotative statements, far from it. It also includes notions of "know-how," "knowing how to live," "how to listen" [*savoir-faire, savoir-vivre, savoir-écouter*], etc. Knowledge, then, is a question of competence that goes beyond the simple determination and application of the criterion of truth, extending to the determination and application of criteria of efficiency (technical qualification), of justice and/or happiness (ethical wisdom), of the beauty of a sound or color (auditory and visual sensibility), etc. Understood in this way, knowledge is what makes someone capable of forming "good" denotative utterances, but also "good" prescriptive and "good" evaluative utterances. . . . It is not a competence relative to a particular class of statements (for example, cognitive ones) to the exclusion of all others. . . . Another characteristic meriting special attention is the relation between this kind of knowledge and custom. What is a "good" prescriptive or evaluative utterance, a "good" performance in denotative or technical matters? They are all judged to be "good" because they conform to the relevant criteria (of justice, beauty, truth, and efficiency respectively) accepted in the social circle of the "knower's" interlocutors.[8]

So the truth of the matter is that Lyotard *does not* really preclude the *legitimation of knowledge*, just as he does not preclude an enunciative use of discourse directed to "the truth." His objection is rather that, in so speaking, we should never presume that, by that device, we are exceeding the relativized, preformed, intransparent, nonuniversalizable conditions of custom and inquiry. Also, there may be much more than truth to legitimate. Fine. But in that case, Lyotard fails to show either that science *cannot* avail itself of the same caveat or that knowledge (in the enunciative sense) *can* escape a legitimative critique. Either, therefore, legitimation need not be "objectivist" (in the sense formulated by Bernstein), or else Lyotard cannot distinguish between science and knowledge (or "narrative knowledge," as he sometimes calls it).

Part of Lyotard's extremely gymnastic effort is directed against the absorption of whatever obtains in the real world *within* the determining confines of language;[9] and part of his effort is directed against all forms of privileged and universalized objectivisms. But his mistake remains one of supposing (without argument) that science and legitimation *cannot* be reconciled with the rejection of such objectivisms. We have already examined the matter.

Lyotard's argument would be beneath review, were it not for the fact that, at just this moment, it is increasingly fashionable to (try to) characterize knowledge in a way that escapes the entire encumbrance of language and legitimation. That cannot be done, as far as one can see: *not because there is no world and no aptitude for discerning what is in the world*, but because whatever may be *distributively* claimed about the world and our discerning powers cannot be disjoined from the linguistic categories in which they are framed. It is not just because what is *enunciated* (*énoncé*, in Foucault's idiom) is already languaged and cannot be made to *correspond* to what, distributively, nonlinguistically, is already "there": that is surely the upshot of the entire history of Western philosophy. It would be a complete dead end to reopen the issue, although it is certainly true that its ramifications are not entirely clear. And yet, *that is* precisely what Lyotard is hopelessly and helplessly trying to recover: the *felt* "correspondence" between what is presented or represented linguistically or cognitively and what is "unpresentable" but *real* behind that façade. Hence Lyotard's closing slogan: "let us be witness to the unpresentable."[10]

In fact, this slogan touches on a deeper theme (the express theme of Lyotard's *The Differend*) that captures more what, at the present moment, is meant by "poststructuralism" than by "postmodernism." It refers to the double condition that we cannot "totalize" over all conceptual schemes and that, in actual practice, we always empower a particular limited scheme, that (therefore) marginalizes, suppresses, makes no provision for its own contingent replacement by what may, for various reasons, inscribe quite other categories of importance (*le différend*) than are dreamt of in our ontologies. Two remarks suffice: first, acknowledging the point *is* instructive but never more than a holist insight, one that is incapable of supporting any distributed claim at all (on pain of contradiction); second, that, therefore, *all* enunciative discourse (involving reference and predication) cannot help but risk the tacit limitation the slogan indicates. Hence, the thesis can only enhance the fortunes of relativism; it cannot possibly undermine its legitimacy. For, if it could provide distributed evidence against relativistic or nonrelativistic conceptual schemes, it would violate the very insight that it means to champion: it would have to favor one determinate schema over another.

It would not then bear "witness to the unpresentable." In effect, this is the *reductio* of the entire counterstrategy we are considering.

One final reference will permit us to close the book on Lyotard. The fact is that Lyotard's essay is, in part, intended to subvert the universalist (Enlightenment) pretensions of Jürgen Habermas's traditionalism.[11] According to our own lights, this is an admirable project in itself. But there is no point in throwing the world away merely to gain a march on Habermas, that is, merely to disallow the "treatment of the problem of legitimation in the direction of a search for universal consensus."[12] Nevertheless, Lyotard goes to extraordinary lengths to insist, first (not unreasonably), that "language games [including the game of science] are heteromorphous, subject to heterogeneous sets of pragmatic rules," and then, secondly (preposterously), that the real "end" of science "is paralogy [the search for dissent]."[13] The best that can be said for Lyotard here is that he must be attempting to retrieve a version of Feyerabend's conception of science. That is to say, he does not responsibly meet the second of our constraining saliences, namely, that science is indeed an impressive body of objective knowledge about the actual world. What would paralogy be *for*, if not (if it had any use at all) something dialectically linked to the recovery of truth? Even paralogy is concerned with the issue of legitimation.

V

Having laid all this to rest, we may now press on quite easily to expose the fatal weakness of another extremely popular version of the "deep" relativism that is said to harbor the serious point of Protagoras' challenge. Richard Rorty, unlike Lyotard, claims that we *can* (and should) disjoin the discipline of first-order science from second-order legitimation: we can have the one without the other. His reason, quite simply, is that *every* would-be legitimation *must be committed to privileged, cognitively transparent, ahistorical, context-free, universally exceptionless, timeless, linguistically undistorted, objective, a priori conditions governing meaning, truth, validity, value, and the like.* This is the essential message of *Philosophy and the Mirror of Nature* – what, as we saw, Putnam regards as a "silly" stance.

So Rorty really agrees with Lyotard. Their difference lies in this: Lyotard tries to free knowledge (*savoir*) from the pursuit of truth, because he realizes that that pursuit is inseparable from legitimation;

Rorty wishes to hold fast to science's grip on truth, but he believes that we can do that just when we give up legitimation.

Hence, speaking against Lyotard, Rorty actually says:

> I do not think that such examples of matters of current scientific concern [that is, "undecidables, the limits of precise control, conflicts characterized by incomplete information, 'fracta,' catastrophes, and pragmatic paradoxes"] do anything to support the claim that "consensus is not the end of discussion." Lyotard argues invalidly from the current concerns of various scientific disciplines to the claim that science is somehow discovering that it should aim at permanent revolution, rather than at the alternation between normality and revolution made familiar by Kuhn.[14]

Rorty's point is that Lyotard was driven to his preposterous account – perhaps by Habermas – "by an overzealous philosophy of science [that] has created an impossible idea of a historical legitimation." If we give that up, we give up the need for the excessive correction: "It would be better to be frankly ethnocentric."[15] What Rorty means by this is: first, to give up (with Lyotard) the "metanarratives" of legitimation; second, to accept (with Habermas) the idea that science is a "social practice"; and, third (his own view), to concede that pursuing such practices (and changing them) is merely conforming to the favored tastes of our own bourgeois-liberal Western world.[16] "More than engineering [he says] modern science is ... not ... an ahistorical teleology – e.g., an evolutionary drive towards correspondence with reality, or the nature of language – but ... a particularly good example of the social virtues of European bourgeoisie; ... modern science will look like something which a certain group of human beings invented in the same sense in which these same people can be said to have invented Protestantism, parliamentary government, and Romantic poetry."[17]

But that won't do at all. For one thing, Rorty clearly means to allow *some* sort of critical and rational reflection *on* the promising direction of the practices in question, particularly science; for another, he simply homogenizes the question of just *how* this critique should proceed when applied to the *different* practices he has in mind. His advice seems to boil down to a single undifferentiated *laissez-faire* tolerance. Hence, *if* legitimation were characterized in a way that did not depend on certain narrow prejudices (listed just a moment ago), then Rorty (rather like Lyotard) would have to admit its recoverability, its special pertinence, and its special discipline. In that case, once again, "deep" relativism would be defeated out of its own mouth. It is simply preposterous to suppose that the practice of science is, *given its objectives*, methodologically and critically not really different from the invention of the practice of Protestantism and Romantic poetry; and it is equally preposterous to suppose that the best way to pursue the objectives of science, as with the objectives of Protestantism and Romantic poetry, is indistinguishable in rational ways from *whatever* obtains under the conditions of *laissez-faire* tolerance. The theory seems to be little more than a cheerful sort of intellectual bankruptcy. *Otherwise, surely, it is itself a very poor legitimative bet.*

VI

What begins to dawn on us is the validity of the charge that one cannot escape the self-referential paradoxes, *if* one espouses "deep" relativism rather than "robust" relativism. For either "deep" relativism is nothing but relationalism (for instance, by way of an "ethnocentric" reading of truth) or else it is entirely irrelevant to the issue (for instance, by way of the inapplicable doctrine of the "differand"). Possibly the most influential recent author responsible for generating the "deep" paradoxes was Michel Foucault. There is every evidence that, toward the end of his life, Foucault became quite troubled by these paradoxes but never managed to escape them. He was never willing to be quite so blithe, however, as to suggest that they could be safely ignored.[18]

The essential paradox in Foucault is simply this: for Foucault, "truth" is both an artifact of social history and a *sui generis* property of discourse about such history and the world. But, of course, it cannot be both in the same sense. The first theme is meant to smash the pretense that truth may be cast in correspondentist terms – a theme Foucault came to see could be effectively construed as an application of Nietzsche's conception of the relation between truth and power.[19] The second conveys Foucault's most professional sense of actually constructing confirmable histories or "objective" *genealogies*:

> Let us give the term *genealogy* to the union of erudite knowledge and local memories which allows us to establish a historical knowledge of struggles and to make use of this knowledge tactically today.... Genealogies are, therefore, not positivistic returns to a more careful or exact form of science. They are precisely anti-sciences. Not that they vindicate a lyrical right to ignorance or non-knowledge; it is not that they are concerned to deny knowledge or that they esteem the virtues of direct cognition and base

their practice upon an immediate experience that escapes encap-
sulation in knowledge.[20]

Foucault's point is that genealogy – the kind of *knowledge* that
genealogy provides – has an emancipatory function, belongs to "the
insurrection of knowledge ... opposed primarily not to the contents,
methods or concepts of a science, but to the effects of the centralizing
powers which are linked to the institution and functioning of an organ-
ized scientific discourse within a society such as ours."[21] But this *is* to
instantiate the paradox, *if* knowledge is, in some sense, a mere "thing," a
product of the history of subterranean powers that we cannot completely fathom.

Foucault is obliged to argue at cross-purposes, then. On the one
hand, "genealogy" (as opposed to "archeology") is emancipative, "external" in its intention *vis-à-vis any* "hierarchical order of power associated with science." In this sense, it is its *active* rather than its *cognitive*
stance that is decisive.[22] On the other hand, genealogy is an enunciative
discourse actually capable of exposing the truth about such regimes of
power; in that sense, its intended (emancipative) *use* is more or less
irrelevant to its cognitive status – where, now, it *is* its cognitive role that
counts. In the one account, "knowledge" is an inseparable artifact of
"power" (by way of a Nietzscheanized expansion of broadly Marxist
themes); in the other, it is the very mark of our discursive capacity to be
"objective" about, *to have "knowledge" of*, such *epistemes* – hence, to
be free, *in some sense*, from the power constellation it exposes.

In short, Foucault needs two sorts of "knowledge," more or less as
Lyotard did, though for opposing reasons. For Foucault will have none
of Lyotard's yearnings for "direct cognition" and the "unpresentable."

Once we have all this in order, we can identify Foucault's paradox
easily enough. On the one hand, "Truth is a thing of this world: it is
produced only by virtue of multiple forms of constraint. And it induces
regular effects of power. Each society has its regime of truth, its 'general
politics, of truth: that is, the types of discourse which it accepts and
makes function as true."[23] On the other hand, genealogy is "a form
of history which can account for the constitution of knowledges, discourse, domains of objects etc., without having to make reference to a
subject which is either transcendental in relation to the field of events or
runs in its empty sameness through the course of history."[24]

But, of course, Foucault never locates *his own discourse* in relation
to these contrasting views, never shows us how to reconcile them, any
more than Rorty or Goodman when similarly confronted by opposing,
disparate, incommensurable practices and beliefs. Surely, in this regard,

though his account is historically more profound, Foucault's attempt at resolution is infinitely weaker than Quine's or Goodman's. Still, as we have seen, those thinkers are much too clever in avoiding a simple capitulation to the self-referential paradoxes.[25]

One way of resolving Foucault's paradox, then, simply requires that we acknowledge that Foucault is not tampering with the meaning of the alethic truth-values ("true" and "false") at all; he is, rather, attempting to place the practice of making and confirming truth-*claims* within the radicalized space of contingent *epistemes* ("regimes of truth"). Wherever Foucault is tempted to combine the two (as admittedly does happen: "Truth is a thing of this world"), he veers in the direction of rela-tionalism and incoherence; but wherever he himself makes bona fide truth-claims about what transpires *within* his constructed *epistemes* ("genealogy"), he simply utters claims of his own that, as he rightly anticipates, are subject to the same sort of forces as the claims he con-siders. In formal terms, there is no difference between the epistemic contingencies Foucault examines and those that were once wrongly thought to render the sociology of knowledge incoherent. What is at stake is *not* the redefinition of truth but the appreciation of the com-plexities of reliably confirming truth-claims within a transient, histori-cized, tacitly preforming, intransparent *episteme*, that, on a plausible (inductive) bet, we have good reason to believe will affect the fortunes of our own claim as it can be shown to do in the case of any other claim. Reflexivity, here, is not incoherence.

VII

There are many other manifestations of "deep" relativism. One can see, however, that they cannot possibly succeed. They all produce a form of the self-referential paradoxes because they fail to grasp the profundity of the two sorts of salience with which we began this last bit of analysis. The important point to rescue from the hubbub of all these confron-tations is simply that escaping from the paradoxes does not require reinstating objectivism, traditionalism, cognitive privilege, apriorism, exceptionless invariances of a legitimating sort, or anything of the kind. What we have called robust relativism is entirely capable of avoiding those disorders. That's what the opponents of relativism (the "deep" relativists) have failed to see.

So we have come to the end of the argument. We have vindicated the option of relativism and the heritage of Protagoras. And that's not an easy thing to do.

Notes

1 See Hilary Putnam, "Why Reason can't be Naturalized," in *Philosophical Papers* (Cambridge: Cambridge University Press, 1983).

2 For a good sense of what is meant by enunciative or constative discourse, see J. L. Austin, *How to Do Things with Words* (Oxford: Clarendon Press, 1963); and Michel Foucault, "The Discourse on Language," trans. Rupert Sawyer; published together with *The Archaeology of Knowledge*, trans. A. M. Sheridan Smith (New York: Harper and Row, 1972). For a sense of why such discourse must incorporate referential and predicative acts, see, further, Joseph Margolis, *Texts without Referents; Reconciling Science and Narrative* (Oxford: Basil Blackwell, 1988), chapter 7.

3 Jean-François Lyotard, *The Postmodern Condition: A Report on Knowledge*, trans. Geoff Bennington and Brian Massumi (Minneapolis: University of Minnesota Press, 1984), pp. xxiii–xxiv.

4 Here it is worth noting that Lyotard takes up the paradoxes of the theory of types applied to the famous story of the lawsuit Protagoras' student Euathlus proposed to face him with. Lyotard's analysis leads him to the notion of a *differend* (*le différend*): "A case of differend [he says] between two parties takes place when the 'regulation' of the conflict that opposes them is done in the idiom of one of the parties while the wrong suffered by the other is not signified in that idiom." See Jean-François Lyotard, *The Differend: Phrases in Dispute*, trans. Georges van Den Abeele (Minneapolis: University of Minnesota Press, 1988), pp. 6–14. The citation is from §12. Here, Lyotard clearly agrees with our point about the context-determined and (in that sense) prejudiced nature of the rules of argument.

5 Lyotard, *The Postmodern Condition*, p. 18.

6 *Ibid.*

7 A ramified version of this argument, with respect to transcendental (or legitimative) arguments, is given in Joseph Margolis, *Pragmatism without Foundations; Reconciling Realism and Relativism* (Oxford: Basil Blackwell, 1986), chapter 11.

8 Lyotard, *The Postmodern Conditions*, pp. 18–19. It seems not unreasonable to read this as linked in Lyotard's mind with Protagoras' view, since he specifically notes that, in the Greek world, this practice is "called [the] mode of legitimating ... opinion" (p. 19). (He refers, of course, to Parmenides.)

9 See Jean-François Lyotard, *Discours, Figure* (Paris: Klincksieck, 1971).

10 Lyotard, *The Postmodern Condition*, p. 82. Cf. the entire discussion of the arts in the appendix: "Answering the Question: What is Postmodernism?" trans. Régis Durand. The entire essay is an attempt to read Kant's notion of aesthetic judgment in the spirit of something like Merleau-Ponty's *The Visible and Invisible*. That is, it is preoccupied with the *nostalgia* for a direct encounter (prethematized) with reality taken distributively (that is, impossibly).

11 See Jürgen Habermas, "Modernity – An Incomplete Project," in Hal Foster

(ed.), *The Anti-Aesthetic* (Post Townsend, Wash.: Bay Press, 1983) and *The Philosophical Discourse of Modernity: Twelve Lectures*, trans. Frederick Lawrence (Cambridge: MIT Press, 1987).

12 Lyotard, *The Postmodern Condition*, p. 65.

13 *Ibid.*, pp. 65–6.

14 Richard Rorty, "Habermas and Lyotard on Post-Modernity," *Praxis International* IV (1984), p. 33. Cf. also, Richard Rorty, *Philosophy and the Mirror of Nature* (Princeton: Princeton University Press, 1979).

15 Rorty, "Habermas and Lyotard on Post-Modernity," p. 35.

16 Ibid., pp. 35–6, 41. Cf. Richard Rorty, "Solidarity or Objectivity," in John Rajchman and Cornell West (eds), *Post-Analytic Philosophy* (New York: Columbia University Press, 1985).

17 Ibid., p. 36.

18 I have it, I may say, on the basis of a conversation with a former student of Foucault's that, in his later years, he was very much concerned to reconsider the problem of legitimation and of transcendental arguments. He apparently felt it was necessary, but he could not recover a ground sufficiently consistent with what he had already written to permit him to explore the matter productively.

19 See, for instance, Michel Foucault, "Nietzsche, Genealogy, History," in Donald F. Bouchard (ed.), *Language, Counter-Memory, Practice; Selected Essays and Interviews by Michel Foucault*, trans. Donald F. Bouchard and Sherry Simon (Ithaca: Cornell University Press, 1977).

20 Michel Foucault, "Two Lectures," *Power/Knowledge: Selected Interviews and Other Writings 1972–1977*, ed. Colin Gordon, trans. Colin Gordon et al. (New York: Pantheon, 1980), pp. 83–4.

21 Ibid., p. 84.

22 Ibid., p. 85.

23 Foucault, "Truth and Power," *Power/Knowledge*, p. 131.

24 Ibid., p. 117.

25 One could go on multiplying cases, but the main lines of objection are reasonably clear. Perhaps it would be enough to observe that Foucauldian-like paradoxes are unavoidable wherever one *tries to reduce enunciative discourse to a mere datum, caused or produced or generated within a domain about which objective reports of just such data are always eligible.*

Two further instances may be mentioned to fix the point. There is an interesting new book by Barbara Hernnstein Smith, *Contingencies of Values: Alternative Perspectives for Critical Theory* (Cambridge: Harvard University Press, 1988), that introduces relativism in the following way: "At the most general theoretical level, the relativism exhibited by this study is not a 'position,' not a 'conviction,' and not a set of 'claims' about how certain things – reality, truth, meaning, realism, value, and so forth – really are. It is, rather, *a general conceptual style or taste*, specifically played out here [in a number of important ways shadowing the intention, though not the actual strategies, of those already examined]" (p. 151). The qualifications are worth reviewing, but we have no space to pursue the matter here.

Suffice it to say that Smith's orientation permits her to say that "the social, political, and communicative dynamics of verbal or other overt *judgments* and, accordingly, the structure and operation of their *justification* can be reconceived along other lines [than the canonical objectivist ones]. Specifically ... justifying a particular judgment to those whose welfare is one's responsibility ... may be conceived as *making as explicit as necessary to them the various considerations that produced that judgment* ... stopping not when the explication hits 'objective' rock bottom but when it turns the trick, that is, *secures their acquiescence*" (p. 160).

But this misses the point, of course, of the self-referential paradoxes and slights our first (and even our second) salience. It also tends to replace *cognitive* questions with *causal* questions. But it fails to take note of the fact that causal questions *are* cognitive questions. That is, Smith does not quite locate her own discourse within the space of argument any more than Foucault does. We may simply add here that it is, precisely, the Edinburgh sociology of knowledge that has systematically attempted to replace cognitive questions with causal ones. See, for instance, Barry Barnes and David Bloor, "Relativism, Rationalism and the Sociology of Knowledge," in Martin Hollis and Steven Lukes (eds), *Rationality and Relativism* (Cambridge: MIT Press, 1982). Cf. also, David Bloor, *Wittgenstein; A Social Theory of Knowledge* (London: Macmillian, 1983), particularly chapter 9 for a short glimpse of the argument; and Barry Barnes, *T. S. Kuhn and Social Science* (New York: Columbia University Press, 1982). There is also, of course, a strong naturalizing tendency in Quine, but it is not intended to support the sociology of knowledge. See W. V. Quine, "Epistemology Naturalized," in *Ontological Relativity and Other Essays* (New York: Columbia University Press, 1969). See, also, Clifford Geertz, "Anti Anti-Relativism," in Michael Krausz (ed.), *Relativism: Interpretation and Confrontation* (Notre Dame: University of Notre Dame Press, 1989), which seems to have influenced Smith.

12

A Last Word

I

Recall, finally, that we have never denied that it was possible to abandon or restrict the scope of excluded middle (both bivalence and *tertium non datur*) and to reject every form of cognitive privilege without subscribing to relativism. Quine argues in just that way. He is, in fact, the principal advocate of the nonrelativist alternative, *if* we read him as holding that, wherever *we* invoke relativistic truth-values, there is "no fact of the matter," no truth-like values of any kind to be assigned.

We saw that such a reading was not entirely satisfactory because, first, on Quine's own view of the analytic/synthetic distinction and of holism, it would be impossible to deny convincingly the relevance of truth-like values for one set of claims and then affirm their relevance for another, where there was no grammatical or empirical basis on which to fix a principled demarcation between the two; and because, second, Quine's own insistence on the role of science in deciding questions of truth leads one to believe that he was genuinely attracted to some form of relativism. Of course, Quine never defends relativism. He avoids it. But he avoids it at a very heavy price. The story helps to spell out the difference between the relativist's and anti-relativist's "temperament."

Quine's treatment of the relevant issues requires the admission of truth-value gaps and the radical uncertainty of a demarcation between sets of asserted sentences over which bivalent values effectively range and sets over which they have no application. His use of Pierre Duhem's scientific holism is conceptually flawed because he relativizes (where Duhem does not) all distributed conceptual distinctions and truth-claims to the *totality* of possible experience – which is cognitively inaccessible. One see this, for instance, in the following pronouncements:

Occasion sentences and stimulus meaning are general coin; terms and reference are local to our conceptual scheme[1]

– which promises *some* cognitive weighting to "stimulus meaning";

The stimulus meaning of "Bachelor" [say] cannot be treated as its "meaning" by any stretch of the imagination, unless perhaps accompanied by a stretch of the modulus [that is, "the length of stimulations counted as current ... count([ed]) as specious present"][2]

– which brings both stimulation and modulus, relevant for truth-value assignment, *within* the pale of analytical hypotheses;

Where cultural contrasts begin to be threatened with meaninglessness is rather where they depend on analytical hypotheses[3]

– which retreats from even admitting the intelligibility of systematically conflicting conceptual schemes, whether in one's home language or in the field linguist's space;

Everything to which we concede existence is a posit from the standpoint of a description of the theory-building process, and simultaneously real from the standpoint of the theory that is being built[4]

– which confirms the impossibility of fixing any favored reference point for reliably testing truth-claims within, and with specific reference to the determinate structures of, an *en bloc* holism, including the very length and locus of the specious present;

We have no reason to suppose that man's surface irritations even unto eternity admit of any one systematization that is scientifically better or simpler than all possible others.... Scientific method is the way to truth, but it affords even in principle no unique definition of truth[5]

– which confirms Quine's strong commitment to truth-values but admits truth-value gaps, hence the question of abandoning excluded middle.

Faced with the need to make a straightforward commitment on the relativism that looms, Quine says the following:

Have we now so far lowered our sights as to settle for a relativistic doctrine of truth – rating the statements of each theory as true for that theory, and brooking no higher criticism? Not so. The saving consideration is that we continue to take seriously our own particular aggregate science, our own particular world-theory or loose total fabric of quasi-theories, whatever it may be.[6]

But here Quines makes no provision at all for the difficulties mentioned.[7] On the contrary, he stonewalls and even flirts with something close to relationalism. After all, what could *he* possibly mean by "our own particular world-theory"? His argument disallows any principled distinction between inter- and intralinguistic synonymy and translation[8] and any cognitively reliable partition of the *en bloc* range of experience with respect to which truth-value assignments may be differentially affected.[9] In a word, Quinean holism admits piecemeal truth-gaps but cannot account for the demarcation on which they rest. Aggressive readers will say at once that to admit that much *is* to subscribe to relativism. More thoughtful readers will say only that to admit that much is to make it impossible to disallow relativism an equal inning with its opponents. Still more thoughtful readers will say that, dialectically, relativism cannot fail to appear to be the stronger doctrine.

II

Nevertheless, Quine shows the way, or a way, a way to avoid relativism. He makes it stick by desperate measures. He seems to be advising us to admit truth-value gaps *wherever the relativist applies his counter-theory*.

But think about that a bit. A viable relativism must: (1) restrict the range of application of excluded middle at least; and (2) reject all forms of cognitive transparency and privilege to which (1) applies. Yet, taken together, (1) and (2) still fall short of relativism. Quine shows us a way of precluding relativism consistently with (1) and (2): simply admit truth-value gaps wherever apparent claims would, on a bivalent model but not now, yield incompatible truths.

But if, contrary to his intention, we treated Quine's notions of the indeterminacy of translation and the inscrutability of reference as *permitting* truth-value assignments *jointly* to claims in accord with competing parsings of the world (rather than disjunctively: allowing truth-value gaps), then Quine *would* indeed *be* a relativist. We are not pressing the point here. What we want to understand rather is just what

210 A LAST WORD

the essential difference is between the relativistic and nonrelativistic "temperaments" in reading (1) and (2). The argument, after all, is already in.

The tell-tale clue in Quine is this: he admits truth-value gaps first, and then he disallows them. One might easily see in this the incipience of Rorty's notorious ethnocentrism. But that would be a mistake, that is, a mistake in interpreting *Quine*, though it may well be *Rorty's* reading of Quine. Rorty's liberal *laissez-faire* policy would apparently recognize that other societies have every right to ignore discrepancies between "our own particular world-theory or loose total fabric of quasi-theories" with respect to which their own truth-"practice" obtains – just as we do – or else that they have the right to accommodate the effect of those perceived differences on grounds of what would be persuasive only *internal* to *their* own frame of reference. But how *can* we individuate "their" frame of reference and "ours"?

Here Quine shuts truth-ascriptions down altogether; for his part, Rorty risks relationalism directly. When Quine says there's "no fact of the matter," a much-neglected equivocation arises: what he says could mean that, where factual questions rightly obtain, there is no way of actually determining the truth though truth is rightly pursued (the pertinent truth-value is "indeterminate": gaps *do* arise for a bivalent logic); or, alternatively, it could mean that it would be a mistake to suppose that a factual question ever arises there at all (there *are* no truth-value gaps to consider: bivalence remains perfectly intact).

One of Quine's solutions offers a nonrelativistic reading of (1) and (2) that adversely affects excluded middle; the other offers another non-relativistic reading that apparently does not restrict excluded middle at all. *Neither* is believable, because Quine's holism and his rejection of a principled analytic/synthetic demarcation make both solutions little more than arbitrary ways of blocking relativism.

Rorty asks us to favor "our" own practice, knowing full well that there are *other* alternatives. Hence, following Rorty: should an incompatibility arise and should we fall back merely to our own "truth," it would at once be impossible to avoid relationalism; on the other hand, should we attempt to weight the merits of the competing opinions in any way, it would then be impossible to avoid admitting the relevance of second-order legitimation.

In that sense, we may offer Rorty no more than a choice between two different forms of incoherence; and we may offer Quine no more than a choice between two different forms of arbitrariness. (For, on Quine's view, if there is "no fact of the matter," then *there are no truth-value gaps*; and if there are no gaps, then excluded middle is not affected. But then, there *are* "places" where apparent questions of truth arise – where, that is, some would say that Quine admits gaps by way of either of his options, whereas they, relativists and nonrelativists alike, would not favor such gaps.)

III

It is certainly not part of the sense of (1) that the mere advocacy of a many-valued logic entails abandoning excluded middle altogether or embracing relativism. For instance, the introduction of probabilized truth-values is not relativistic. On the contrary, what is "probably true" may well be false, for all we know, *sans phrase*. In probabilistic contexts, "true," we say, is not detachable from its epistemic or evidential ground, which accounts for its many-valued nature.[10] We therefore do not contradict ourselves in admitting that it is probably true (in some measure) that "Nixon knew about Watergate in advance" even though it is also probably true (in some measure) that "Nixon did not know about Watergate in advance." There are no necessary self-referential paradoxes in this seeming analogue of relationalist views of truth. Nor, for similar reasons, would there be for any epistemic practice confined to how things transiently "appear" to us (Protagoras' option, on the classical view).

Neither (1) nor (2), then, nor (1) and (2) taken together, entails relativism. But then, neither relativism nor anti-relativism is conceptually unavoidable in any sense that respects the developing argument of this account. That's to say: one can always formulate an internally coherent and philosophically responsive form of each. Quine, as we have just seen, constructs a formally consistent anti-relativism.

IV

The point of worrying Quine rests with its not being enough to be consistent. One has also to avoid mere arbitrariness. Once Quine's radical *holism* is conceded (a holism, unlike Duhem's,[11] that brooks no principled demarcation between analytic and synthetic truths), and once the cognitive *intransparency* of the world is conceded (certainly a correlate of that holism, though it may also be independently affirmed), it becomes impossible to proceed non-arbitrarily to fix *the modulus of the specious present (of any length, for any society, for any set of intercommunicating societies)* relative to which a relativistic reading of *any* of the

first-order scientific questions Quine considers *could be disallowed* in
principle or by dint of dialectical advantage.

Quine, as we saw, goes to desperate lengths to avoid relativism by
introducing truth-value gaps at the critical juncture. Given his holism,
his exposé of the "dogmas" of empiricism,[12] his support of "analytical
hypotheses," Quine obviously risks truth-value gaps *everywhere*. At
that point, the relativist regains the high ground; for *he* insists that,
wherever the anti-relativist presses his advantage, *he* will either win
outright or produce a stalemate more convincing than his opponent's
claim or at least confirm the conceptual viability of his own claim. In
that sense, Quine's strategy is a metonym for an entire family of anti-
relativisms and a test of the coherence and dialectical force of relativism
itself.

All this may be put in a different way. Quine's holism amounts to a
proposal – not an argument – that offers a context for conditions (1) and
(2), which bear on every pertinent argument. The proposal is this: (3)
affirm opacity everywhere. (3) provides a completely opaque holist
sense for all the distributed sorts of intransparency that could be collected under (2) – a context, therefore, for all possible contexts of
discourse. As relativists, we may go along with Quine, except that we
must be careful never to permit (3) to yield *any* differential results
regarding alethic or epistemic or ontic policies. For Quine, however,
what characterizes (3) bleeds into the space of (2). In effect, Quine
cheats, though he is not formally inconsistent. First, he permits any
well-formed sentences to service truth-claims; then he reconsiders, he
introduces truth-value gaps *here and there*; and *then* he denies that the
contexts in which such gaps apparently obtain are contexts in which
the question of truth-value assignments arises in the first place. So the
maneuver is a little labored. Relativism is precluded but never shown to
be incoherent. Fine.

V

"Opacity" (3) is a blunderbuss term. Once adopted, (3) subtends every
possible thesis about man's condition in the world. "Opacity" is not
a determinate thesis as it stands. It only expresses a global sense of
whatever would pit our sort of relativism against Quine's sort of anti-
relativism at every possible point of contest.

The puzzles at (2) and at (3) inevitably tend to be the same, but there
is a division even so. Certainly, the rejection of apodicticity, correspondence, foundationalism, essentialism, progressivism, inductivism,

possible-worlds semantics, universalism, totalization, and similar doctrines tend to collect rather naturally at (2); but historicity, particularly
the radical historicity of concepts and human existence, horizonal blindness, preformation and the prethematized world, the tacitly artifactual
nature of human persons, undifferentiated holism, perspectivism (in
Nietzsche's sense), genealogy (in Foucault's), the primacy of *praxis* (in
Marx's sense), and similar doctrines tend to cluster more at (3). They
also infect the themes of (2), of course, and are legitimately collected
there as well. The difference is roughly this: those puzzles that are more
strongly associated with (3) tend to yield resolutions that are nearly
always open to a winning form of robust relativism: witness Quine's
peculiarly arduous maneuvers regarding holism; whereas puzzles more
narrowly associated with (2) yield solutions that are more nearly balanced as between nonrelativism and relativism.

We are speaking here more of temperamental differences among
philosophers than of specific arguments about contested questions. But
those differences are hardly negligible: there are no arguments that are
ultimately separable from these "temperamental" complications, and the
complications themselves are not merely ornamental or rhetorical in a
pejorative sense. They collect the inexhaustible sources of our most
inclusive visions of the world, from which *every* determinate quarrel is
drawn.

For instance, when we observed quite early in this account that
Robert Stalnaker took it for a certainty that there were just two truth-
values, we could be fairly sure that he would not provide any play for
doctrines favorable to the relativist's position. The "possible-worlds"
strategy of semantic analysis, we may say, would so extend the reliability of some epistemic practice (functioning rather like an analogue of
Quine's specious present) – although Quine himself would not favor
possible-worlds talk – that it would be extremely difficult to find *any* of
the puzzles we have collected at (3) taken seriously enough by Stalnaker
that it might be thought necessary to resolve them satisfactorily *before*
or *while* continuing with the possible-worlds scenario answering
puzzles at (2). This is not to say that Stalnaker must address *Quine's*
question regarding the specious present, or that his own program entails
a similar question, or that it is without merit because it does not address
issues of the sort suggested. No, it is just that the seeming smoothness
and pertinence of Stalnaker's use of "possible worlds" depends on *not*
raising any of the questions connected with (3), with regard to recommending (*not* legitimating) a possible-worlds semantics. Should they
be raised? Well, the argument here is that they should; that they *are*
raised and are as quickly smothered; and that, if they were explicitly

confronted, then a possible-worlds semantics would be seen to be decidedly vulnerable – hospitably so for the fortunes of relativism, in particular, for a relativistic reading of (1). What, after all, should we mean in speaking of "all possible worlds" under conditions of severe intransparency?

VI

In short, some philosophers ignore in this way a *source* of argument that affects the persuasiveness of argument itself, though it does not bear in a determinate way on its perceived piecemeal rigor. It tells us something about the relevance of the particular forms of rigor we prefer. Quine is rigorous enough, but is what he says entirely relevant or telling with regard to the deep questions we find posed *within* the questions he explicitly raises? Rigor, we may say, is an "internal" question, that is, a question internal to some tacit context of contexts, and "temperamental" preferences concern how our holist perspectives collected at (3) affect the formulation of the distributed issues of (2).

The point may be nicely illustrated by a brief scan of Jaakko Hintikka's possible-worlds semantics. First of all, Hintikka maintains that "the theory of reference is ... the theory of meaning for certain simple types of language ... the usual reasons for distinguishing between meaning and reference are seriously mistaken."[13] This, of course, is directly opposed to Quine's "cleavage" between theories of meaning and theories of reference;[14] although one might well argue that the attack on the analytic/synthetic dogma and the advocacy of holism may require something closer to Hintikka's claim, and yet also Hintikka's own claim may be thought to place his semantics under the burden of responding to the effect of something like Quine's holist constraints. Secondly, Hintikka does not restrict quantification or reference to actual individuals even where he requires reference to the same individuals in different possible worlds.[15] Thirdly, beliefs about particular individuals, whether actual or possible, entail quantifying in opaque contexts, in which, moreover, such individuals are said to be identical in different possible worlds.[16] Roughly, of course, we must be able to reidentify the same individual in different contexts of discourse; in particular, Hintikka proposes a set of "individuating functions" (semantic or meaning functions) in virtue of which, in principle, the same individual is assigned to every world in which it exists.[17] And fourthly, Hintikka takes it that if one has a belief about a particular individual, one must be able (and apparently must believe that he is able) to characterize that individual uniquely. So he says for example:

> If it is true to say that *a* has a belief about *the particular individual* who in fact is Smith, [say,] then *a* clearly must believe that he can characterize this individual uniquely. In other words, he must have some way of referring to or characterizing this individual in such a way that one and the same individual is in fact so characterized in all the worlds compatible with what he believes. This is precisely what the existence of *f* amounts to, [*f* is a member of the set of individuating or meaning functions that pick out an individual in different worlds: "names or individual constants of a certain special kind, namely those having a unique reference in all the different worlds we are speaking about" that satisfy cross-identification across possible worlds]. If no such function existed, *a* would not be able to pick out the individual who in fact is Smith under all the courses of events he believes possible, and there would not be any sense in saying that *a's* belief is *about* the particular individual in question.[18]

The trouble with Hintikka's careful account is reasonably plain. For one thing, as we have already seen in connection with Quine's notion of "pegasizing" and "socratizing," there just *is* no sense in which man has or can have God's knowledge of all possible worlds *in virtue of which he can uniquely characterize any particular individual*.[19] This is, in fact, in accord with what we took to be the minimal conditions of relativism. For a second, Hintikka extends a possible-worlds semantics in such a way that the very identity of individuals across possible worlds depends on speakers possessing individuating meaning functions that just *do* pick out individuals rigidly in the possible worlds in which they exist. Under (2), certainly in accord with (3) (but doubtless not in accord with some (3') in which, say, we *could* approximate to God's competence), such a strategy would not be available to actual speakers, and any particular such strategy would make no sense to particular speakers in terms of their own fragmentary information. For a third, Hintikka does not really consider the puzzles of opacity (3) bearing on our intentional constructs as, say, affected by the historicity and temporal contingency of our conceptual schemes, by conceptual incommensurabilities and the radical division of cultural labor, by the role of blind or impenetrable contexts, by the absence of any approximative approach to a totalized scheme of meaning functions suited to the individuals referred to in ordinary discourse. And for a fourth, it is just counterintuitive to suppose that the identification of actual individuals *logically depends* on our being able to identify them successfully in all possible worlds.

It appears that, for Hintikka, "our concept of an individual" and of the truth of a belief about that individual depends on "our ways of cross-identifying members of different 'possible worlds'" and on that individual's satisfying what is affirmed of it (in a given world) in the other possible worlds in which it exists, where the "individuating functions" by which that condition obtains "are . . . certainly . . . created by men."[20] Hintikka's entire program arises within the contingencies of our own *Lebenswelt* or *Lebensform*, but he does not appear to address the implications of that dependency. We are, of course, claiming that to do so would be to yield considerably in the direction of a relativism of the sort we have been favoring.[21] Also, Hintikka's confidence here is obviously more a "temperamental" than an argumentative matter, though to put the issue thus may wrongly encourage just the bifurcation between (2) and (3) – or between (2) and any other (3') that could also be said to signify a context of all contexts – that we mean to avoid.

VII

There is, actually, a critical observation that Husserl makes about the *Lebenswelt* that affects the prospects of any semantics that would resist relativism. It is, as we shall see, curiously related to Wittgenstein's notion of plural *Lebensformen*, from which, distributively, we cannot exit but which, also, we cannot directly explore as plural. It is also related to Heidegger's notion of the "concealment" of alternative possible "unconcealed" worlds through the "unconcealment" of the apparent world we inhabit. And yet, of course, Husserl's theory was taken to be sympathetic with a possible-worlds semantics and to have succeeded in obviating relativism.[22] The "plurality" of the *Lenbenswelt* raises serious doubts about that prospect.

What Husserl says is this (we have already had occasion to cite it): "The world [the lifeworld, the world-horizon] does not exist as *an* entity, as an object, but exists with such uniqueness that the plural makes no sense when applied to it. Every plural, and every singular drawn from it, presupposes the world-horizon."[23] Nevertheless, there can be no doubt that *this* thesis is drawn from Husserl's reflecting on the historically contingent *plural* life–worlds of ordinary human existence – roughly, the plurality of different actual societies sharing different sets of common practices.[24]

Remember that, in closing this account, we are merely trying to understand the "temperamental" motivation for relativistic and non- or anti-relativistic points of view. It is clear that if Husserl were to claim apodictic invariances ranging over all possible empirically divergent conceptual schemes, he would have to disjoin the study of the transcendental *Lebenswelt from* the contingencies of the "natural" *Lebenswelt* into which, one of its plural manifestations, we are all born. He does indeed attempt to disengage the life-world thus, for he goes on to say: "The life which effects world-validity in natural life world-life does not permit of being studied from the attitude of natural world-life. What is required, then, is a *total* transformation of cognitive attitude, *a completely unique, universal epoché.*"[25]

However, *if* phenomenological reflection on natural life-worlds, intended to arrive at the "completely unique, universal epoché" Husserl speaks about, is the same cognitive capacity that functions "naturalistically" (even if it is now to be applied to different projects), and if it is encumbered by the same constraints collected under (2) and (3) that affect all other cognitive endeavors, then it is quite impossible that the required "total transformation" take place: Husserlian phenomenology must be subject to the same prospect of relativism that naturalistic inquiry is. This is, in fact, a very large part of the import of Heidegger's and Merleau-Ponty's naturalizing of phenomenology, as well as of those recent tendencies among Husserlians (for instance, those favored by J. N. Mohanty and Dagfinn Føllesdal) that find Husserl himself much less committed to an apodictic phenomenology than had been previously thought.

In any case, the point of Husserl's insisting that the *Lebenswelt* cannot be individuated at all is the same one we noted in Quine's insistence that we inhabit "one" world: all intelligible discourse is a candidate for inclusive understanding; nothing can be left out. In that sense, there can be no alternative to the expanding horizon of inclusive understanding; and there is no sense in which there is "one" such understanding among many. But *that has nothing to do* with the determinable prospects of formulating concepts adequate to "all possible worlds" or necessary for all human understanding, or with escaping the threat of conceptual incommensurabilities or horizonal limitation or historicized divergencies and contingencies. There *is* no point at which Husserl's phenomenological ideal can be pursued *progressively* with regard to the cognitive capacities of human inquiry – without finding the suitable puzzles of (2) that can be answered sufficiently well to recommend the lifting of (3); and there may be no convincing way of treating the *contexted* solutions at (2) as leading to the *contextless* work of phenomenology by which the puzzles at (3) can be put to rest.

Here, we are merely interested in the extraordinary lengths to which Husserl was willing to go, even in the late *Crisis* volume, in order to secure his "completely unique, universal epoché." He obviously could not rely on the natural sensory "ego" or ordinary inquiring subject; and so he had to invent an extraordinary subject equal to the task, *somehow* the same in every natural person:

> Only by starting from the ego [Husserl says] and the system of its transcendental functions and accomplishments can we methodically exhibit transcendental intersubjectivity and its transcendental communalization, through which, in the functioning system of ego-poles, the "world for all," and for each subject *as* world for all, is constituted. Only in this way, in an essential system of forward steps, can we gain an ultimate comprehension of the fact that each transcendental "I" within intersubjectivity (as constituting the world in the way indicated) must necessarily be constituted in the world as a human being: in other words, that each human being "bears within himself a transcendental 'I'" – not a real part or a stratum of his soul (which would be absurd) but rather insofar as he is the self-objectification, as exhibited through phenomenological self-reflection, of the corresponding transcendental "I." Nevertheless, every human being who carried out the epoché could certainly recognize his ultimate "I," which functions in all his human activity.[26]

This remarkable passage (and similar ones) has to be read to be believed. But although it is hardly necessary for the advocates of possible-worlds semantics to subscribe to Husserl's formula, they must have some comparable (if leaner) source of confidence, if they intend to totalize over a set of meaning functions adequate for capturing God's mind.[27]

Doubtless there is no mere argument that will change such opposed temperaments as the relativist's and the non- or anti-relativist's. Why should there be? What we require, and what we now have evidence of, is a sense of the coherence and viability of relativism and of the fairness of its claim to a measure of dialectical power equal to or sometimes greater than that of its opponents. What we do not adequately understand (philosophically) is how "temperamental" differences regarding (3) – or regarding some alternative holistic vision (3') – affect the distributed disputes of (2), so that those disputes remain palpably productive, dialectically worth pursuing. The answer clearly has to do with our sense of the gathering force and promise of competing ways of formulating puzzles regarding (2) under the temperamental influence of (3) or some similar vision. Our arguments here, therefore, are perpetually indirect and perpetually hostage to our doubts about their circularity. But that itself is a consequence of favoring the spirit of (3).

This, then, is the truth about relativism.

But having said that, let us remember what we have demonstrated. We have distinguished alethically between relationalism and robust relativism. We have admitted the reflexive incoherence of relationalism and shown that robust relativism is not subject to the disorder of the other. We have drawn both options from the same ancient Protagorean source, shown them to be distinct and independent of one another, and applied them in increasingly complex epistemic and ontic contexts: most notably, in contexts in which ontic invariance can no longer be assumed (protagoreanism), in which conceptual divergence and incommensurability obtain (incommensurabilism), and in which the intentional properties of cultural phenomena and their inherent alterability under interpretation and historical change are admitted (ontic relativism). We have placed the entire question within a comprehensive philosophical contest that concedes the inseparability of alethic, epistemic, and ontic reflections, eschews all forms of cognitive transparency and ontic fixity, and acknowledges ultimate "temperamental" differences (myths of the context of all contexts) within the play of which philosophical quarrels continue to be pursued as before.

We have shown that the enlargement of our vision, by way of abandoning or restricting bivalent truth-values and admitting the coherence of incongruent truth-claims (the minimal definition of relativism: LF) need not threaten at all the fair sense in which the serious inquiries of science and other disciplines do constitute a stable yet profoundly contestable – historicized – *episteme*, the best (by our lights) that we can as yet construct. We have also shown that the entire endeavor is inherently incapable of totalizing over all possible conceptual schemes, and so cannot fail to "omit" what is not yet explicitly conceptualized or not yet perceived to have been conceptualized (poststructuralist concerns about *l'autre*); but that that holistic defect cannot be made to bear in a distributed way on the cognitive fortunes of any body of truth-claims. And we have shown that neither relativistic nor nonrelativistic accounts of truth are conceptually unavoidable, that we can always construct (at a price) nonrelativistic analogues of robust relativism, but that it also always remains a matter of reasonable bet as to which of such options are to be preferred. We have, in short, shown that the legitimation of relativism is entirely possible, plausible, favored at the present time, and certainly not a conceptual disaster. But also, having doggedly confined ourselves to the truth about relativism, we have had to admit in silence that there are larger truths and larger quarrels that relativism itself invokes. Possibly the occasion will arise ...

Notes

1   W. V. Quine, *Word and Object* (Cambridge: MIT Press, 1960), p. 52.
2   Ibid., p. 42 in the context of p. 28; cf. also, pp. 33, 43.
3   Ibid., p. 77. See, also, W. V. Quine, "On Empirically Equivalent Systems of the World," *Erkenntnis* IX (1975), p. 328.
4   *Word and Object*, p. 22.
5   Ibid., p. 23.
6   Ibid., p. 24.
7   Cf. ibid., §11.
8   Cf. for instance ibid., p. 79.
9   Cf. for instance ibid., pp. 275–276.
10 See Carl R. Hempel, "Inductive Inconsistencies," in *Aspects of Scientific Explanation and Other Essays in the Philosophy of Science* (New York: Free Press, 1965).
11 It may be useful to remark here that Duhem's holism is a holism of *all* perceptual phenomena, where the difference between perceptual and logical distinctions is preserved; whereas Quine's holism erases any such disjunction within its own space. So Duhem says, closing a famous account of his: "Despite Kepler and Galileo, we believe today, with Osiander [Andreas Hossmann] and [Cardinal] Bellarmine, that the hypotheses of physics are mere mathematical contrivances devised for the purpose of saving the phenomena. But thanks to Kepler and Galileo, we now require that they save *all the phenomena* of the inanimate universe *together*." See Pierre Duhem, *To Save the Phenomena: An Essay on the Idea of Physical Theory from Plato to Galileo*, trans. Edmund Doland and Chaninah Maschler (Chicago: University of Chicago Press, 1969), p. 117. See, also, *The Aim and Structure of Physical Theory*, trans. Philip P. Wiener (Princeton: Princeton University Press, 1954), particularly chapter 7.
12 Cf. W. V. Quine, "Two Dogmas of Empiricism," in *From a Logical Point of View* (Cambridge: Harvard University Press, 1953).
13 Jaakko Hintikka, "Semantics for Propositional Attitudes," in *Models for Modalities: Selected Essays* (Dordrecht: D. Reidel, 1969), p. 87.
14 W. V. Quine, "Notes on the Theory of Reference," in *From a Logical Point of View*, particularly p. 130. Hintikka makes the point explicitly.
15 Hintikka, "Semantics for Propositional Attitudes," p. 98.
16 Ibid., pp. x–xiii.
17 Ibid., p. xi.
18 Ibid., p. 104.

19 Leibniz had grasped the problem already. See Benson Mates, *The Philosophy of Leibniz; Metaphysics and Language* (New York: Oxford University Press, 1986), chapter 7. Cf. also, Joseph Margolis, *Texts without Reference; Reconciling Science and Narrative* (Oxford: Basil Blackwell, 1987), chapter 7.
20 Cf. Hintikka, "Semantics for Propositional Attitudes," pp. 108–9.
21 This goes some distance, we may say, to meeting objections to the antirealist's (or relativist's) questioning of a "realism about worlds." Cf. Graeme Forbes, *The Metaphysics of Modality* (Oxford: Clarendon Press, 1985), chapter 4.
22 See David Woodruff Smith and Ronald MacIntyre, *Husserl and Intentionality: A Study of Mind, Meaning, and Language* (Dordrecht: D. Reidel, 1982), chapter 7.
23 Edmund Husserl, *The Crisis of European Sciences and Transcendental Phenomenology: An Introduction to Phenomenological Philosophy*, trans. David Carr (Evanston: Northwestern University Press, 1970), p. 143.
24 For example, cf. ibid., pp. 132–5.
25 Ibid., p. 149. Cf. also, pp. 150, 151–2.
26 Ibid., pp. 185–6.
27 See, for instance, Alvin Plantinga, *The Nature of Necessity* (Oxford: Clarendon Press, 1974); also, Margolis, *Texts without Referents*, chapter 4.

Index

Page numbers in bold type indicate definitions